SHARING THE CITY

Community Participation in Urban Management

JOHN ABBOTT

Earthscan Publications Ltd, London

To my beloved wife

Ania

First published in the UK 1996 by
Earthscan Publications Limited

Copyright © John Abbott, 1996

All rights reserved

A catalogue record for this book is available from the British Library

ISBN: 1 85383 328 2 Paperback
ISBN: 1 85383 323 1 Hardback

Typesetting and figures by PCS Mapping & DTP, Newcastle upon Tyne

Printed and bound by Biddles Ltd, Guildford and Kings Lynn

Cover design by

For a full list of publications please contact:
Earthscan Publications Limited
120 Pentonville Road
London N1 9JN
Tel. (0171) 278 0433
Fax: (0171) 278 1142

Earthscan is an editorially independent subsidiary of Kogan Page Limited and
publishes in association with the WWF–UK and the International Institute for
Environment and Development.

Contents

List of Illustrations

FIGURES

TABLES

List of Acronyms

AHC	Amsterdam Home Committee
AKRSP	Aga Khan Rural Support Programme
ANC	African National Congress
BESG	Built Environment Support Group
CBO	Community-based organization
COSATU	Congress of South African Trade Unions
CUAVES	Comunidad Urbana Antogestionaria de Villa El Salvador
FUNDASAL	Salvadorean Foundation for Development and Low-Cost Housing
IDT	Independent Development Trust
IFP	Inkatha Freedom Party
IIED	International Institute for Environment and Development
ILGS	Institute for Local Government Studies
ILO	International Labour Organization
IMF	International Monetary Fund
NGO	Non-governmental organization
NUM	National Union of Mineworkers
ODA	Overseas Development Administration
OECD	Organization for Economic Cooperation and Development
PEBCO	Port Elizabeth Black Civic Organization
PHC	Primary Health Care
PRA	Participatory Rural Appraisal
PWV	Pretoria–Witwatersrand–Vereeniging
RDC	Reconstruction and Development Committee
RRA	Rapid Rural Appraisal
SACC	South African Council of Churches
SANCO	South African National Civic Association
SINAMOS	National System for the Support of Social Mobilization
TPA	Transvaal Provincial Administration
TRAC	Transvaal Rural Action Committee
UN	United Nations
UNCHS	United Nations Centre for Human Settlements (Habitat)
UNICEF	United Nations Children's Fund
UNRISD	United Nations Research Institute for Social Development
WHO	World Health Organisation

Acknowledgements

First and foremost I wish to thank my wife Ania for her support and encouragement, and for helping me to understand such a complex subject. A book such as this one, which transcends desciplines, evolves over many years and receives inspiration from many different sources. I have been fortunate in those years to be able to interact with many wonderful people across a wide spectrum covering academics, professionals, educationalists, community activists and leaders, and ordinary people. I have been fortunate to gain experience across a range of activities within the development arena. It is in the communities themselves, however, that I have learnt the most, witnessing the power of patience, politeness and tenacity when faced with attitudes of intransigence and lack of understanding from those in a position of power and authority. It is there that the key to successful community management in South Africa lies. Among the many people I have met I would like to mention, and to thank, two in particular. The first is Mr Zwane, the civic leader of KwaThandeka, who led by example and showed me that wisdom does not always come from academic learning. The second, posthumously, is Mr Majola, the civic leader of Bruntville in Natal. He and his family were victims of the South African struggle for peace and security, all of them murdered to try to prevent the democratization of the development process.

Among academics and professionals I would particularly like to thank Mary FitzGerald, who taught me the theory and practice of non-directive community development; Professor Dan Smit, who helped to bridge the gap between engineering and planning; and David Marsden, for helping to provide an international perspective. Finally, I would like to thank Jonathan Sinclair Wilson of Earthscan for his support and encouragement.

John Abbott
December 1995

PART

Historical Analysis of Community Participation

1

Introduction

COMMUNITY PARTICIPATION AND URBAN MANAGEMENT

Although the rate of urbanization has increased dramatically in the South over the past 20 years, the capacity of governments to support this urban growth has decreased. Various attempts have been made to address this dichotomy, but without success. Nor is there a consensus on the best way to solve the problem. The World Bank supports increased involvement by the private sector, whereas non-governmental organizations (NGOs) and community-based organizations (CBOs) are beginning to see community management as a way forward. Whatever their policy preference however, all of those concerned with the process recognize that the solution must involve local communities. The growing acceptance of this view brings the management of the urban environment into line with other sectors of international development, in which the importance of community participation has long been perceived, but it also brings with it the same problems. There is still no clear understanding of what constitutes meaningful and effective community participation. Many workers have analysed the subject of community participation in a variety of different contexts, but in spite of this it is still true to say, as Midgely did in 1987, that there is 'no rigorous academic foundation for the whole topic of community participation'.[1]

The lack of a theoretical basis for community participation is particularly important in urban management for several reasons. Firstly, the whole debate exists within a clearly defined political structure, namely that of local, or municipal, government. This immediately raises the issue of the relationship between participation and democracy. Secondly, there is the mix between public and private services which constitutes modern local government. The participatory process which suits one of these may not be appropriate to the other. Thirdly, there is the geographical spread and the difficulty which this poses in defining communities and their boundaries. This has particular relevance to several of the physical infrastructure services. Finally, there is the level of technology involved. A modern city has a sophisticated support system in terms of the engineering equipment employed, the level of technical expertise and the computer-based systems of management. Widening the scope of the decision-making process therefore constitutes a complex task.

Under these conditions there has to be a clear and mutually agreed understanding, among all parties concerned, about the meaning and scope of community participation. Much has been written on this subject, but it still remains to be collated and structured in a cohesive way; this is the aim of this book. By taking existing material and integrating it with new research, a participatory framework for urban management has been developed.

Urban management in a changing world is an integral part of a wider development process. To create a structure for participation in urban management it is first necessary to create a structure which explains community participation as a process in its own right. Only when the complexities of the participation process have been unravelled can the role of community participation in urban management be fully understood.

NATURE OF COMMUNITY PARTICIPATION

Community participation is relevant in every sector of development, whether it is education, health, conservation, agriculture, or water and sanitation. When it is practised successfully it transforms programmes and provides the critical component which can promote sustainable development. In a world of rapid change, effective and meaningful community participation is a fundamental basis of security, either of the individual or of the state. A clear understanding of the nature of participation is central to the search for peace, social justice and democracy.

As with any concept which has strong social and political implications, it is often convenient for those who interact with the process to interpret it in a way which meets their own interests, as well as their own particular perceptions. Thus, for example, development professionals working in developing countries might see community participation simply as a way of mobilizing community support for projects; NGOs in the field, as well as CBOs, may see it as a vehicle through which local communities can take control of the development process and bring about sweeping political change; development agencies may see it as a method of improving project performance, whereas many governments and civil servants view it simply as threatening and subversive.

Self-interest alone cannot explain the degree of divergence of the different interpretations. The reality is that the whole basis of community participation lacks a cohesive, academically rigorous, conceptual structure within which implementation can be placed. Instead, the process of learning about community participation has been organic, based on extensive experience. This in turn has created an empirical base for the practice of participation. There is nothing inherently wrong with empirically derived systems, provided that they operate within a cohesive framework which can provide collation of data, the systematic collection of evidence and the production and dissemination of widely agreed practices. This has never been the case with community participation, although it is essential for an activity which is practised by such a wide and diverse variety of professionals (from anthropologists and political scientists through sociologists and social workers to architects, planners and engineers) in different cultures and political systems, and which extends through a multitude of different sectors and can operate at a variety of different points in the development cycle.

These are not the only complications. There are other reasons why community participation cannot operate in a conceptual vacuum. Two levels of participation – the conceptual theory and the practical implementation – are interdependent. Without a conceptual structure within which the case study material can be placed in context, there is no means of relating projects to each other, of understanding fully why projects succeed or fail or of knowing what practices should be followed to ensure success in different contexts. The purpose of this book is to address these questions, firstly in general terms and then specifically from the perspective of urban management. The objective is to place existing practice in context but, more importantly, to create a structure for the logical development of community participation programmes which will be applicable to urban environment.

ANALYSING THE PARTICIPATORY PROCESS

The lack of cohesion between the theoretical and practical components of community participation can be traced back to the fundamental problem of trying to make community participation into a component of the development process. In 1955, the United Nations (UN) defined community development, which was then the widely accepted expression of community participation, as 'a process designed to create conditions of economic and social progress for the whole community with its active participation'.[2] The problem with trying to do this is that 'the extent to which participation can be inserted into development strategies depends on what is meant by the term, and . . . it is apparent that no clear consensus exists'.[3] In spite of this, researchers have continued to seek the relationship and to define community participation accordingly. The result has been that most theoretical work on community participation has attempted to fit it into a pre-defined role which is more a reflection of the researchers' own philosophies than a genuine attempt to define its theoretical basis. The result has been that 'unlike most other ideas in development studies, popular participation has not been subject to careful academic scrutiny'.[1]

The irony is that the seeds of a cohesive participatory structure do exist in published work. To assemble these ideas, however, requires a different approach. Community participation is an extremely complex puzzle to unravel. What is needed is an analysis of the individual pieces and the inter-relationships between them. This book integrates previously published work with the author's own work in the field across several different disciplines and attempts to build a complete picture of the community participation process. To check the validity of the results, four criteria have been defined against which the ideas being developed were measured. These are rationality, context, practical implementation and applicability.

Rationality

The work should be theoretically sound, academically rigorous and have a logical and coherent structure. There are several reasons why this work has not been adequately carried out before. The term community participation has a multiplicity of interpretations and, as a result, is heavily value-laden. The primary cause of confusion lies, not with the concept of community participation itself, but rather with the inability of the western system of categorization by generic specialization to deal with concepts which span currently defined disciplines. Furthermore, in spite of the rhetoric in support of participation, it has never been considered sufficiently important to warrant the establishment of a specialist programme.

This point can be illustrated by looking briefly at possible academic bases. Should it be in the school of social work, on the basis that one of its roots - community development – is based there? This is unlikely to be successful. On one level community development has been discredited as a form of community participation in developing countries because of its failures in the 1950s. On another level much of the practical work on participation takes place in the development arena, where few practitioners are social workers. Perhaps development studies then? Again, only a few practitioners pass through this school, and the fact that the subject is not 'mainstream' could be disadvantageous.

The reality is that community participation exists wherever there is a practical discipline working with people on the ground. Thus it is to be found in projects in fields as diverse as health, urban management, agriculture and forestry, water and sanitation provision and education. Each area of application has taken the subject and provided its own interpretation and its own definition. Unfortunately, this ad hoc approach has led to frustration and a general lack of progress in the field. The result is that 'participation [has become] an indispensable part of any programme or project, coming from sources as varied as national governments, UN agencies and non-government organizations',[4] yet no single body can provide a description of the process which is acceptable to all the others and which enables the large body of material on the topic to be integrated.

This study attempts to take community participation out of the system of academic categorization which underpins the conventional educational structure and to show that the subject spans many disciplines. As a result it deals with the subject itself and does not accept that community participation can be defined sectorally. There may be facets which link specific aspects with particular sectors, but these should then be explained in terms of a general theory. This approach is particularly important for the application of community participation in urban management because there it will be required to overcome the strongly entrenched interests of local governments.

Context

The analysis of community participation should be able to place the process within a wider context in a coherent and logical manner. This is implicit in earlier work, but has rarely been successful. The first description of this wider surround was the economic development paradigm. This proved inadequate and was overtaken by events, as described in Chapter 2. The second was the project environment. This proved even less satisfactory, as it opened the way to a multiplicity of interpretations. Unfortunately, those who controlled the international funding system supported this surround, primarily because it could be linked with a quantifiable product, eg a water supply or health clinic, and could be controlled by the project cycle. The result was that community participation was increasingly seen as a means of ensuring a satisfactory end-product.

What happened then was in effect a digression from the main debate about the nature of the surround (Chapter 3). The role of community participation described here was opposed, mainly by those people linked to UN organizations, who argued for the supremacy of social goals in development. This led to a polarization between the two groups which was expressed through the means and end analysis. Researchers moved away from the issue of the surround, to explore the individual conceptual aspects of community participation, which resulted in diverse explanations, definitions and models and served to obscure the search for a coherent structure. With hindsight it can be seen that this drift was inevitable, as meaningful objective debate was impossible. This was partly due to the misunderstanding of the nature of development itself, but the major constraint which prevented this debate from happening was the over-riding influence of the Cold War. The debate about the role of community participation raised fundamental questions about the causes of poverty, the role of development and the basis of democracy. Instead of seeing this as an important international debate, these issues were seen as challenging the political and ideological base of the superpowers. It became impossible to develop economic and social policies related to development without these being either consigned to a political pole or adopted by one of them. The result was a capitalist–communist conflict which pre-defined the wider arena and translated itself directly into a series of dualities on the ground. These might be state and community, oppressor and oppressed, landed and homeless. Each sector tended to create its own duality.

Without the constraints which were imposed on independent analysis as a result of the Cold War, it becomes possible to view participation outside the notion of a duality and to recognize the wide variety of participatory processes. These processes exist and have validity in their own right, yet they are also an integral part of something outside themselves. The term environment is the most precise expression to describe those collective factors which influence different approaches to community participation and within which the different approaches are situated. It is also confusing, however, because of its physical interpretation. As the development process becomes increasingly integrated with the physical environment, so will the state of the physical environment become an increasingly important factor influencing the community participation process. For this reason the term 'environment' will be limited here to the physical environment, whereas the term 'surround' will be used to describe the wider condition.

Practical Implementation

The theory of community participation should incorporate a practical implementation strategy. All work on community participation has had to address this aspect of participation. The result has been a series of specific approaches, first community development, then political empowerment and now community management. None of these approaches is complete in itself, because they have not related back to the wider surround. This leaves us unable to deal with the fundamental contradiction which exists between theory and practice.

As a result, practice often attempts to be politically correct, an objective which it can never fully achieve. It is relatively easy to define what is ideal, or even appropriate, but another to make it work. The first notion exists in a conceptual state, a form of virtual reality, whereas the second has to operate in real time; it is theoretically possible for the two ideas to converge, but the role of money in development prevents this from happening. The first state can determine a cost, but the second has to work with money, and money has a time value. This is a difficult enough concept in itself, but it is compounded by the way in which it interferes with what should be purely social judgements. Yet it is a central feature of development and has to be dealt with. Once money is allocated, the passage of time changes its value and this has to be compensated for in the development activity. One change is inflation, the fact that the cost of the same product after a period of time has increased, but there are other aspects to time value. Money is a commodity which is available for a limited period and has to be used during that period. This in turn provides a constraint on time, a constraint which is disruptive to the achievement of social goals.

Because early work could not integrate the participation process in the wider surround, and consequently could not deal with these inherent contradictions, it created its own explanation of them. It defined the relationship between the community and the activity as a duality. The early approaches to community development and empowerment could not explain participation adequately in terms of a reality. The strength of community management, and the reason why it is now becoming so popular, is that it appears to provide a solution which finally integrates the two, although community management does not satisfy the other criteria described here. This book shows that community management, although having an important role, also has major limitations.

Applicability

The final criterion is that the structure should be applicable to any situation. None of the existing approaches meets this criterion, although the structure proposed here appears to do so. Clearly, this claim is difficult to justify until sufficient case study material has been analysed. Therefore two alternative methods have been proposed and used here to test its validity; both of these are retrospective tests. The first is based on the principle that if the structure of the process has been accurately described it will, in turn, explain and incorporate existing approaches to community participation. The basis for this is the assumption that, if these approaches work in certain situations, then they must in fact form part of that wider structure. Community development, political empowerment and community management, and where and how they fit into the wider structure, are analysed and explained. The second method looks at existing, well-documented case studies which involve community participation as a major component. Ten of these are analysed and a satisfactory explanation is provided for the historical development of each.

LAYOUT OF THE BOOK

The book is divided into three parts. The first part traces the historical development of community participation in a post-Cold War context. As a result, the evolutionary process can be analysed more objectively, as pre-defined socio-political pre-conditions, such as the creation of a construct based on a pre-determined definition of community participation, are no longer required. What then becomes evident is the degree to which these pre-determined views actually shaped the evolution of community participation.

The second part of the book takes all the existing work and, through the use of comparative analysis, develops a surround which accommodates all the existing approaches. Once this is in place, it is possible to create the wider structure which explains the relationship between the participatory process and the different activities which form the basis for development. From this structure urban management is shown to involve a wide and complex range of participatory mechanisms. It is also shown to operate on two distinct levels. Such a theoretical structure is central to an understanding of community participation. Unless it can be implemented, however, it is inadequate. This is the purpose of the third part of the book, which is concerned primarily with participation in the urban environment. Here the implementation of the community participation process is evaluated from several different perspectives and attention given to the specific roles of some of the key actors, specifically CBOs, NGOs and development professionals. This part links theory with practice and identifies the main factors which determine the success of the participation process in urban management.

Community Participation and Economic Development

BACKGROUND

The current approach to community participation is strongly empirical. The result is that, although there is 'an extensive, if not overwhelming literature . . . which defines, surveys and analyses the experience of community participation',[1] most publications are detailed case studies which document implementational aspects of community participation. There is very little about the wider conceptual issues and that which does exist is diverse and poorly integrated. The result is a distorted perception of community participation.

Community participation cannot operate in a vacuum. It is true that, at a community level, there is a growing understanding of the way in which community needs are analysed, trainers trained and educational programmes implemented.[2,3] Without a conceptual structure in which to place the case study material in context, however, there is no means of relating projects to each other, of understanding fully why projects succeed or fail or of knowing what practices should be followed to ensure success in different contexts.

This is a pragmatic view. There is a more fundamental reason for adopting an integrated approach. This is summarized by Freire in his analysis of what constitutes meaningful change in society. He argues that

'men's actions consist of action and reflection: it is praxis; it is transformation of the world. And as praxis, it requires theory to illuminate it. Men's activity is theory and practice; it is reflection and action. It cannot . . . be reduced to either verbalism or activism'.[4]

The current emphasis on the empirical as the basis of community participation practice is leading to a repetition of old mistakes. New approaches are being developed which have many of the flaws seen in earlier approaches which are now discredited or discarded. This is particularly true of the new approach of community management.

One manifestation of this failure to integrate theory and practice is found in the way that researchers have treated the historical analysis of community participation. There is a small number of workers who have developed conceptual ideas to explain community participation. The early analysis of the relationship between community participation and economic development theory was one of these. This provided a theoretical justification for providing communities with a central role in the development process, which was necessary to counter the prevailing view and change thinking about development in bodies such as the World Bank. However, the way in which this linkage was developed and used was seriously flawed and the validity of the relationship was never analysed in depth. Parts which were deemed useful, and which satisfied emotional rather than analytical criteria, were carried forward and became established thinking. Other parts, which may have had an equal or greater importance, but which did not fit changing perceptions, were discarded.

To understand community participation fully it is necessary to understand its relationship with the wider political, economic and social environment in a structured way. The linkage between participation and economic development theory was the first attempt to consider participation in such an environment. It was flawed, but it also had important insights which were never fully recognized. This makes it a useful point from which to begin the exploration of the role of community participation in society.

CONVENTIONAL ECONOMIC DEVELOPMENT THEORY

There was a major shift in thinking about economic theory after the Second World War. On the one hand there was a view that there existed 'a large measure of agreement among economists in all countries [of the West] on the fundamental theoretical aspects of their subject'.[5] This was the classical interpretation which related primarily to the fields of equilibrium analysis and associated subjects.[6] There were other areas where far less was known. For example, 'The analysis of the factors affecting the level, efficiency and growth of resources in an economy was outside the scope of the deliberation of economic theorists'.[7] There was a growing recognition of the need to broaden the subject of economics to take account of these and other issues. This was true for all countries, but has particular significance in the 75 per cent of the world which was known as 'underdeveloped'.

Not only were many of these countries moving towards independence, which required a new understanding of how they might integrate into a new world order, but many were also exploring different economic systems as an alternative to western capitalism, and in particular those based on Marxist economic theory. To the major western countries of Europe and the US economics and politics could not be separated. A Marxist economy was synonymous with a communist country. If the western countries were to prevent the spread of communism and encourage western style 'democracy', this could not be done by force alone. Capitalism would have to provide a realistic economic alternative and demonstrate that it provided a better vehicle for generating wealth. To do this it required a theoretical basis which could be used to sell capitalism to less-developed countries. The result was the modernization theory of economic development.

MODERNIZATION THEORY

Modernization theory uses western society, and particularly the US, as a role model and argues that all societies shift from the traditional and primitive to the modern through a series of clearly defined stages of economic growth. This is not a new concept. In the nineteenth century the members of the German historical school of economics were developing theories which 'formed a basis for further discussion of problems of economic stages in Germany and, to some extent, elswhere'.[8] What was different about the approach after the Second World War was its global perspective and the way in which it divided the world into two dominant categories of developed and underdeveloped.

The basic problem was defined by researchers such as Liebenstein[9] and Nelson[10], with the latter describing it in the following way:

> The malady of many underdeveloped economies can be diagnosed as a stable equilibrium of per capita income at, or close to, subsistence requirements. Only a small percentage, if any, of the economy's income is directed towards net investment. If the capital stock is accumulating, population is rising at a rate equally fast; thus the amount of capital equipment per worker is not increasing. If economic growth is defined as rising per capita income, these economies are not growing. They are caught in a low level equilibrium trap.[11]

Lewis[12] argued that the key to achieving meaningful levels of development lay in understanding how the capitalist countries moved from low to high levels of saving and investment. As it was applied to countries in the South, Lewis' analysis 'implies that the opportunities for worthwhile investment exist; it is the capital which is lacking. . . what is needed is a massive investment over a short period to raise income levels above the containment rate'.[13]

This analysis was over-simplistic. It was left to the economic historian Rostow to develop a comprehensive model of economic development which appeared to explain this transition and which, in turn, provided the theoretical foundation for modernization theory. In the first instance he argues that 'The process of economic growth can usefully be regarded as centring on a relatively brief time interval of two or three decades when the economy and the society of which it is a part transform themselves in such ways that economic growth is, subsequently, more or less automatic. This decisive transformation is here called the take-off.'[14] Rostow then went on to expand this into a general model, saying that 'It is possible to identify all societies, in their economic dimensions, as lying within one of five categories: the traditional society, the pre-conditions for take-off, the take-off, the drive to maturity, and the age of high mass-consumption'.[15]

The traditional society is that in which the 'structure is developed within limited production functions'.[16] Although there could be improvements in productivity, there was a ceiling resulting from 'the fact that the potentialities which flow from modern science and technology were either not available or not regularly and systematically applied'.[17] In this statement, Rostow identified his role model clearly and unequivocally and classified all countries outside western Europe and the US, excluding communist states, as traditional societies.

The second stage of economic growth

> 'embraces societies in the process of transition . . . [wherein] the preconditions for take off were initially developed, in a clearly marked way, in Western Europe of the late seventeenth and early eighteenth centuries'.[18]

The take-off is described by Rostow as

> 'the great watershed in the life of modern societies [when] the forces making for economic progress . . expand and come to dominate the society. Growth becomes the normal condition. Compound interest becomes built, as it were, into its habits and institutional structure'.[19]

The fourth stage was the drive to maturity, which Rostow argued took place approximately 60 years after take-off, and this would then be followed by the age of high consumption.

Although Rostow stated that 'the stages-of-growth are an arbitrary and limited way of looking at the sequence of modern history',[20] he also states that they 'constitute an alternative to Karl Marx's theory of modern history',[21] and he subtitles his book a non-communist manifesto. His ideology was stated clearly when he said that 'These stages are not merely descriptive . . . They have an inner logic and continuity. They have an analytic bone-structure, rooted in a dynamic theory of production'.[22] The result of positioning the book in this way meant that modernization theory was no longer simply a work of economic theory; instead, it became part of the ideological struggle to exert the dominant influence over the developing world by western countries.

This wider framework was given credence by the development of a social theory to support it, thereby providing a much wider socio-economic theory of development in the South. It was Max Weber who developed the notion of the Protestant work ethic and he progressed from this to draw other conclusions about the social structure of modern industrial and bureaucratic society. Building on these ideas, Talcott Parsons and his followers in the US developed a description of the important social and cultural characteristics which differentiate the social structure of modern industrialized societies from that of traditional societies.[23] Parsons saw the cultural system as fundamental and argued that there are changes in what he defined as pattern variables which were required for development to occur. In a traditional or community-based society he identified these pattern variables as being affectivity, diffuseness, particularism and ascription. He then tried to show how they shift over time when creating a modern society to become affective neutrality, specificity, universalism and achievement. Thus, for example, there have to be changes in the roles and the relationship between people, creating a change from affectivity to neutralism. In a modern western society people fit specific roles, in their jobs, for example, whereas in a traditional society there are strong emotional and cultural associations linked with positions, eg a tribal chief. So in a western society a job is taken out of the emotional and cultural environment and de-personalized.

So the goals of development as he saw them were:

- social, described as the integration of society;
- political, summarized as the need for the society to work for the attainment of goals; and
- economic, requiring adaptation to the new requirements.

All of these are based on the role model of a typical western society. Their primary importance, however, was to emphasize the need for structural change in society as a pre-condition of economic take-off. Not only was this important in the anti-communist struggle, but it also provided the theoretical justification for western governments and multilateral agencies to interfere with the social and cultural society of countries in the name of economic development. As Kindleberger argued dismissively in reports to the World Bank in the 1950s.

> 'These [ideas] are essays in comparative statics. The mission is to bring to the underdeveloped country a notion of what a developed country is like. They observe the underdeveloped country. They subtract the latter from the former. The difference is a program'.[24]

Even when the limitations of this simplistic interpretation were recognized, this did not force a radical rethink, simply a change of emphasis. Instead of a generalized western model the focus switched more specifically to the US model. There, support for modernization theory could be built on example, rather than disparaging and dubious comparisons. McLelland switched the focus of analysis from the society to the individual. He stressed the importance of individualistic achievement and linked this with economic growth.[25] He argued that

> 'the connection seen by Max Weber between the Protestant Reformation and the rise of the entrepreneurial spirit ... can now be understood as a special case, by no means limited to Protestantism, of a general increase in achievement produced by an ideological change. The profit motive ... turns out on closer inspection to be the achievement motive'.[26]

The result is that 'In its most general terms, the hypothesis states that a society with a generally high level of achievement will produce more energetic entrepreneurs who, in turn, produce more rapid economic growth'.[27] Coupled with this, Hoselitz, in different research, explored the nature of the entrepreneurial function and, by comparing the personnel guiding a corporation to the collective equivalent of the individual entrepreneur in early capitalism, argued for the need for an entrepreneurial group.[28] Together these two ideas form the theoretical basis for the trickle-down concept which was to form part of the new intellectual basis for modernization theory. This proposed that if there was a group that was dynamic and entrepreneurial, then the spin-off from the wealth that they created for themselves would then trickle down to other parts of society.

Unfortunately, this concept was also used to support the notion of an elite which was not limited to capitalist entrepreneurs. Instead it could be made up of traditional leaders, colonial administrators, revolutionary intellectuals or nationalist leaders. Whatever that dynamic leadership consisted of, they could still motivate development. This notion has no support in the earlier work and is implicitly refuted by Hoselitz.[29] It is, however, important when examining the criticism of modernization theory from a community participation perspective. It is the justification of an elite, as much as the more widely proclaimed criticism of the failure of the trickle-down effect to materialize, that motivated the desire for a change in the role of the poor and the fundamental purpose of community participation. As Moser argued

> 'the growing pre-occupation in recent years with the more specific questions of popular participation must be seen within the more recent context of increasing discontent with established "modernization" economic development strategies . . . to provide for adequate redistribution of resources, sufficient employment or basic needs'.[30]

COMMUNITY PARTICIPATION AND MODERNIZATION THEORY

From its origins in the eighteenth century in the UK and the US, community development evolved into a branch of social work with a clearly defined role. It provided limited social support, through the medium of individual community development workers, to improve the personal well-being of people in impoverished working class communities. This continued to be its function when it was exported to the colonies and it was able to perform this task with reasonable success within the paternalistic structure of the colonial administration.

The difficulty came when bodies such as the UN, viewing those same countries as emergent independent nations, began to redefine the role of community development and express this in terms of wider social and political goals, rather than specific community needs. In this capacity it was envisaged that 'Community development is a process designed to create conditions of economic and social progress for the whole community with its active participation'.[31] In broadening the scope of community development in this way the UN was the first to view community development as synonymous with community participation,[32] a metamorphosis which was to be the root cause of the misunderstandings surrounding community participation over the next three decades.

This role as a vehicle for social and economic change for people in developing countries was later justified by researchers, such as Nkunika, on the basis that 'the term participation is frequently used with connotations of a long socio-historical tradition, and understood to be civil involvement in political life'.[33] This interpretation, which took community development out of context, was an ambitious objective. With hindsight, it is clear that such high expectations would be difficult, if not impossible, to meet. This proved to be so. The result was the application of a form of participation which was inappropriate to the needs of communities at that time.

Gilbert and Ward state that 'In preparation for the eventual independence of its African and Indian colonies the British employed community development as a method of encouraging the growth of political democracy and local initiative'.[34] However, this became seen by many parties, particularly those struggling for independence, as 'quite explicitly an attempt to create plausibly democratic institutions without serious dislocation to the vested interests of the status quo'.[35] In some areas it became used as a tool for neo-colonial expansion,[36] whereas in others 'the primary motivation was to promote political democracy and the integration of the poor into society [not as a worthwhile objective in itself but] in order to counteract the spread of communism'.[37] The problem of using community development as a tool of policy without a clear understanding of its historical role and purpose meant that 'the community development process itself was open to abuse, either through co-option by privileged groups, or through destruction by those same groups, to whom it posed a threat'.[38]

Given this background, the criticisms which were levelled against community development were well founded. Thus 'CD [community development] hardly ever faced up to the differences in interest that could exist between different members of the "community" that was to be "developed", notably in terms of their control over opportunities to make a living'.[39] Further, 'The community developers achieved little because they disregarded inequality, conflict and power relations'.[40] In other words, they did not put community development into context.

A clear pattern may be discerned in this increasingly strident criticism. Placed in a role for which it was never intended, community development was unable to resolve the wider social issues and in many instances became a vehicle for manipulation and community control. This perceived failure of community development coincided with a time of growing disillusionment with the strategies of modernization theory. As a result, community development became associated with the elites who were the main beneficiaries of those strategies and the two (community development and modernization theory) became inseparably linked.

This interpretation created a paradox. If community development had failed, and community development and community participation were synonymous, then community participation had failed. To resolve this, community development and community participation had to be separated. The UN recognized that 'the major weakness of community participation lay in its emphasis on mobilization rather than participation . . . Community groups have rarely been given the power to choose how they should be involved'.[41] This provided the key to separation. It was the specific approach to participation, constituted as community development, which was considered to be the cause of this failure to achieve economic and social progress, rather than the principle of community participation itself. This laid the foundation for a new, more appropriate approach to community participation, based on the concept of community power and control.

AN ALTERNATIVE THEORY OF ECONOMIC DEVELOPMENT

It was stated earlier that modernization theory uses western society as a role model, but it also goes much deeper. For it takes as the status quo the economic structure which existed in the late 1940s, using the relative economic conditions of the different geographical regions of the world as the starting point for a new economic policy. The political basis for modernization theory was set by Truman in 1949, when he stated that 'We must embark on a bold new program for making the benefits of our scientific advances and industrial progress available for the improvement and growth of underdeveloped areas'.[42]

This world view was increasingly questioned by a body of economists who saw economic history from a different perspective, namely underdevelopment theory. This rejects the notion that economic theory can begin from an arbitrarily defined day 1. Instead, it argues that countries are the way they are today because of past events. This argument is well developed by Rodney. He argues that

> 'Obviously underdevelopment is not absence of development, because every people have developed in one way or another and to a greater or lesser extent. Underdevelopment makes sense only as a means of comparing levels of development...A second and even more indispensable component of underdevelopment is that it expresses a particular relationship of exploitation, namely the exploitation of one country by another'.[43]

Development and underdevelopment 'have a dialectic relationship one to the other . . [and that] Western Europe and Africa had a relationship [which long preceded colonialism] which ensured the transfer of wealth from Africa to Europe'.[44] International trade was an extension of European interests. A three-way trade was set up between Europe, Africa and the Americas. Europe (and later the countries of North America) supplied the vessels and dictated the terms of trade, which operated in the following way:

> 'When Europeans reached the Americas, they recognized its enormous potential in gold and silver and tropical produce. But that reality could not be made a reality without adequate labour supplies. The indigenous Indian population could not withstand new European diseases such as smallpox, nor could they bear the organized toil of slave plantations and slave mines, having barely emerged from the hunting stage...At the same time Europe itself had a very small population and could not afford to release the labor required to tap the wealth of the Americas. Therefore, they turned to the nearest continent, Africa, which incidentally had a population accustomed to settled agriculture and disciplined labor in many spheres. Those were the objective conditions lying behind the start of the European slave trade, and those are the reasons why the capitalist class in Europe used their control of international trade to insure that Africa specialized in exporting captives'.[45]

Effectively, 'the exploitation of Africa and African labor continued to be a source of capital to be reinvested in Europe'.[46] In Africa the loss of such a large percentage of the fittest and most able-bodied population had a major impact on the capacity of Africa to develop internally.

This condition of dominance and control was institutionalized by colonialism, but it also changed its form. As Rodney illustrates, 'slavery is useful for the early accumulation of capital but it is too rigid for industrial development'.[47] Europe used its power to suppress all indigenous development and to create subservient economies. In Africa this resulted in a dependency of colonized on colonizer. In Latin America a different scenario developed. Much of the easily accessible wealth had been used up. In addition, there had been a far greater rate of colonization than in Africa. The result was the formation of a two-tier culture in which there was a peasant class which derived, not from early feudal society, but from a condition of slavery and inferior social status. A form of segregated development took place which had many similarities with South Africa but was less obvious because it lacked the institutionalized racial structure.

DEPENDENCY THEORY

Marxist development theory integrates underdevelopment into its own economic model. Dependency theory treats it differently. Thus Freire describes underdevelopment as representing

> '*a limit-situation characteristic of societies of the third world ... which cannot be understood apart from the relationship with dependency...The task implied by this limit situation is to overcome the contradictory relationship between these "object"-societies and the metropolitan societies; this task constitutes the untested feasibility for the third world*'.[48]

Dependency theory does not seek to justify revolutionary action in terms of the righting of past wrongs. What it does is to use the historical development of society, which views the world dualistically as a developed centre with a dependent periphery, as the theoretical basis for a more radical transformation of society.

Dependency theory, coming after the failings of modernization theory had started to become apparent, made strong use of comparative analysis. A good example of this is Frank's critique of modernization theory,[49] which contains both empirical and theoretical components. Empirically he argued that the pattern variables which Talcott Parsons identified simply do not fit the real world. To give one example, many of these pattern variables described as being traditional can still be found in the US. In addition, he challenged the idea that development happens by diffusion from the west. Modernisation theorists see capital and technology being transferred into the developing world in order to help generate development. Frank showed that in fact there is on the one hand a net outflow of capital from the South to the North and on the other hand that technology flows are heavily controlled.

From a theoretical basis Frank showed that modernization theories ignore the structure of societies. The dualist approach neglects the real linkages between the traditional and modern sectors. On a policy level, whereas a modernist would argue that if we could change the pattern variables in a society then development would happen, Frank argued that this is blatantly not so and that changes in pattern variables will not lead to development. Contact with the west had not led to development in the past. This is where the second aspect of modernization theory became important, namely the issue of entrepreneurs. The US role model was a land of apparently unlimited resources, particularly by comparison with the technology available to exploit those resources at the time. The accumulation of wealth by individuals did not therefore restrict the opportunity of other members of society. It also took place over a prolonged period. This was not a valid model for development after the Second World War. The bulk of wealth-generating resources was already controlled by western countries, whereas the opportunities provided for wealth generation through the exploitation of new technologies lay in the future. In this situation wealth was most easily achieved at a local level through political power. Kerr's hypothesis of beneficial elites proved invalid. Instead, the control of power by local privileged elites created increasing economic and technological dependence. It was this changeover to the local privileged elites which provides the linkage with the social analysis of Freire and which led in turn to the growth of *conscientisacion* (a term which 'refers to learning to perceive social, political, and economic contradictions, and to take action against the oppressive elements of reality'[50]) and empowerment as new forms of community participation.

COMMUNITY PARTICIPATION AND DEPENDENCY THEORY

Freire analysed society in terms of a dualistic model in which a minority, termed oppressors, controlled the majority, who were oppressed. He saw education as the key to effecting the transformation of society by overcoming the fear of freedom and building self-respect. He argued that 'The oppressed, having internalized the image of the oppressor and adopted his guidelines, are fearful of freedom. Freedom would require them to eject this image and replace it with autonomy and responsibility'.[51] Coupled with this is the conviction that

> 'every human being, no matter how ignorant or submerged in the culture of silence he may be, is capable of looking critically at his world in a dialogical encounter with others. Provided with the proper tools for such an encounter, he can gradually perceive his personal and social reality as well as the contradiction in it, become conscious of his own perceptions of that reality, and deal critically with it'.[52]

This led to the concept of *conscientisacion*.

Conscientisacion thus became a form of community participation to be seen in juxtaposition to community development. This led to the notion that

'At a working level, two main strands [of community participation] can be distinguished: (1) the community development movement, with its heyday in the 1950s and early 1960s: and (2) the concern with community involvement through conscientisacion, a mainly Latin American phenomenon of the 1960s and early 1970s'.[53]

The linkage between *conscientisacion* and empowerment is more complex. Empowerment as an objective of community participation developed its conceptual form in the 1970s, driven by world bodies such as the ILO, UNICEF, UNCHS and UNRISD, on the basis that such action would encourage meaningful change in society[54] and enhance the satisfaction of basic needs.[55]

In support of the latter, Shepherd states that the ILO encourages the use of the term to allow it to confront questions of power both ideologically and in its dealings with governments. He then states that

'decision making processes are the most obvious instances of the exercise of power. Therefore if participation in decisions can be broadened or made effectively representative, this means that power is being shared and that groups formerly excluded from the exercise of power are included'.[56]

Having made this statement, however, the ILGS report goes on to say that 'at government level too much participation may be considered to undermine the capacity for development by putting too much strain on national resources or institutions'.[57] This raises for the first time the idea that there might be too much participation, ie a point beyond which community participation becomes self-defeating.

In an attempt to clarify the meaning of the term empowerment, UNRISD defined empowerment as 'the organised efforts to increase control over resources and regulative institutions in given social situations, on the part of groups and movements hitherto excluded from such control'.[58] The framing of this definition provided a focus, namely control as an objective in its own right, which had been missing previously. This made the concept of empowerment more tangible. Within the context of socio-political change in Latin America during the 1970s, and particularly the emphasis on urban development (this issue is discussed in greater detail in Chapter 6), this also brought empowerment more closely into alignment with the concept of *conscientisacion*, which provided the final break with community development.

PARADIGM APPROACH MODEL OF DEVELOPMENT

The relationship between community participation and economic development can best be described in terms of a hierarchical structure, with the economic paradigm forming the wider context within which a specific approach to community participation operated. In this hierarchical relationship, community development came to be recognized as an approach to community participation which operated within the paradigm of modernization theory, whereas empowerment was the approach which operated within the paradigm of dependency theory.

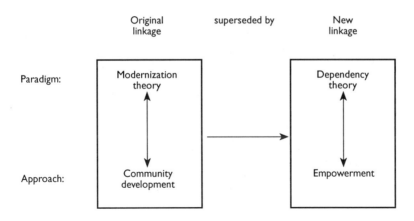

Figure 2.1 *The paradigm approach model of community participation*

Furthermore, on both levels there is a notion of one being superseded by the other. Thus in the wider context the dependency paradigm superseded the modernization paradigm, whereas at the working level empowerment superseded community participation. This relationship is illustrated in Figure 2.1.

The relationship between the paradigm of economic development and the community participation approach represents a model of the participation process in the sense that 'it represents a tentative description of what the system might eventually look like and suggests possible relationships between variables'.[59] Because of the strong linkages which exist between the two levels it has been termed the paradigm approach model of community development.

Unfortunately, there was no attempt to develop the model further into a full theory. To a large extent this was due to changes taking place in the wider arena of development, which are discussed in the next chapter. As a result, the model declined in importance, although it was never formally rejected. The outcome, which reflects the empiricist tendencies described earlier, is unfortunate for several reasons. On the one hand, the model provides an important insight into the relationship between community participation and the wider surround which was never fully explored, but which is central to creating a full theory of community participation.

On the other hand, researchers have carried forward from the model two concepts which have since become the central tenets of community participation thinking. Because of the lack of critical theoretical analysis these have never been challenged, yet both are seriously flawed. This in turn has created a major constraint on subsequent objective analysis. The two tenets, which are described further here, are:

- that a new and seemingly more appropriate approach to community participation supersedes the previously accepted approach; and
- that the central feature of the community participation process is a duality between the community and the state.

The Notion of Supersedence

Whereas the economic model underlying modernization theory is predictive, that underlying dependency theory has a much greater element of analysis. Thus it is able to bolster its argument by pointing to the real failures of modernization theory, particularly the absence of an obvious trickle-down effect and the growth of despotic elites. Unfortunately, the same process of critical analysis was not applied to the associated forms of community participation. Instead, the same result was assumed through association. The result was to create a linear mode of thinking about community participation.

The logical outcome of this linear thinking, based on the superseding of one approach by another, is that there is a single universal approach to community participation. Such an approach should meet the needs of communities in all countries and under all circumstances. Support for this interpretation is to be found in later work on the subject,[60,61] and continues through to the present time, with the latest example of this type of thinking illustrated by the debate on community management.

This line of reasoning is both simplistic and fundamentally flawed. The argument depends for its logic base on the scientific interpretation of the hypothesis operating once removed from the subject in question. In its subsequent application to community participation this requires 'inappropriate' forms of participation, of which the most clearly defined example is community development, to be discredited and superseded. If this is really so, and if community development has been superseded by empowerment, then there should be evidence of a gradually diminishing role for community development. In practice the converse is true. There is strong evidence, detailed here, that community development is still being practised successfully and, furthermore, is growing in popularity.

In developed countries community development has evolved and retains not only its identity but also its relevance as a primary vehicle through which social change is enacted at a local level. The strength of community development in this regard can be seen from the wide range of papers on the topic, which:

- debate this relevance of community development;[62]
- highlight the fact that academic departments of community development continue to exist in many developed countries; and
- indicate that both institutions and programmes are expanding in countries such as, and diverse as, Australia[63] and Hungary[64].

It is possible to argue that there is a difference between the North and South in terms of economic development and that this difference is the factor which dictates the success or failure of community development. If valid, this would be compatible with the paradigm approach model of community participation. Support for this view comes from Oakley and Marsden who, in discussing the failure of conventional economic models in the 1950s and 1960s, talk of community participation 'as it is applied to developing countries'.[65] Even if this argument is accepted, it does not explain why community development succeeded in the North when it is based on the same community development approach which had failed in the South.

This is no longer the only contradiction. In the past ten years there has been increasing evidence of a resurgence of interest in, and support for, community development projects in less developed countries. This evidence indicates that the application of community development to these countries can be effective under specific circumstances. Based on their work in India, for example, Jones and Wiggle strongly support the community development approach, but within a specific context, in this case a rural/village situation. Here, they argue that 'with a high level of political support, it [community development] could become the major agency for social and economic development'.[66] This optimistic view is itself based on firm evidence of success, clearly illustrated by Midwinter when he states that 'Community development has a superb record globally of highly successful projects'.[67] This is further supported by Nigerian case studies,[68,69] which reflect the success of community development as an approach to improving quality of life in meeting specific, clearly defined goals.

The second problem with this notion of supersedence is found in its expectations of the new approach, whether this is empowerment or, more recently, community management. This can only be achieved by limiting the definition of community control to a narrow interpretation which distorts the true meaning of community participation to reflect the needs of specific situations or specific interest groups. Thus empowerment, for example, depends for its success on the existence of the state–community duality discussed in the next section. In other situations where the relationships are more complex, the empowerment approach can also fail. What emerges from this analysis is a different interpretation of the relationship between different approaches to community participation. There are situations where each can be shown to fail. The issue is no longer whether a specific approach is now more universally applicable. Instead, it is which factors make different approaches appropriate in different situations. This notion of an approach being appropriate was recognized in some of the research on community participation. Thus Oakley and Marsden state that 'the search for more appropriate styles of development is fundamentally linked to what has been termed dependency theory'.[70] This lesson has since been forgotten.

The Concept of a Duality

Conscientisacion/empowerment grew out of dependency theory. In its application it was strongly influenced by a specific component of that wider theory, derived from Freire's concept of the oppressor/oppressed duality. With urbanization as the focal point of struggle in Latin America during the 1970s this concept was applied, for example through the work of Castells,[71] to the confrontation between the state, as oppressor, and the urban disenfranchized poor, as the oppressed. In this way it moved across to development generally to become a central tenet of community participation. This was reinforced by the superseding of community development, with the associated implication that community participation could not function satisfactorily when operated as an integral part of the state structure. Thus community participation, in its ultimate form, becomes a struggle to give rights to communities and to enhance the power, the self-confidence and the self-respect of communities. The result, which in this instance refers to local development but can be extended to other areas, is summed up in the following way:

> 'the two fundamental actors in local development processes are the local governments and the local communities. But"'community and bureaucracy are two evidently antithetical styles of social organization" [...], which serve to distinguish the two major protagonists in planned development, the people and the state'.[72]

This is the basis of the duality.

However, in accepting this notion of a duality as a fundamental tenet of participation, researchers have made a mistake which recurs repeatedly throughout the history of community participation. An important concept (in this instance the nature of the relationship between oppressor and oppressed) has been adopted as a universal truth without due regard for context. Freire was writing of a state (Brazil) which was not only strongly authoritarian but which, under its various military dictatorships, has long practised a form of discrimination. In dealing with this situation, Freire developed theories of antidialogical and dialogical action. This describes the mode of operation of an oppressive elite, through use of the tools of antidialogical action: conquest; divide and rule; manipulation; and cultural invasion. It also describes the converse, whereby people define and control their own destiny through dialogical action: co-operation; organization; cultural synthesis; and unity for liberation.

Nowhere in Freire's work is it implied that the oppressor/oppressed relationship is a feature of all government/citizen interactions. In adopting this type of duality as a basic tenet of community participation, researchers have taken a specific situation and generalized the condition. They no longer tested it within the framework of the paradigm approach model, however, because the development arena which was evolving during the late 1970s and 1980s had itself changed. Community participation was now operating in a different environment and was forced to respond to that environment. It was the use of these two tenets of participation, operating in and reacting to this new environment, which created the next phase in the analysis of community participation.

Community Participation in Project-Based Development

TRANSITION FROM ECONOMIC DEVELOPMENT PROGRAMMES TO PROJECT-BASED DEVELOPMENT

The interpretation of development at the core of the paradigm approach model was based on the primacy of economic growth, which in turn focused on the growth of two economic sectors, agriculture and industry. In arguing for a changing paradigm, proponents of dependency theory were less successful in influencing world opinion about a change in economic policy than they were in influencing a change in the perception of community participation. Although there was widespread recognition that modernization theory had failed to produce the conditions for take-off, western countries refused to accept the failure of the policy itself. Instead they saw the problem in terms of a lack of capacity to absorb the financial investment and the technology, a viewpoint which could be justified on a theoretical level by the social theories of Parsons[1] and others. What needed to be changed were the mechanisms of transfer and the institutional capacity of developing societies, and the key to affecting this change was the international aid programme.

While this debate was taking place, there were other international forces at work, which also influenced the change in development thinking. These grew out of a concern for the social realities of the less developed countries. Driven by the UN, these can be traced back to the first *Report on the World Social Situation*, published by the UN in 1952,[2] which led, ultimately, to the *Proposals for Action* of the First UN Development Decade (1960–1970). This proposal argued that development was not just growth, but growth plus change, stating that 'Change, in turn, is social and cultural, as well as economic, and qualitative as well as quantitative . . . The key concept must be improved quality of people's life'.[3]

These two strands of thought, arguing, respectively, for the primacy of economic and social goals, reflect an ideological clash between international organizations. The first is represented by the World Bank and the IMF, as representatives of western capitalist governments, whereas the second is represented by the various implementing agencies of the UN, and reflects the broader representative nature of that organization. The

debate was central to the new ideas which emerged on community participation during the 1970s and 1980s, but the way in which this occurred
was fairly complex. The logical starting point to begin the analysis is with
the donor countries' response to the failure of modernization theory.

Multilateral aid programmes, channelled initially through the World
Bank but later expanding to other regional banks, were established to
provide vehicles for the transfer of international development capital.
These were supplemented by significant amounts of bilateral aid, supplied
by individual western/OECD countries.

In the 1960s, when the objective of development was economic growth,
the way in which this objective was pursued was through the medium of
structured economic plans. Little[4] has shown how recipient countries were
encouraged by the donors to produce these economic plans, which would
set out the main problems and objectives in quantitative terms and then
relate the means, usually a set of coherent projects and other expenditure
to those problems, to the ends. Everything was spelt out in detail and
related to external assistance. Once plans were submitted these could be
studied by the donors, who would consider not only the urgency of the
problem, but also the feasibility of achieving the objectives of the plan
within the given time. They then looked at the relationship between the
internal and external inputs to see how much support for the plan was
generated internally. To an extent they would also consider how these
plans related to their own political goals and ideologies and this would
often be done in an interactive form with different donors keeping in close
touch with each other about the plans which needed aid. On the basis of
these factors donors would make their decision about how much to
support and for what period of time. There were also other factors involved
in reaching this decision, primarily the degree to which the donor country
or, in the case of the multilateral agency, the interests of international
capital, would benefit from the plans.

Underlying this approach to economic planning was a fundamental
assumption that the country or, if it was local, the body responsible for
carrying out the economic plan, had the human resources to carry through
that programme. This meant both an understanding of and a capacity to
deal with all aspects of the programme cycle. However, many of the
countries did not have that capacity and the money was subsequently
perceived by donor agencies to have been 'wasted', at least in terms of the
economic development objectives. Little shows succinctly how this was
particularly the problem with aid to Africa in the late 1950s and early 1960s,
the period representing the transition from colonial administration to
independence.[5]

In an attempt to overcome this problem there was an increasing shift
towards giving aid for projects. The relationship between projects and
development programmes is complex. All development plans can be
defined in terms of a variety of projects which make up a substantial
component of that plan and it is difficult to determine precisely where one
ends and another begins. In India, for example, the aid would often be
project-based, but it always took place within the context of a wider plan,
and the Indian programmes of that time were probably the most successful

in their ability to integrate the two and achieve at least partial implementation of the economic plans that they had put forward.

This was not so everywhere. In Africa, development planning had a poor track record and the projects and programmes increasingly diverged from each other. The funding of projects as objectives in their own right grew as agencies recognized the ease with which projects could be quantified. In this way donors could, in theory, obtain a better measure of the success of their aid. There was also the benefit that the projects had a clearly defined end-point, which was attractive to donors from a financial planning and budgetary perspective. This was the first step in the transition. At this stage, although there was a growth in the number of projects, these remained predominantly within the economic sectors of agriculture and, to a lesser extent, industrialization.

The second factor influencing the change in the structure of the development process was the role of the UN. On one level the UN had been encouraging the search for a broader definition and understanding of the development process through the proposals for action in the First and Second Development Decades. Thus services and infrastructure, for example, were still neglected by the development programmes of the time and there was a need to rectify this. There was also another level, however, where the UN was working through individual agencies to address specific global problems. Of these agencies the most important was probably the WHO. The importance of these bodies was not only that they were motivated by social needs rather than economic concerns, but also that they were sectorally driven. Thus they opened up new sectors which were not directly economically based and, through their achievements, highlighted the potential of sectoral programmes. This also laid the foundations for the introduction of the Basic Needs Approach.

Meanwhile the donor agencies, led by the World Bank, were attempting to rationalize their own strategies for moving forward. These were predominantly reactive in nature, being influenced on the one hand by the lack of success of modernization strategies and on the other by the growing demands for recognition of the importance of social factors in the development process. In 1969 the ILO created a World Employment Programme and accumulated large amounts of evidence that social restructuring, particularly in land reform and economic redistribution, was necessary if jobs were to be provided for most people.[6] This coincided with a shift in the World Bank's thinking about the effectiveness of aid funding. Against the background of the widespread failure of modernization, there was also the danger of increased radicalization within the less developed world, and an increase in the number of countries which were already undergoing revolutionary change. The World Bank, with its base in the capitalist economies, had to find ways to counteract this. McNamara's speech to World Bank directors in Nairobi in 1973 launched that so-called 'period of new-style projects'[7] in human resources development and poverty alleviation, looking at the areas of health, education, nutrition, family planning as well as a new approach to rural development. The World Bank thus began to recognize and take on board the idea that development constituted more than simply economic development – that it also had a social component. Its solution to this problem was to divert part of its funding across from conventional economic development programmes into sectoral sub-projects. This satisfied the twin goals of ensuring that these projects remained as the component parts of the wider development programme, while at the same time acknowledging the importance of social factors in that wider programme.

This was the state of play when, in 1975, the General Assembly of the UN requested a programme which would achieve the social objectives of development more effectively than the International Development Strategy adopted in 1970.[8] The response to this request was the Conference on Employment, Income Distribution and Social Progress, organized by the ILO in 1976, and the result was a programme of action for what later became Basic Needs.[9]

The importance of this Programme of Action was the way that it started by placing everything within the context of strategies and national development plans and policies, arguing that they 'should include explicitly as a priority objective the promotion of employment and the satisfaction of the basic needs of each country's population'.[10] At the same time there was a strong sectoral emphasis which was finally made explicit by the inclusion of services in the definition. Thus

> 'Basic needs, as understood in this Programme of Action, include two elements. First, they include certain minimum requirements of a family for private consumption: adequate food, shelter and clothing, as well as certain household equipment and furniture. Second, they include essential services provided by and for the community at large, such as safe drinking water, sanitation, public transport and health, education and cultural facilities'.[11]

The way in which the programme was described made it acceptable in principle to all parties and, for the first time, created a common vision of development. Unfortunately, this agreement did not extend to a common strategy on implementation.

The Basic Needs Approach expanded the concept of development by sectors significantly and was able to sell this concept by defining service provision as an objective in its own right. It was less successful, however, in marketing its view of programmes. Philosophically, the Basic Needs Approach pursued the UN agency stance on the centrality of national programmes. Donor agencies, however, which had already had serious problems with the programme approach within the context of economic development, found it even more of a problem when extended to social goal orientated sectoral programmes.

By this stage the original interpretation of development, which focused on economic growth, was severely under stress, but by no means universally discredited. Instead, the effect of the stresses was to pull the strategy in two different directions, indicated by phases I and II in Figure 3.1. The World Bank and other bilateral agencies were moving increasingly towards a project base, but attempting to retain the new social components within the umbrella of economic development. The UN organizations, on the other hand, were attempting to broaden the scope of development into a number of different sectors, but sought to retain a programme-based approach.

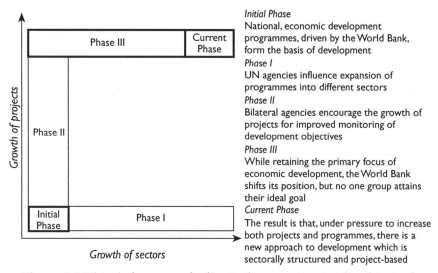

Figure 3.1 *Historical pressures leading to the current project-based sectoral system of development*

The adoption of the principle of Basic Needs, as an integral part of the development process, highlighted the disparity in their respective approaches. It also brought community participation to the centre of the development debate for the first time. The ensuing debate on community participation created a new shift, shown as phase III in Figure 3.1, which dictated the future direction of the development strategy for the next 15 years.

The programme of action had attempted to satisfy the needs of all the major international actors. It put Basic Needs within a wider development programme, yet stressed the importance of service provision across a wide range of sectors. It highlighted the centrality of social development and community participation in the wider development process, while talking of the importance of economic growth and seeing employment as a means and an end. However, it did not say how the potential contradictions inherent in addressing such a multiplicity of objectives might be met. The result was a major difference in interpretation. The Basic Needs Approach provided the justification for development by sectors, by defining service provision as an objective in its own right, and this view prevailed. It was less successful in arguing its case for the second policy, namely the centrality of the programme-based approach.

Donor agencies already had severe problems with this approach, as discussed earlier. The concern became even greater when it extended to incorporate socially driven programmes. The Basic Needs Approach appeared to provide an alternative solution because, as the prevailing argument went, Basic Needs could be interpreted quantitatively, in terms of access to water, for example, or the number of clinics. In other words, the programmes could be turned into a series of projects with a quantifi able output.

This interpretation of Basic Needs has been strongly criticized, with justification. Thus Wisner argues that 'Despite its forceful words . . . [it] was sufficiently vague to be seen as supporting either the strong [empowerment] or weak [manipulative participatory development] schools of thought on the BNA'[12] and he went on to say that 'It adopted a working definition of need and a core list of needs, which became an excuse for technocratic donors to limit their commitment to basic needs while continuing to promote export led growth'.[13]

This line of argument is itself as ideologically driven as the World Bank approach it is criticizing. It ignores the external influences placed on bodies such as the World Bank. The reality is that there is a problem in defining what constitutes success once the definition of development moves outside the simple one of economic growth. The only way that could be found to do this, at the time, was by quantifying output. This was not a problem limited to the World Bank. In 1977 the WHO's World Health Assembly endorsed a programme of *Health for All by the Year 2000*, which included among its goals

> 'Primary health care is available to the whole population, with at least the following:
> • safe water in the home within 15 minutes walking distance and adequate sanitary facilities in the home or immediate vicinity;
> • local health care, including availability of at least 20 essential drugs, within one hour's walk or travel. . .'[14]

In addition, the whole nature of the economic debate itself had undergone a significant shift since 1945 and this had also influenced thinking. In 1950, economists relied heavily on empirical data and economic theory was strongly qualitative. At that time it has been argued that

> 'The analysis of the factors affecting the level, efficiency and growth of resources in an economy was outside the scope of the deliberations of economic theorists. The discussion was generally at a high level of abstraction, so much, indeed, that the principle long-term determinants of income and wealth, such as the factors underlying the growth of capital, the size of population, the attitude towards work, saving and risk-bearing, the quality of entrepreneurship and the extent of markets, were considered as institutional forces or facts given, as data, to the economist'.[15]

This was to change significantly over the next 25 years, but the underlying uncertainty remained and caused a greater emphasis to be placed on physical inputs into the development process which could be measured clearly in monetary terms.

So although the superficial debate may have been about whether development was constituted as economic growth or social upliftment, there was a fundamental difference emerging which related to the form of measurement of output. Economists were moving away from qualitative criteria and increasingly towards a quantitative mentality, where they were supported by a strong technocratic component within the donor agencies and the UN organizations. Seen in this light, the Programme of Action in a sense consolidated the moves which had been taking place over the previous 15 years. From an extreme where development was defined in terms of national goals and objectives, it moved to the opposite extreme, to be broken down into constituent parts, both by sector and by project.

Although not all organizations followed this route (the ILO, for example, continued to operate through national programmes), it became the dominant strategy. Essentially, development had been re-defined and this provided the new environment which shaped the second wave of conceptual thought on community participation. This was a sectorally driven project-based environment in which community participation would focus on project implementation.

COMMUNITY PARTICIPATION IN A MULTI-SECTORAL, PROJECT-BASED SURROUND

By the time the programme of action was introduced, the ILO was able to say that 'A basic-needs-orientated policy implies the participation of the people in making the decisions which affect them through organisations of their own choice',[16] and to have this statement accepted in principle by all parties. The problem was how to follow the principles through to implementation. The pointer to answering this question was found in the health care sector. As early as the 1950s there had been a recognition, on the part of the WHO, that the mass campaigns, such as those against malaria, could only succeed if they had the support of a comprehensive health care system which could reach the most remote rural areas.[17] This could not be achieved within a reasonable time frame, or an affordable budget, unless there was a fundamental change in the structure of the health care system, which, until that time, had been based on the western model of centralized curative centres with highly qualified staff.

The alternative was to change the focus from curative to preventative medicine. For, as Gish pointed out, 'the majority of deaths in the Third World are due to preventable conditions of childhood lived in poverty and malnutrition . . all closely related to the management of the physical environment'.[18] What was needed was a new structure capable of providing basic health care services, a conclusion which was supported by UNICEF from experience of its Mother and Child health initiatives of the 1960s. There followed a series of international studies and meetings, which culminated in the primary health care (PHC) strategy approved at the Alma Ata conference of 1978. In this strategy, PHC was defined as

> 'essential health care based on practical, scientifically sound and socially acceptable methods and technology made universally accessible to individuals and families and at a cost that the community and the country can afford ... It forms an integral part both of the country's health system, of which it is the central function and main focus, and of the social and economic development of the community'.[19]

The change of focus to one emphasizing community participation brought to the fore the issue of context. In the paradigm approach model, the specific approach to community participation had a clearly defined surround in which it operated, namely its associated paradigm of economic development. With the move away from development as a national programme towards a project-based system, this changed and the surround actually became the project. It was in this context that the two core issues which had been brought forward from the paradigm approach model became critical. The two tenets were (1) that a new and seemingly more appropriate approach to community participation supersedes the previously accepted approach and (2) that the central feature of the community participation process is a duality between the community and the state.

The new health programmes reinforced the notion of empowerment acting within a sector. Supported by the theoretical analysis which underlay *conscientisacion*, these programmes provided the role models which reinforced the notion of a duality to the extent that it became an implicitly accepted parameter of community participation for the next 20 years. At the same time the dominance of empowerment as an objective of participation modified the notion of supersedence and replaced it by the concept that there was a single dominant form of community participation. The way in which this was achieved was through a definition of participation, the most common of which is provided by the UNRISD. This states that community participation is a process 'designed to increase control over resources and regulative institutions, on the part of groups and movements of those hitherto excluded from such control'.[20]

Although widely accepted, support for this definition was not universal. Its support base was found predominantly among social researchers and practitioners, and community organizations. There were others, primarily those who continued to support the centrality of economic growth as the basis of development, who saw it as idealistic or even subversive. In his analysis of participation, Paul produced a second definition which was founded more firmly in development projects and provided a less threatening view of the process. In this definition, participation was described as

> 'an active process by which beneficiary/client groups influence the direction and execution of a development project with a view to enhancing their well being in terms of income, personal growth, self-reliance or other values they cherish'.[21]

In producing this alternative definition Paul may have questioned the political nature of the statement, but he accepted the principle that the definition is central. This in turn reinforced the validity of the notion of a single universal form and provided the basis for a new, alternative model of community participation constructed around the definition. The second step was the construction of a framework to translate the definition into practical reality. The problem was that there were two bases for this model, competing for dominance.

The Development of the Conceptual Framework

In a review of approaches to community participation in rural development, prepared for the ILO, Oakley and Marsden brought together what they termed working statements from a number of sources. These 'emphasize the conflicting range of interpretations, which themselves reflect the dominant paradigms of development thinking internationally'.[22] The various statements were then grouped into four broad categories,[23] which they label: collaboration–input–sponsorship; community development (effectively self-help); organization; and empowering. In practice, these four categories can be further consolidated, with the first two being sub-sections of community development and the second two sub-sections of empowerment. The important point about these categories is that they all view community participation in terms of relationships which apply to development programmes.

The move towards a project-based, sectorally driven development process shifted the focus of community participation to a much more basic level. Whereas development programmes provided a mechanism to explore the interaction between the state and the community, development projects introduced a new variable. The project was a defined, tangible entity. This produced a new three-way relationship of state, community and project. With a multiplicity of projects deriving from a wide variety of sectors and serving so many different objectives, the understanding of what constituted the community participation process became significantly more confused.

The first problem was that of terminology. In this new situation it was difficult to describe exactly what constituted community participation. Moser argued that the range of different definitions was the primary reason for the spreading confusion.[24] In making this statement (about different definitions) there is a valid assumption that a definition should capture the essence of what is central to community participation. However, this fails to recognize, and take account of, the degree of subjectivity that existed in the analysis of the topic. Community participation as a notion is itself multifaceted and various workers have used different terms, not only to focus on diverse aspects of it, but also to impose their own view as to what constitutes the central feature of the participation process. In doing this they defined their own key terms and expressions, occasionally using a previously quoted term but giving it a completely different meaning. These various terms included: definitions;[25] objectives/goals;[26] purposes/objective;[27] kinds of participation;[28] methodology;[29] and working statements.[30]

This problem of conflicting terminology was partially resolved in 1987 by Paul. The basis for his analysis was derived from a review of World Bank experience with community participation in 50 projects selected from the sectors of urban housing (18 projects), health and nutrition (15) and irrigation (17).[31] The value of Paul's work lay in his approach, which was from a wholly analytical perspective, the first work to approach the subject in this way. His first step was to draw a clear distinction between the terms 'definition' and 'objective', as the inter-changeability of these two terms had been an ongoing source of confusion. Having done this, the second step was the desegregation of intensity, ie the degree to which the people affected become involved in those projects, from the objectives of the project. He argued that 'While CP [community participation] can be used for any or all of these (sic) objectives, it may vary in the intensity with which it is sought in a particular project or at a particular stage of the project'.[32]

In addition to rationalizing terminology, Paul was also the first to define a comprehensive conceptual framework for community participation. Thus 'the multiplicity of approaches to an interpretation of CP [community participation] in the literature and the world of practice can be better understood within this analytical framework [ie the conceptual framework]'.[33] This term conceptual framework is defined here as those elements of community participation which define the central features of the process forming the basis of the project implementation programme.

Although he may have resolved the problem of terminology, Paul's approach did not provide the definitive conceptual framework. Instead, his description of the terms intensity and objectives served to re-open the ideological debate. To understand how an alternative framework emerged in spite of this detailed analysis, it is necessary to explore the terms intensity and objectives in greater detail.

Intensity of Community Involvement in the Participation Process

In 1969 Arnstein[34] wrote a paper which set out a novel concept, describing participation in terms of the degree to which people were involved in the projects and programmes which affected their lives. To explain how this worked she produced a typology of eight levels of participation which, for illustration purposes, she arranged in the ladder pattern illustrated in Table 3.1.

Arnstein described participation in terms of a series of increasingly meaningful inputs into the decision-making process, with each rung corresponding to the extent of citizens' power in determining what she called the 'end product',[35] and which could be either a project or a programme. Although Arnstein's ladder gained a limited following in certain countries in the South,[36,37] the more common response was to dismiss it as simplistic and paternalistic. As Peattie argued, 'this [ladder of citizen participation] is not a helpful way to try to understand citizen participation in the Third World'[38] and that 'citizen power is more complicated than a simple transfer of power from top to bottom'.[39]

Table 3.1 *Eight rungs on a ladder of citizen participation*

Degrees of citizen power
8 Citizen control
7 Delegated power
6 Partnership
Degrees of tokenism
5 Placation
4 Consultation
3 Informing
Non-participation
2 Therapy
1 Manipulation

Source: Arnstein (1969)[34]

However, this is to ignore the underlying influence that the typology has had on conceptual thinking. Firstly, it served to reinforce the notion of the duality, emphasizing that participation is 'of the governed in their government'.[40] Arnstein argues for the need for less privileged citizens to have power, and that 'It is the redistribution of power that enables the have-not citizens, presently excluded from the economic process, to be deliberately included in the future'.[41] She also states that

> 'The justification for using such simplistic abstractions is that in most cases the have-nots really do perceive the powerful as a monolithic "system", and the powerholders actually do view the have-nots as a sea of "those people", with little comprehension of the class and caste differences between them'.[42]

Secondly, it introduced, for the first time, the concept which was later to form the basis of intensity, namely that there are different degrees to which people can become involved in decision-making processes. Paul took this notion and placed it at the centre of his conceptual framework, although he limited the number of options to four: (1) information sharing; (2) consultation; (3) decision-making; and (4) initiating action.[43]

The third important aspect of Arnstein's work related to the way in which she viewed power, which is very different to that of *conscientisacion* and empowerment. This has major implications for the debate about power and control which will be discussed in detail in Part 2 of the book.

The final reason for the importance of Arnstein's work stems from the way in which she places power within the framework of a continuum. Arnstein argued that, for example, although she has shown eight rungs on the ladder, 'In the real world of people and programs there might be 150 rungs with less sharp and "pure" distinctions among them'.[44] What Arnstein has done here is to introduce the concept of a continuum whose opposite poles are manipulation and community control. The notion of a continuum became the third accepted tenet of community participation.

The real problem that most researchers have is with the concept of intensity itself. This is seen as an implicit contradiction when used in the context of community participation. The reason for this can be found in the debate on the third key term, that of objectives.

OBJECTIVES OF COMMUNITY PARTICIPATION

The move towards a project-based approach to development opened up the debate on the purpose of community participation. Each project is different and will have unique features, but this was not an insurmountable problem in itself. It was transformed into a serious problem by the rapid expansion of sectoral interests that had accompanied the move towards project-based development. Thus the debate which had taken place over many years in the health field was repeated in each of the different sectors. This process of reinventing the wheel was due in part to the narrow sectoral focus which is a product of the western educational structure. It also reflected the fundamental division between those who saw economic improvement as the primary objective of development and those who considered social well-being as the fundamental purpose. In the paradigm approach model the relationship between the government and the governed represented a natural duality which, in simplistic terms, provided a natural cleavage between these two camps. Those supporting the economic argument saw the government as the primary agent, whereas those with a predominantly social objective supported a community-driven approach. With the increasing trend towards project-based development a new variable was introduced and this simplistic division was complicated. It became necessary to consider the relationship between the state, the community and the project. The way in which this was done was to subsume the project within the existing duality, and the vehicle for achieving this was the means and end hypothesis.

In 1983, Moser argued that 'the extent to which participation can be inserted into development strategies depends on what is meant by the term and it is apparent that no clear consensus exists'.[45] However, she then goes on to say that, although it was not useful to provide a list of definitions in the abstract, 'an important distinction can be made, within the spectrum that exists, between those which identify participation as a means and those which identify participation as an end'.[46] Moser then clarified this statement with the following description:

'This distinction between means and end clearly has important implications for the way in which community participation is evaluated in projects and programmes. Where participation is interpreted as a means, it generally becomes a form of mobilisation to get things done. This equally can be state directed, top down mobilisation (sometimes enforced) to achieve specific development objectives, or bottom up voluntary community based mobilisation to obtain a larger immediate share of resources. The most frequent constraints of participation as a means are operational obstacles such as inadequate delivery mechanisms, lack of local structures of local coordination, while evaluation is concerned with the measurement of quantitative results of specific development objectives, rather than the extent of real participation. Where participation is identified as an end the objective is not a fixed quantifiable development goal but a process whose outcome is an increasingly meaningful participation in the development process. Where the real objective of participation is "to increase control over resources and regulative institutions in given social situations, on the part of groups and movements of those hitherto excluded from such control" [as in the UNRISD definition quoted earlier], there is an inevitable sharing and then transfer of power involved as social groups deliberately attempt to control their own lives and improve their living conditions. In this context tensions can develop between the state, trying to promote participation to achieve centrally decided objectives, and the "hitherto excluded" groups who in the process of participation are trying to increase their control over resources. Where participation is identified as an end, the constraints on participation are structural—national and local institutional opposition which most frequently react oppressively if any real transfer of power occurs, and in reality determine the limits of participation. Evaluation of participation as an end is complex, since it is essentially the evaluation of a non-material and non-quantifiable process. Ultimately it is an evaluation of the transfer of power and poses the question as to whether authentic participation can only occur when there is a redistribution of power'.[47]

Although clear in its distinction between the two interpretations of community participation, the practical application of this idealistic differentiation is more complex. As Moser herself admitted later, 'as with any dualistic division, this one between participation as a means and participation as an end is mechanistic and limited in its applicability'[48] and then goes on to say that 'In reality it is not the evaluation of participation either as a means or as an end which is important, but the identification of the process whereby participation as a means has the capacity to develop into participation as an end'.[49] This still does not address the practical problem of how projects operated in this way should be implemented.

Paul tried to address this practical problem by viewing the participation process from the perspective of the project (and coupling it with the variable of intensity). Thus he identified a total of five potential objectives for the project, namely '(i) project cost sharing; (ii) improving project efficiency; (iii) increasing project effectiveness; (iv) building beneficiary capacity; and (v) empowerment'.[50] To place these within the context of community participation, Paul placed the different objectives and levels of intensity, together with what he termed the instruments of community participation, within a three-dimensional matrix (Table 3.2), stating that 'the three dimensions are inter-related and that there are certain combinations of these dimensions which are more likely to be consistent and hence more effective (for community participation) than others in a given project context'.[51] This provides the first definition framework model of community participation.

Clearly, this approach is presenting a different view to that of the means and end, which is strongly community-orientated. This reflected a growing concern during the 1980s about the apparent inability of the empowerment approach to translate itself into practice through projects. Thus Paul, for example, states that of the 50 projects which he evaluated, only three could be identified which had empowerment as their basic objective.[52] In her monogram, published in 1989, there is an implicit recognition of this criticism of empowerment, which Moser tackled by taking a selection of contributions to the participation debate which dealt with the objectives of community participation, including that of Paul, and constructing Table 3.3. By showing how the different views are related, this is shown to be a justification for the basic principle of means and end. This is a weak argument intellectually. Its strength lies in taking the moral high ground, ie arguing that, ultimately, community participation as an end can be the only correct form of participation.

This is an interesting argument. Having made this statement, and drawn in both the UNCHS and a complex conceptual framework such as Paul's to support it, Moser justifies the retention of the means and end duality as the only basis for defining the functioning of community participation in a project environment. Furthermore, by recognizing that it may take time to achieve participation as an end, Moser provides a valid reason why there are so few projects implemented which have empowerment as their objective, as empowerment-based projects may have difficulties in achieving their goal immediately. The result was the creation of two conflicting conceptual frameworks, one based on three elements of objectives, intensity and instruments, and the other based solely on objectives.

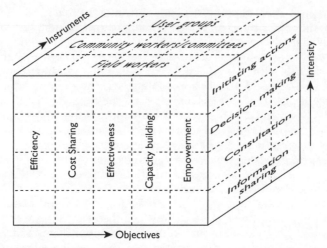

Figure 3.2 *Objectives, intensity and instruments of community participation*

Table 3.2 *Categorization of objectives of community participation*

Oakley and Marsden, Moser	Paul	UNCHS
Means	Project cost sharing Improving project efficiency Increasing project effectiveness Building beneficiary capacity	Means to improve project result Building self reliance, co-operative spirit
End	Empowerment	Right and duty to participate

Source: Moser (1989).[53]

EMERGENCE OF A DOMINANT CONCEPTUAL FRAMEWORK FOR COMMUNITY PARTICIPATION

In Arnstein's original work, the intensity of community involvement was the basis of community participation; a one-dimensional process in which the levels of intensity were defined along a continuum. By incorporating objectives, Paul produced a much more flexible structure which explained the process of participation in projects fairly comprehensively. With the inclusion of instruments, Paul produced a model which appeared to incorporate all the important variables of the process as he saw them.

Paul's conceptual framework was important in several respects. It clarified the confusion over terminology. It brought together the multiplicity of objectives into a unified structure and clearly distinguished the level of community input (intensity) from those objectives. Finally, it attempted to create a model of community participation which was independent of the ideological debate, based on analysis rather than socio-economic theory.

This attempt at impartial analysis is also the major flaw in Paul's work. Community participation does not exist in a vacuum and the relationship between those governing and those governed is a critical facet of any debate on community participation. By limiting himself to objective analysis, Paul's framework fails to address the central issue of who decides. Who decides the objective for a specific project? Who decides the level of intensity? Who chooses the instruments of community participation? The reality is that Paul has not been objective in his analysis. Instead he has brought forward a value system, which is that of the World Bank. The whole structure of analysis is geared to project implementation, and community participation was seen from that perspective. This is evident in the initial definition. Whereas the UNRISD definition speaks of control over resources and institutions, Paul talks of influencing the direction and execution of development projects. This is the language of the development agencies.

The second failing of Paul's model stems from a misunderstanding of the nature of a participatory model. Paul places his three 'dimensions of participation' in a matrix structure.[54] This may be useful for illustration purposes, but it is misleading. The different forms of objective, intensity and instrument do not link together in this way. Nor does Paul make any attempt to explain how the three dimensions might function interactively. In fact, he specifically states that on a given project there may be several forms of the different dimensions at work. Finally, it is not even clear whether the different forms of the three dimensions are discrete or form part of a continuum, as Moser assumes. This is an important question which is not addressed by Paul.

Essentially what Paul has done is to examine many projects and, from his analysis, shown that different objectives, levels of intensity and instruments can exist. In doing this, and categorizing the three elements, he has produced an important tool for evaluating community participation in projects. However, there is also an implicit assumption that the results form the basis of an applied model which is required to be predictive and constructive. This is an invalid assumption (see Chapter 8). He has not provided a basis for implementation and it is not a planning tool, although it may be a planning aid. So although it is a useful analytical tool for evaluation, it is not a model for community participation.

The alternative basis for a conceptual framework model is very different. Moser saw that the question of who decides was central to the participation debate. Her hypothesis addresses the question by dismissing the notion of intensity completely, on the grounds that the people affected should be those who make the decisions. The only critical issue is therefore to decide on the objective. Once a list of objectives has been identified (eg as in Paul), then the framework can be further simplified by placing the different objectives into one of two categories: those which support community empowerment and control (the end component of the framework) and those which do not (the means component).

From a theoretical perspective, the arguments in favour of the means and end duality are weak in two respects. The first is the logic of the construct itself. Moser built her argument around Table 3.2, and reiterated Paul's statement that his objectives lie along a continuum.[55] As mentioned in the previous section, this is a questionable interpretation. It does not follow, for example, that Paul's objective of effectiveness is naturally closer to empowerment than is the objective of efficiency. It may be valid to argue that the achievement of effectiveness is more likely to require a higher degree of community involvement than does the achievement of efficiency, but that is a different issue. The second weakness lies in the construct's total disregard for other factors, such as the surround (see Chapter 8). There is no recognition that this might play a part in the process, or even influence the degree, of community participation. The use of means and end is reductionism in extremis.

In spite of these weaknesses, however, the means and end duality has a number of attractions. The first is the pure simplicity of the idea of participation as an end, which is easily understood as a concept and has therefore had a powerful influence. The second is the way in which intellectual and moral arguments are combined. Thus there is a sense throughout that it is morally correct for poor and disenfranchised people to take responsibility for decisions which affect their lives. As a result empowerment is seen as the only possible form of participation. This presumption is justified by the definition, around which the whole argument in favour of means and end is built, and therefore it is not seen to need further elaboration; hence the integration of definition and conceptual framework into a single model. However, this model as it stands does not deal with the practicalities of implementation. Its primary purpose is to provide the conceptual framework from which a practical model can be constructed.

COMMUNITY MANAGEMENT

As Moser recognized, projects may be multifunctional, and she saw the need to make the transition from a point where the objective of the project was means-orientated to one which was ends-driven. There is a further problem associated with projects. Once they are in place they have to be operated and maintained, requiring skills, materials and equipment to be paid for. This is where community management appears to provide an answer to both of these problems and thereby provides the final component for the definition framework model of community participation.

Most projects which involve community participation are small and clearly defined, eg schools, village water supplies and rural forestry programmes. By involving communities in the decision-making process around a project, and giving them responsibility for the ongoing management of the project, a sense of ownership is instilled, opportunities for wider community contributions are opened up and the likelihood of long-term success for the project is enhanced. Community management is the implementation strategy which links these two aspects of project development together. In doing so it provides for the implementation of sectorally based projects, within a definition based on increased community empowerment and control over resources, and using as a conceptual framework the dualistic, means and end interpretation of community–project interaction.

To some researchers community management is community participation in its final, evolved form.[56] This is simplistic, however, and, in accepting this view, proponents of community management are making the same mistakes that were made with the earlier acceptance of political empowerment. They are taking an approach which works in specific situations and making it a universal model without giving due consideration to the context and surround. This can be seen from a brief analysis of the historical development of community management.

It is sometimes forgotten that community management is not a stand-alone term. The full description is community-based resource management. Furthermore its origin, like those of other approaches, is geographically specific, originating in South-East Asia. This has several implications. The first relates to the object of the approach, ie the resource. Of primary importance in this regard are land and water. These provide the basis for economic rural development. The importance of this will be shown later. The second relates to area and demography. Thus Korten sketches the background motivation for community-based resource management in the following way:

> 'Public development efforts of the past few decades have seen increasing extension of state authority **throughout Asia** [emphasis inserted by this author] into affairs once the preserve of local authority and control . . . All too often however, in its enthusiasm for modernizing and rationalizing resource management, the state has underestimated the extent and capacity of the system by which people have learned through long and difficult experience to manage locally available resources to meet their own self-defined needs'.[57]

So community-based resource management is intimately linked with the utilization of tacit knowledge. The use of tacit knowledge is critical, but it needs to be recognized that the knowledge base discussed here was built up to deal with rural areas of relatively high density. Other areas of the world have drastically changing demographic conditions which make some of this knowledge obsolete. In the Maputaland region of South Africa, for example, the use of tacit knowledge cannot prevent the depletion of the last remaining mangrove swamp. The ability of local people to obtain a sustainable yield from the swamp has been overtaken by increased human and cattle population.

The third implication is political. Several countries in South-East Asia have been successful in promoting rapid economic growth while maintaining an authoritarian political regime. The encouragement of community-based resource management does not imply any increase in political power. Community management operates with the consent of government and does not fully grasp the political aspect of government/ community relations. It also needs to be recognized that many community management projects relieve central government of the burden of finding additional funds for operating costs and are therefore strongly supported, particularly when they involve non-contentious issues. Further, community management generally operates within a clearly defined project context focused on one specific sector. As projects grow and involve multiple choices or scarce resources, community management moves into a new and untested area for which it is ill-equipped. Its ability to deal with multi-sectoral problems is similar. It has provided some important answers, but still leaves many questions unanswered, particularly those which affect the relationship between parties in situations where the community cannot be so easily defined.

IMPLEMENTATION STRATEGIES BASED ON THE MEANS AND ENDS CONCEPTUAL FRAMEWORK OF COMMUNITY PARTICIPATION

Community management is not the only implementation strategy which meets the UNRISD definition requirements. There is also a second strategy. In community management, the community takes primary responsibility for motivating, defining and controlling the project, with the approval of government. One alternative is for the community to follow the same route, but independently of or in defiance of government. An example of this is San Salvador housing projects in El Salvador (this case study is discussed in more detail in Chapter 6). This is a confrontational approach which is based on dividing all actors into two camps; those who support the community project and those who oppose it, and is a development of the political empowerment approach to participation described in the previous chapter.

What has evolved here is a model that has strong similarities with the earlier paradigm approach model. Community management operates for projects in ways which are similar to the way in which community development operates in social programmes. Both focus on communities. The major difference is that whereas community development is based on the active support of government, community management is built around passive support. On the other hand, the Villa el Salvador project, which is also community-based, can also be described in many ways as a classic empowerment approach, but operating within a project-based environment.

This analysis reinforces the argument that classic approaches to community participation have a strong tendency to reduce the interaction with the community to a duality. The paradigm approach model was able to define this in terms of the relationship between the government and the governed, in which any activity became simply a vehicle for playing out this interaction. Initially, the move towards project-based development introduced a third variable (the project) which complicated this relationship. The way this was overcome was to change the focus to one based on a duality between the community and the project, summarized so clearly by the means and end hypothesis.

There is no doubt that the approach of community management can and does work, but its application is not universal. It therefore falls into the same category as community development and empowerment. There are situations where it is appropriate, but others where it cannot operate. To understand what defines an appropriate situation for any of the various approaches, it is first necessary to break out of the constraint imposed by viewing community participation as a duality. This can be done by opening up and exploring the interaction as a three-way relationship between government, community and project.

Community Participation and Local Government

INTRODUCTION

Most published work which deals with the theoretical construct of the community participation process can be related to either the paradigm approach model or the project-based model of participation. The one characteristic which is shared by these two models, and which in turn creates a linkage between the different strands of research, is the notion of a duality and the ongoing attempts to reduce the participation process to this state. This is most commonly expressed either as a duality centred around power relationships, eg between governing and governed, oppressor and oppressed (the first model), or as a relationship between the community and a project (the second model). Even where researchers look at specific problems which operate outside these models they still attempt to describe relationships in terms of dualities, eg the community and the planner,[1] the community and the World Bank, the community and the NGOs. It is as if development comprised a hub (the community) with a series of radiating spokes which connect the hub to satellite stations.

In the wider arena which comprises the global physical environment, this type of thinking is rapidly being superseded by a recognition of the inter-relatedness of activities, actors and interests. No one part can function without its operation affecting all the other parts. This, coupled with the failure of existing development strategies for developing countries, and the end of the Cold War, will cause a profound change in the essential nature of the development process over the next decade. This is turn will necessitate a reversal of the trend towards increasing desegregation of development programmes into ever smaller, discrete projects. There will be an increasing recognition of the need to look at how projects interact and to build this interaction into the planning process. This will also necessitate increased cross-sector activity.

These changes are already taking place. The growth of the Global Environment Facility is one example of this change, although this body has so far failed to recognize the full implications of what such cross-sectoral activity involves, in terms of issues such as democratization and community participation, particularly in its biodiversity programmes.[2] The changing profile of the UN is another example of this trend. Although the change from a strong development base to an emphasis on peacekeeping and disaster relief is intended to reflect the changing nature of the world after the collapse of the Soviet system, it also reflects the UN's own failure in development. In particular, its strong sectoral bias has proved to be incapable of changing to meet the need for cross-sectoral development.

Coupled with these changes is the remodelling of the role of national governments. On one level there is a trend towards more open and democratic government. A report on democratic trends classified countries according to whether they have free and fair elections, protection of civil liberties, multi-party legislature, an uncontrolled press etc, and classified them accordingly as free, partly free or not free. A total of 74 were classified as free, 63 as partly free and 53 as not free, most of the last category being in Africa.[3] Many of those in the first two categories would have been classified as not free ten years ago, and several of these were the target government in political empowerment struggles. Hence there is a new political arena developing in which to place community participation. At the same time the nature of government is changing and becoming more complex, influenced to a large degree by the growth of new technologies, although it is also facing up to new economic realities. It is working from a relatively smaller resource base, in terms of available per capita expenditure and the amount which can be bought for this amount of money. These problems are causing stresses in the structure of government which are being felt everywhere, but are particularly acute in the less developed countries, where they are accompanied by a lack of human resources.

All of these changes affect communities and require an effective community participation strategy if they are to succeed. The present indications are that this is not happening. The most vocal solution to the current crisis, driven by the multilateral development and finance agencies and some western countries, is privatization. The World Bank, for example, argues that countries need to free themselves of many traditional roles in nationalized industries. Thus they need to:

- manage infrastructure like a business, not a bureaucracy;
- induce competition – directly if feasible, indirectly if not; and
- give users and other stakeholders a strong voice and real responsibility.[4]

The areas concerned are those most closely linked to community involvement and the result is yet another redefinition of the role and nature of community participation, this time in a predominantly urban context. Communities are being redefined as collections of individual consumers, able to achieve participation through the market place. This narrow view of participation has already been attempted through the privatization programme in the UK and has failed. It has resulted in a reduced level of accountability and a widening of the gap between rich and poor. If this is the situation in a country with a high GDP, then its impact on countries with a low GDP, where the power of the consumer is minimal, could be disastrous.

There is a need to assess and, if necessary, counter this move towards an unfettered global market place, which can only exacerbate the North–South divide. At the same time, a balance between the public and private sectors must be encouraged. Community participation is the key to achieving this balance, but this requires a much clearer understanding of the role and nature of community participation than has existed to date. It requires an understanding of the way in which a community, comprising perhaps only a few hundred people, can interact at a variety of levels which extend from their own small area through to the national and international arenas.

The starting point in building this understanding begins with the relationship between the community and the government. Community participation in many ways challenges the western system of democracy generally, but particularly the Westminster system. This is not to say it seeks to replace the system, but it does seek, at the very least, to supplement it and possibly to change it. The debate on extra-parliamentary activity is not new. In the UK:

> 'The Skeffington Report includes many of the arguments of the participatory school in stressing the need for involvement outside elections and emphasising the educative role of participation ... [which] would also seem to oppose the view of the representative school, (eg Dahl) in seeing the complexity of society in requiring more, not less, participation'.[5]

This approach has been rejected and the government argues strongly that the expression of people's views should take place through parliament. Yet the same government, in its aid programmes which have a strong bias towards community management, is imposing on developing countries a form of extra-parliamentary community involvement which it refuses to accept in its own country.

This is a perspective which earlier research has failed to address satisfactorily. Why is there such a need for extra-parliamentary participation in countries which are either free or partly free? One argument is that, with limited resources, communities have to become actively involved in managing projects if they are to improve their situation. This is essentially a means approach to community participation. Yet those same researchers will argue, on an intellectual level, that they support empowerment and the ends approach. This is a contradiction. The reality is that the question of why community participation is necessary in free and partly free societies has not been addressed in any detail. That is the purpose of this chapter, because it is only when this is understood that it is possible to understand the nature of the contradictions in the existing approaches to community participation.

Essentially, governments everywhere are suffering from a crisis of confidence because they are no longer able to meet the rising expectations of their citizens. Although there are exceptions, most countries are undergoing a structural change from high growth, resource consuming societies to managed growth, managed resource societies. Clearly the stresses on government will be greatest where people do not have a high standard of living, as this is where the pressures will be greatest, but the underlying problems are the same. All levels of government will be affected, but the effect will be greatest at a local level, as this is where the resource constraints affect people's lives most directly. This explains the centrality of community participation in urban management. This chapter explores the changes taking place at local (municipal) government level and takes South Africa as a case study.

MUNICIPAL GOVERNMENT IN LESS DEVELOPED COUNTRIES

At the municipal level the issue which reflects these concerns, and which can therefore be used to explore the nature of the changing relationships, is that of the provision of physical infrastructure. There are three major systems of local government structures in less developed countries. Two of these are strongly influenced by colonial occupation by the British and the French. The third is that used in Latin America, which is similar to the US model, but with a Spanish influence. There are many differences between them.[6] However, in terms of the relevance to this debate, the two major differences between them are (1) the relationship between the legislature and the executive and (2) the relationship between central and local government.

On the first, 'Latin American municipal governments tend to organize themselves politically between the executive and the legislative. The first is usually assigned to a single body (the mayor or intendent) and the second to a collective body (a council chamber)'.[7] Often 'the legislative body is subordinate to the municipal executive'.[8] In terms of the relationship between central and local government, the Latin American system has two characteristics. The first is a linkage between the legislative side of municipal government and party machines,[9] based on a system of patronage. The second is the strong influence of what Herzer and Pirez call the dominant sector of local society over the executive and employees, whose careers are often dependent on being receptive to this sector.[10]

The French system also has a dual elective system, which is dominated by the chief executive (the mayor) but, in terms of the relationship between central and local government, the linkage (with the system as operated in developing countries) is much more bureaucratic. Thus 'The devolution of power to local government (in francophone countries) . . . operates within a well established financial and administrative system that continues to maintain tight control [from the centre]'.[11]

Under the British system the two arms of the local authority are more distinct with 'the [elected] legislative arm (or council) concerned with policy formulation; and the executive arm concerned with the implementation of the policies and composed of administrative and professional staff'.[12] On the relationship between central and local government the British system is different again from the other two. Here '. . . a number of important Anglophone countries [among developing nations] already enjoyed a considerable degree of financial freedom as well as a wide range of permissive functions at the level of local councils'.[13]

The case study material used to explore the changing structure of local government is drawn predominantly from South Africa. This country is generally similar to other anglophone colonies, which operate 'an urban administration system . . . derived from the British local administrative system'.[14] However, in its local government reform of 1982, in which it attempted to establish autonomous Black Local Authorities to manage the African townships, the government set up a structure which was similar to the form of government operated in Latin America. This makes it a useful study area for the exploration of municipal government. The theoretical analysis then uses the British based model of local government, but the findings and conclusions are considered to be relevant to different operational systems.

Before the Royal Commission of 1925–1929, most of the functions of local government in Britain had related to social infrastructure such as education, watch committees, small holdings and care of the mentally defective. This emphasis on social services remains strong in England (for example, following the local government reforms of 1974, the provision of social infrastructure again became the dominant function) and this influences the way in which many British researchers view local government in less developed countries (as illustrated by the earlier quotations).

The incorporation of physical infrastructure management into the local authorities arises from two distinct roots, one in public health and one in transportation. As a result of an investigation into the poor laws in the mid-1880s a relationship began to emerge between disease and the urban environment. This was established as an incontrovertible link by Chadwick's report of 1842.[15] Chadwick recommended improved sanitation (water supply and sewerage) controlled by a central authority. This mobilized local authorities who, although balking at the cost of service provision, were not prepared to have centralized control for fear that this would mean the loss of local government.[16] The result was the Public Health Act 1875, in which local government retained the management of water supply and sanitation, but central government took legislative responsibility.

Transportation was different. Here, according to Onslow, it was only the county councils and the metropolitan boroughs (cities) which were involved heavily in physical infrastructure (meaning in this instance roads and drainage).[17] In this instance it was the growth of (mechanical) vehicular traffic after the First World War which forced a restructuring of the system. The integration and rationalization of all physical infrastructure was finally addressed in the final report on local government reform and three broad technical functions of the large authorities were recognized: roads and bridges; public health; and housing.[18]

In parallel with the debate on management control was a second debate on the financing of infrastructure. With the debate on water supply and sanitation in the mid-1840s, the choice was 'between a joint-stock company deriving its income from those who used its services and a public authority financed by all through the rates and backed by legal statute'.[19] The second option was chosen, although those joint-stock water companies which had already been formed were granted licence to continue. The financial arrangements were codified by the second report on the reform of local government.[20] The major implication of this decision was the separation of the source of income (rates) from the sources of expenditure. The practical result of these local government reforms was the concept of government management by line function, with the key areas being administration (town clerk), finance (treasurer) and physical infrastructure (town engineer). Although powerful in their own right, the latter two were nonetheless subservient to the first.

The local government structure which was set up in the anglophone colonies was based on this model and remains substantially unchanged. However the functional nature of local authorities in less developed countries has changed significantly since then. Thus, as Bubba and Lamba state, 'The main function of local authorities [in less developed countries] is the provision of basic services'.[21] Such a dramatic change must affect local government capacity, particularly when it is accompanied by severe resource constraints. This chapter examines the implications of this change in emphasis, not only on local government, but also in terms of its effect on community participation.

It is important for the development of this argument to examine briefly structures of local government and the differences between local government in developed and less developed countries. The relationship between the local authority, as the statutory agency responsible for urban infrastructure provision, the infrastructure itself, and the different actors involved in the process of providing and operating that infrastructure is discussed. The implications of managing an urban system with a high technical component can then be evaluated.

ROLE OF INFRASTRUCTURE IN MUNICIPAL GOVERNMENT

The increasingly dominant role that infrastructure provision plays in local government in less developed countries can be illustrated by two significant indicators: (1) community needs and priorities; and (2) local government income, expenditure and employment patterns.

On the first of these Stren states that the

'combination of rapid urban population growth, superimposed on a small urban base, is unique to black Africa as a region. In combination with severe economic decline during the 1980s, these two demographic forces have enormously increased the pressure for urban services, particularly in the largest cities across the continent. This "squeeze" between burgeoning urban populations and the services they need is already one of the dramatic crises of the late twentieth century'.[22]

He goes on to state that

> 'Perhaps the most noticeable and enduring problem is the absence or inadequacy of necessary supporting infrastructure and social amenities in most urban areas. Water supply, sewers, roads, electricity, health facilities, and social services are overloaded and unreliable... the environment is dangerously polluted ...[and] a high proportion of roads are in a state of disrepair ...'.[23]

Lee-Smith and Stren have quantified this crisis. After reiterating that 'African cities have been undergoing a serious "service squeeze", according to which larger and larger urban populations are receiving fewer of the services they need, on a per capita basis'[24] they state (quoting Kulaba) that

> 'Dar es Salaam ... during the mid-1980s, was unable to spend more than the equivalent of $5.80 per capita [per annum] on urban services... [while] Nairobi ... [had] an estimated annual expenditure of $68.00 per capita during the same period'.[25]

In respect of the second indicator, this time in a South African context, Figure 4.1 shows the structure of Johannesburg City Council in 1992. Six of the eight strategic business units are concerned either directly with infrastructure provision or with the wider urban physical environment (education and health are the responsibility of the provincial government in South Africa and consequently have a negligible effect on this structure). Of the 21,266 employees, 12,896 are employed in these units. In addition, a significant proportion of the 2352 support staff could also be allocated (in terms of budget) to services for these units.[26] Thus approximately two-thirds of the staff are involved with physical infrastructure and the physical environment. In terms of expenditure, spending on activities related to physical infrastructure provision accounted for in excess of 70% of the total capital expenditure in 1991–1992, and approximately the same in terms of operating expenditure.[27] This was the situation before Johannesburg was formally merged with Soweto. After merging, and particularly when additional informal settlements are included, these percentages are likely to exceed 80%.

Two important points emerge from this analysis. The first relates to the central role of physical infrastructure in urban management. If participation in urban management is to be meaningful, it has to address the issue of participation in the hard area of physical infrastructure. Unless this is done, participation remains selective and therefore prescriptive[28] (this will be illustrated further by the case study of FUNDASAL in El Salvador, discussed in Chapter 8). The second point is that physical infrastructure is still perceived as a collection of services. This cannot always be totally avoided. However, there is a need to develop more integrated approaches to infrastructure provision, particularly in respect of the participatory process. This issue will be explored at some length in the second part of the book.

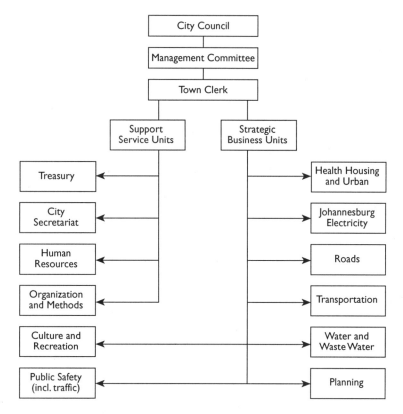

Figure 4.1 *Management structure of Johannesburg City Council*

CONCEPT OF LOCAL GOVERNMENT AS A SUPPORT STRUCTURE FOR THE PROVISION AND MAINTENANCE OF INFRASTRUCTURE

In its idealized form, which was approached briefly by some developed countries in the period after the Second World War, the success of infrastructure as a technical and social service has four facets.

1   There is an accepted, and broadly acceptable, system of local representation, which enables people to express their views and exercise their influence. This facet represents legitimacy of the local government structure as a whole.

2   The financial cost, although significant, is within the means of most of the population, and mechanisms exist for helping those who cannot afford to pay, so that no one should (at least in theory) be forcibly removed from their homes or even lose the use of the services because they cannot afford to pay service charges. The money to operate this local authority is not necessarily collected locally, but

    may be provided by central government. This is the affordability facet.
3   There is an adequate support system for infrastructure operation in terms of management, financial and technical expertise. This facet is described as the institutional capacity.
4   The infrastructure services provided represent the optimum technical solution which provides maximum user convenience. Thus people do not have to worry about the nature of the service, as it does not require them personally to input more than the minimum effort. An example here is the flush toilet. Consumers are rarely interested in the waste water treatment plant unless it is in their immediate vicinity.

These four facets of legitimacy, affordability, institutional capacity and user convenience are all under stress in anglophone countries in Africa, including South Africa. It is this stress which is exposing the weaknesses and deficiencies of local government structures in those countries and encouraging the move towards greater community participation. Thus any analysis of community participation in local government in these countries has to address the impact of this stress. One way to do this is by exploring the way in which a local authority actually supports the provision and maintenance of infrastructure.

Departments within local authorities are traditionally seen as having independent line functions, but these are primarily operational structures. If the local authority is viewed from a different perspective, namely in its role as a provider and manager of physical infrastructure services, then this structure is inappropriate. A more logical view is one which depicts the functional nature of the system more effectively. This is illustrated in Figure 4.2. To supply and manage services, the local authority is provided with legal responsibility (from central government) for the provision of various services and is mandated by the users (rate-payers) to do this. This is the political centre which then regulates three separate management functions.

The first function is to plan, design and develop both the urban environment and the infrastructure to support that environment. This requires a level of technical expertise, a part of which may be found outside the organization (ie with professional consultants and contractors). The second function is the effective management of the infrastructure and the regulation of the urban planning process. This requires adequate human resources across a range of areas (eg technical, financial and managerial). The third function is that of financial planning. This in turn has two components, the raising of capital and amortizing of the loan and the provision of funds for ongoing management.

This concept of functional centres highlights the importance of a variable which had not previously been considered in any detail, namely the role of different actors in the development process. In developed countries, under the British local government system described earlier, the role of the actors can be clearly defined. Here the local council and its officers dominate the decision-making process, constrained only by the limitations imposed by central government in terms of legislation and the specific authority's own financial capacity. This control exists because the

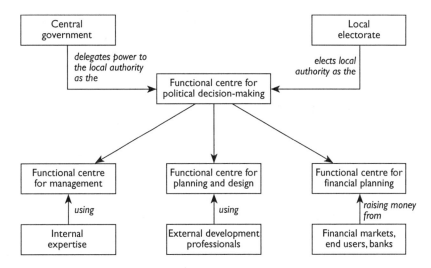

Figure 4.2 *Functional centres for the provision of urban infrastructure in developing countries*

local authority has, at least in theory, both *de jure* and *de facto* power, the latter arising from its financial independence and the credibility of the process through which it is elected. Thus although it may be influenced by other parties, such as financial institutions, it cannot normally be dictated to by them.

Coupled with this definite control there is an adequate supply of skills to manage the infrastructure once it is built. This means that the other actors have specific roles. Thus the consulting planner or engineer, for example, has a clear brief, namely to produce a technical design using, in the engineer's case, the best available technology. This is done in the knowledge that the operation and maintenance of the project will be handled by the local authority and that the latter has the capability to carry out that function. The technical professional must then ensure only that the construction cost is minimized and that the project, as built, meets the technical specification. In South Africa these roles change and this affects the capacity of the local authorities to carry out their functions effectively.

These functional centres represent four components of the management structure for urban infrastructure. Each of these components then has a critical facet of management associated with it, which summarizes the quintessential reasons for the success of the urban management system in developed countries.

1   The political centre. There is an accepted, and broadly acceptable, system of local representation, which enables people to express their views and exercise their influence. This facet represents the legitimacy of the local government structure as a whole. In South African towns this was achieved artificially by excluding the majority of the population who might oppose the system.

2   The financial planning centre. The financial cost, although significant,
    is within the means of most of the residents. Again, in South Africa
    this was achieved artificially by excluding the poorer sectors of the
    population. The money to operate this local authority is not
    necessarily collected locally, but may be provided by central
    government. This is the affordability facet.
3   The management centre. There is an adequate support system for
    infrastructure operation and maintenance in terms of management,
    financial and technical expertise. This is the institutional capacity
    facet.
4   The planning and design functional centre. The infrastructure services
    provided represent the optimum technical solution which provides
    maximum user convenience. Thus people do not have to worry about
    the nature of the service, as it does not require them personally to
    input more than the minimum of effort. An example here would be
    the flush toilet, where consumers are not interested in what happens
    to the waste, except perhaps when the treatment plant is in their
    immediate vicinity. This is the user convenience facet of management.

INFRASTRUCTURE PROVISION IN LESS DEVELOPED COUNTRIES

The description just given represents an idealized situation. In the UK, where
the model originated, 'the twentieth century saw a steady transfer of
functions from local to central government',[29] which accelerated after 1974.[30]
Before 1974, however, the provision of urban infrastructure was probably
the least affected of the local authority's services (in terms of managerial
responsibility) and this is also true for many less developed countries,
including white South Africa. From the perspective of infrastructure
provision, this idealized situation is considered a valid base from which to
begin the comparison with the *de facto* situation in less developed countries.

The international literature quoted highlights two key issues, namely,
institutional capacity and financial capacity, and views these as the major
problems of local government in less developed countries. However,
following the construct developed earlier that infrastructure is becoming
the dominant component of local government, this leads to a different
perspective, which is supported by the South African case studies.

The reality is that all four facets of the provision and implementation of
urban infrastructure described earlier (legitimacy, affordability, institutional
capacity and user convenience) are under pressure in anglophone countries
in Africa. As such, they may be termed areas of stress in the management of
infrastructure in these countries. In the African townships in South Africa
all four of the facets of urban management came under stress simultaneously with the establishment of self-contained, self-financing black local
authorities. However, it was only when these stresses were analysed in
conjunction with the changing roles of the different actors that the reasons
for the failure of the urban management system became clear.

The most obvious reason for the failure was that the local authority in these areas lacked legitimacy. This lack of legitimacy took two forms. The first was political and is described in detail in the second part of the book. This led to the growth of community-based organizations who challenged the political status quo. The second arose from the inability of the local authority to deliver adequate services. Some reasons for this, which relate primarily to the capacity of the local authority, have been described by Bubba and Lamba[31] when discussing the urban management system in Kenya. All of these reasons are equally valid in South African townships. However, these could be described as internally generated constraints. The South African study identified a second set of constraints which are externally generated.

The effect of the decreasing fiscal base of local authorities, and the subsequent reduction in their financial independence, meant that the leverage of the financial institutions who provide the capital infrastructure projects was greatly increased. This in turn restricted the ability of the local authority to raise further loans through conventional sources. These authorities were then forced to rely increasingly on a limited number of development banks, rather than commercial lending institutions, which increased the external leverage of those institutions even more. Further, once the council structure was weakened through internally generated constraints, more of the parties who previously had a peripheral role in the urban management process, such as parastatals and utility companies, actually became more heavily involved in the decision-making process itself. The lack of legitimacy associated with decreasing power also encouraged the growth of local community-based organizations.

Finally, and of major importance, was the changing role of the technical professionals. The changes taking place in urban management took those professionals beyond technical management and into the arena of decision-making around social issues. In addition, the engineers in particular had to take account of several variables which did not exist before. These included the choice of technical options matched to affordability, the use of different construction techniques (eg labour-intensive construction), and the operation and maintenance capability of the client.

IMPACT OF STRESS AND THE CHANGE IN THE BALANCE OF POWER

These changes relate to a second attribute of the functional centres, which relate to the issue of power. In Figure 4.2 there is a clearly defined power relationship which is consistent with a democratic structure. The changes just described alter the nature of the power relationship significantly. This in turn changes the role of the respective centres from one which is predominantly functional to one where they become loci of power in a struggle for dominance in the decision-making process. The importance of this concept of loci of power emerged from the analysis of the situation in Alexandra township near Johannesburg,[32] which was the focus of a major evaluation exercise to examine the effectiveness of urban upgrading.

Alexandra is an apartheid township, ie it was built for the accommodation of black South Africans who, in the period between 1947 and 1982, were considered only temporary sojourners supplying labour to industry in the country's urban areas. As a result, it was allowed no industry or commerce and was provided only with the minimum of physical and social services. Where it differs from most townships, however, is in its proximity to a major industrial centre, which developed subsequent to its establishment in the northern suburbs of Johannesburg. This made it one of South Africa's most desirable areas for Africans in terms of proximity to work opportunities.

Alexandra was established as a dormitory suburb for whites in 1905, with 338 stands of just over 1 ha in size.[32] When these failed to sell, due to a lack of amenities and the distance from central Johannesburg, it was subdivided into 2308 stands of approximately 1000m², and re-proclaimed as a black settlement in 1912. By 1958 the population had grown to 96,000. Pressure had been building up since the early 1940s to remove the people of Alexandra to Soweto, south of Johannesburg. In the 1960s the peri-urban board responsible for the administration of Alexandra instituted a policy of compulsory purchase of freehold properties, coupled with the forced removal to other townships of those unable to prove ownership, which resulted in a population reduction to 40,000 by 1972. The policy of the government during this period became the conversion of Alexandra into a township of hostels for migrant workers.

This policy was rescinded in 1979, when the government decided that Alexandra would be replanned for the accommodation of (the remaining) landowners and other qualified families. By this time the population had again increased to 90,000. Thus began a protracted struggle between residents and the state, exacerbated by the rent increases of 1993 onwards. In 1986 residents created a zone of people's power in Alexandra, designed to challenge, rather than merely oppose, state power. Street committees and people's courts were formed and Alexandra effectively became autonomous, although this was a temporary situation. The township was rapidly cordoned off, troops were moved in and the local leadership went underground. People's power was finally crushed by the national State of Emergency in June 1986. The re-imposition of state control meant the resurrection of the redevelopment plan, whereby Alexandra would be upgraded to create a model township for qualified residents.

A R150M programme of infrastructure redevelopment was planned, under the nominal control of the Alexandra City Council. However, like many black local authorities, Alexandra suffered from severe resource constraints, both in terms of personnel and access to a strong revenue base. The legal responsibilities of central government were also much stronger than for adjacent white municipalities, which limited their decision-making capacity. There was not always a quorum of councillors available because of resignations through grassroots pressure, which made the role of the chief executive (termed the administrator) more powerful than the town clerk of a white municipality. In addition, the unrest of the mid-1980s placed the township under military control, so that all civic decisions had to be co-ordinated with the military authorities.

As a result, the project was managed by the technical consultant, but strongly influenced by a variety of different parties, many with widely divergent interests and all pursuing their own agenda. These actors included:

- the Alexandra Council;
- the army commander responsible for security in the Alexandra township;
- provincial (ie regional) government departments;
- two adjacent white municipalities;
- central government departments;
- the parastatal electricity supply company;
- two local community civic organizations;
- several local non-political organizations;
- the Development Bank of Southern Africa as a funding agency;
- several sets of development professionals;
- a non-governmental organization, providing support to one of the civic groups;
- the construction company.

The impact of such a proliferation of parties was to fragment the process of decision-making, as the different actors focused on the needs of the four different functional centres as independent problem areas, without reference to the management structure as a whole. This affected the balance of power and control over the decision-making processes around infrastructure provision, leading to a change in the relationship between the various centres to one which is illustrated in Figure 4.3. This change in turn affected the areas of stress described earlier, namely

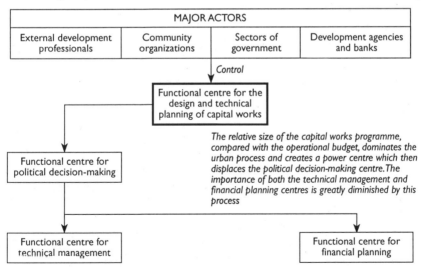

Figure 4.3 *Impact of capital expenditure on the relationship between functional centres*

the facets of legitimacy, affordability, institutional capacity and user convenience. This was exacerbated by the way in which the different actors perceive their own priorities in this changing situation.

Thus the community organizations concentrated on the political centre, where the issue was legitimacy. Implicit in this approach was a perception that creating legitimate structures would also enable people's needs to be satisfied. This assumption was questionable given the resource constraints which existed. The major financial institutions such as the World Bank and, in South Africa, the Development Bank of Southern Africa, have been concerned increasingly with the need to ensure institutional capacity, thereby concentrating on the management centre, and this was clearly illustrated by the Alexandra experience and the priorities set for the evaluation, which was funded by the Development Bank of Southern Africa.

The engineering approach was to concentrate on the issue of affordability, which fell within the financial planning centre.[33] This was also the area of interest of parastatals and utility companies, who were interested in promoting their own particular service. Although concerned primarily with different functional centres, the irony was that all of the different groups actually exercised their influence through actions in the technical planning and design centre, using this functional centre to satisfy their own agenda.

None of these groups examined the effect that the output from this centre had on the constituency that they were all, nominally, serving, ie the community. In taking this attitude they ignored the primary facet of this centre, which is user convenience.

User convenience is a concept used to describe the social, political and cultural acceptability of the project. This view was distorted by the proliferation of the agendas described here, but compounded by a further factor. The South African research revealed a situation where the technical professionals were taking an increasingly dominant role in the decision-making process. Under these circumstances it was their choice of levels of service which drove the debate as the community-based organizations and their advisers lacked the expertise to counter the technical arguments effectively.

It is the combination of all these factors which limits the capacity of a local authority to manage urban infrastructure provision and which leads to the decline of the urban management capacity.

1   The problems with councils described by Bubba and Lamba[34] result in a loss of political credibility.
2   The involvement of different actors in the decision-making moves the focus of the project across to the technical side of the project. Here the council is weak and outside parties are seen to be increasingly responsible for decisions. The community feels excluded, leading to a further loss of credibility, not only of the council but, equally importantly, of the local government system itself.
3   User convenience, which reflects the social impact of the services, has been excluded from the process, preventing the expression of local needs and aspirations as well as control. This alienates the local community even further and makes them more antagonistic to the local authority structure.

IMPACT OF STRESSES ON THE URBAN MANAGEMENT SYSTEM

The South African study of local authorities on which this chapter is based identified four components of the local authority management system as being central to the successful provision and maintenance of physical infrastructure in developed countries, namely, legitimacy, affordability, institutional capacity and user convenience. In the African townships of South Africa, all four of these areas were placed under severe stress simultaneously. This affected the structure of the urban management system in a manner which fundamentally changed that structure. This process of change adversely affects the community in three ways, all of which justify a new role for communities in the management of the urban environment. This can only be achieved through meaningful and effective community participation. The different types of impact are described in the following sections.

Nature of the Decline in the Urban Management System

This complex process, which is illustrated in Figure 4.4, occurred in the following manner. Firstly, the stresses caused a weakening of the political power of the local authority which, because these stresses came from four separate functional centres, could not be solved by addressing problems in only one of them (eg legitimacy or institutional capacity). This initial weakening of the management structure then opened the way for other actors to become involved and strengthened the role that those actors could play in the decision-making process around infrastructure provision. Again, it was the differing nature of the four areas of stress which was a complication, as weaknesses were exposed and actors involved on four different fronts.

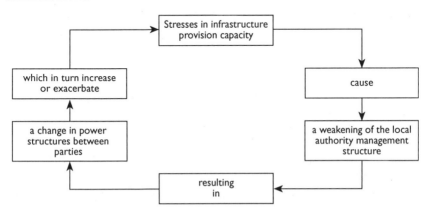

Figure 4.4 *Cycle of local authority fragmentation*

Because these actors had specialist interest and knowledge, once they were in a position to influence decisions they had a tendency to view the problem (of service infrastructure provision and operation) from their own particular perspective. Limited resources meant priority setting in the allocation of resources, but the different actors perceived these priorities differently. In many instances the solution proposed by the technical professionals was that which was implemented.

Not only does this process exclude the community at large, who are the people directly affected by these decisions, but the new decision-making process which results from the growth in the power of external, non-elected actors serves to alienate the wider community from the entire local government process. Hence the four areas of stress, viewed as independent problem areas, become arenas of debate around resources allocation and priorities which cannot possibly meet the needs of all parties. This leads to a vicious circle of local authority fragmentation which explains the political necessity for community participation. This crisis of management also leads to the following two fundamental changes.

Loss of User Convenience

One major difference between urban and rural areas in less developed countries is the differing perspectives on service provision. In rural areas the starting point is generally either negligible or, at best, the most basic of services. This means that any service is likely to represent an improvement on the extant condition. In urban areas the situation is very different. There the basis for measurement is a very high level of service which provides optimum user convenience. New services in poor areas are therefore likely to represent a loss of user convenience, even if this exists predominantly as a perception for people who do not themselves have any services. The debate about affordability, subsidy and levels of service is complex and will be discussed later. The critical issue is that there needs to be a mechanism for reconciling quantitative and qualitative perceptions of services which can only be achieved with the full involvement of the community.

Discrepancy Between Capital and Recurrent Expenditure

In western local authorities the operational budget is significantly greater than the capital budget, whereas the financial capacity of the authority is such that it is capable of motivating financial institutions to allow it full control over the capital budget. In many less developed countries the situation is reversed.

The estimated, internally generated, income of the Alexandra City Council for the year 1990–1991 was R11.0M, whereas the estimated expenditure for the same year was R49.1M, giving a ratio of income to expenditure of 22.5%. Because the central government expected black local authorities to be financially self-sufficient, there was no central government support, but this untenable situation would have to change. In 1990 the council already had an external loan debt of R198M, whereas the accumulated deficit on the operating budget to the end of June 1991 was R117.2M. This situation is not sustainable and the result is twofold. On one level central government becomes the main provider of funds for the operational budget, most of which is spent on salaries and general expenses. More important here, however, is the fact that Alexandra City Council is incapable of generating any income to pay for capital works, making it totally dependent on outside funding. An upgrading budget of R150M therefore becomes the main focus of the struggle for power because it is in determining how and where this money will be spent that the greatest political mileage is to be gained. In this situation the council becomes marginalized, the balance of power changes and the situation illustrated by Figure 4.3 develops.

The functional centre for the design and technical planning of capital works dominates the urban process and creates a power centre which displaces the political decision-making centre. This challenges the basis of conventional democratic structures and demands new approaches to community involvement in the decision-making process. In addition, this situation demands a new approach by community organizations. They can no longer concern themselves with gaining power over decisions affecting capital works alone. The new relationship shown in Figure 4.3 means that the importance of both the technical management and financial planning (for operation) centres are greatly diminished. This was illustrated in Alexandra where the operation and maintenance budget for physical infrastructure was cut by approximately 40% in real terms over the period from 1986 to 1991, a period of intensive spending on capital works. The communities are thus going to have to concern themselves increasingly with the technical aspects of urban management which go far beyond the World Bank notion of residents as consumers.

IMPLICATIONS FOR COMMUNITY PARTICIPATION

Under these circumstances the view that community participation is about community management and control is neither realistic nor feasible. New forms of community participation are required which fall outside those driving the debate in Chapters 2 and 3. To a degree this is now being recognized by the growing support for stakeholder analyses. This appears to provide an implicit acceptance that the duality concept is invalid, although the reality is less sanguine.

The concept of stakeholders flows from work carried out in participatory rural appraisal (see Chapter 13) and is linked to community management. The basis of the concept is that community is a poor word to define an interest group involved in a specific activity. What is needed is to focus more specifically on the target group, who are then considered the primary stakeholders. At the same time the impact of other parties is assessed but, because these are not the recipients, they are secondary stakeholders.

The replacement of the term community by the term primary stakeholder is fraught with pitfalls. Community, for all of its faults, ensures that the debate takes place at a local level. The term primary stakeholder has no such guarantee. The system is being developed by funding agencies in the North, driven by the UK's Overseas Development Administration (ODA), and the aid agencies define who are to be primary and who are to be secondary stakeholders. This has three serious flaws. The first relates to the perception of the ODA. This reflects the views of a specific political party (the Conservative party), which sees a citizen's participatory rights predominantly in terms of a consumer of a service. This means that it has a specific interpretation of the term primary stakeholder, which does not necessarily correspond to that in the country and community concerned.

The second flaw derives from the first, but is wider in its implications. The use of the term stakeholder fails to address the issue of power. The term community has to address the socio-political reality. The term primary stakeholder seeks to operate in a socio-economic environment which excludes political debate. This is in line with the trend towards community management, but it is potentially manipulative of recipient communities and has serious implications for meaningful community participation.

The third, and most serious, flaw in this redefinition of community is the way in which it sees the relationship between the project and the primary stakeholder as pre-eminent. This is an outmoded concept which does not take account of the centrality of sustainability in an increasingly interactive global environment. Primary stakeholders are not limited to those directly affected by the project when that project affects the wider environment. The manner in which primary and secondary stakeholders are defined is therefore invalid. There has to be a recognition that other parties are necessary for the success of major projects, but that they also have interests of their own to put forward which can be equally important. To classify them as secondary is simplistic and inaccurate. There are situations where this type of relationship is valid, but this is not a universally applicable structure.

So new forms of relationship are required. It is necessary to draw the external actors into the system more fully so that they too are made accountable for their actions. In making these changes the community's role will also change significantly. The community is no longer the central focus, but is an integral part of an intricate network which expands outwards into the national and international arenas. This is the basis of the alternative approach to community participation which evolved in South Africa during the early 1990s. This differs significantly from existing approaches and will be termed negotiated development.

This new approach was not limited to municipal government or to physical infrastructure alone. The same circumstances of increased stress and changing power dynamics which brought about this new approach to community participation at a local level were found in many areas of life in South Africa. The problem of achieving biodiversity objectives in rural areas of high population densities, which require multiple land-use practices, was an example of another situation where this approach was practised. Here again the conventional approaches, such as integrated rural development, had failed. Community management was not appropriate, just as it was inappropriate for urban upgrading.

There is now a fourth approach to community participation, which appears to have particular relevance in urban management. Certainly this approach evolved from a need for improved urban infrastructure, unlike the other three, and could therefore be assumed to be the most appropriate. However, it is not the intention of this book to make this claim, ie to say that negotiated development is the only approach, or even the best approach, to community participation in the urban management process, because it too is linked to a specific geographical, cultural and political surround. The reality is that all four approaches to community participation, ie community development, political empowerment, community management and negotiated development, continue to have successful applications.

Given this reality, the accepted tenet of a single universally applicable form of community participation becomes untenable. Its full implications were never analysed and the increasing variety and complexity of situations where community participation is required illustrate this and show it to be flawed. What is required is a new understanding of community participation which places the different approaches in context and links them to given situations in a way which is understandable and predictable. This requires a coherent and replicable structure. Only when this has been achieved can the most appropriate approach be linked to a specific situation. Creating such linkages and developing a coherent and replicable structure forms the basis of Part 2 of the book.

PART

Theory of
Community Participation

Characteristics of Community Development

INTRODUCTION

Part 1 of this book describes three distinct analyses of the underlying causes of community participation. The first describes participation as a response to different global economic regimes; the second as a need for control in a project dominated environment; and the third as a response to the failure of conventional government. Each of these strands highlights important features of the community participation process, but none of them provides a complete analysis. Each is constrained in some way, whether by pre-conceived ideas, be they ideological, economic or rational, or simply by inadequate experience and understanding. This second part of the book seeks to draw out the key features of the different strands and, in conjunction with new research material, show how they can be integrated to produce a common surround which can provide an understanding of the community participation process.

A useful starting point is the original strand, which provided the paradigm approach model. Researchers have drawn two conclusions from this model about the fundamental nature of community participation. The first conclusion was that one form of community participation may supersede another. This later formed the basis for the premise that there was a single, universally applicable form of community participation. The second conclusion was that the central feature of the community participation process comprised a dualistic relationship between the community and the state. Neither of these conclusions is valid. The book identified four different approaches to participation. It showed, and will continue to demonstrate, that each of these approaches is appropriate in different situations.

This new analysis of the paradigm approach model does not invalidate the research behind the model; it simply means that the conclusions which were drawn from that research were flawed, due primarily to the pervasive influence of the global geo-political situation. This political aspect was polarizing the debate and influencing the conclusions. In viewing it from a post-Cold War perspective, it becomes clear that the underlying research is extremely valuable because the paradigm approach model illustrates two important facets of community participation. The first is simply that different approaches to community participation do exist, a simple concept but one with wide ramifications.

The second facet relates to the way in which it places community participation within a wider surround. Where the paradigm approach model failed, and the cause of the misleading hypothesis, was in its choice of that surround. It is the use of an economic paradigm as the basis for describing the surround that is clearly inadequate for this purpose. The critical issue in determining what governs the appropriateness of the different approaches is the nature of the wider surround within which communities find themselves operating.

So what is the real surround and how is this to be identified? The alternative hypothesis, proposed here, is that different approaches are appropriate in different situations. If this is the case, then it follows that an approach which is appropriate in a given situation would be successful. Equally, it would be unsuccessful if applied in a situation which was inappropriate. Existing analysis has focused on the operation of one existing approach (community development) in inappropriate situations, looking at why it fails. This provides a justification for the use of a different approach in those situations, but is not particularly useful as objective research. The alternative is to identify what it is which makes different approaches successful, as this will then provide information on the surround. By doing this for different approaches a broader understanding of the wider surround can be assembled. This is the approach taken here.

To date, four different approaches have been identified: community development, political empowerment, community management and negotiated development. Three of these will be evaluated in the three chapters which follow. The fourth, community management, will not be evaluated separately. However, it will be examined briefly in this chapter, together with community development, and incorporated into Chapter 8, where the findings of the three evaluations will be integrated. In each of the following three chapters the methodology adopted will be the same. The approach will be analysed from a historical perspective and specific characteristics will be identified which describe the important features of the surround within which the approach operates successfully. No attempt will be made at this stage to define the surround; this will evolve from a comparison of the different characteristics of the three approaches. The first approach to be evaluated is community development.

COMMUNITY DEVELOPMENT APPROACH TO PARTICIPATION

Stohr[1] states that community development had its roots in the UK and the US, where there was a need to assist with the social needs of the urban poor in the industrializing cities. These roots were in community work which 'in its modern sense in Britain was begun in the nineteenth century by upper- and middle-class idealists and reformers who sought to ameliorate the often appalling conditions under which working-class people lived in the new industrial towns'.[2] Batten goes on to say that

'Such people's material needs at that time were obvious and specific, and many of them were too poor, too ignorant, and too disorganized to do very much to help themselves. In this context the newly-formed social agencies necessarily took the initiative in planning and providing for people'.[3]

In these developed countries community development has evolved and retains not only its identity, but also its relevance as a primary vehicle through which social change is enacted at a local level. The strength of community development in this regard was discussed in Chapter 2. In making the transfer to developing countries the assumption was made that community development could be applied to a wide variety of projects, without consideration of context. For example, Warren states that

'As a method of bringing about social change, community development serves alike in situations that are predominantly rural and preindustrial and in situations that are urban and industrialised [and, furthermore] community development is a widely applied method of bringing about social change that extends beyond the US'.[4]

This is a historical misconception, which is illustrated by the examples given in Chapter 2.

The reason for this type of misconception stems from the absence of a sound theoretical structure. This is not to denigrate the theoretical work which has been produced by workers such as Batten and Biddle in the UK, and Cary, Sanders and Holdcroft in the US. All of these researchers, however, are working within a specific paradigm which reflects a specific viewpoint of democracy and the relationship between the state and its citizens. Such a perspective might be a convenient starting point for an exploration of the subject, but it tends to pre-determine the causes of failure by linking these to political status. What is needed is to broaden the perspective and identify the features of the approach which are to be found in all successful projects, irrespective of specific relationships, as these are the key issues of universal relevance. The starting point in this search is the theoretical basis of community development.

COMMUNITY DEVELOPMENT THEORY

FitzGerald states that 'The term community development gives a form suited to the twentieth century to [the] long-standing tendency of membership of a group to act together to improve the life-style of the group as a whole'.[5] Whereas previously this may have occurred through movement to new areas or emigration, this became increasingly difficult over time and greater emphasis has, therefore, been placed on in situ improvement. It is this specific focus on internally generated improvement which links community development so strongly with the concept of self-help.

Unfortunately, people attempting to improve their existing situation have limited freedom to act independently. Communities, and particularly urban communities, are increasingly constrained in their freedom of action by bureaucracies of government authorities and by external economic forces. It will be shown later that the major failing of community development has been its inability to explore this relationship between community and government in detail and in an objective manner. Instead the debate has focused almost exclusively on the needs of communities as semi-independent entities. As an example, Moughtin *et al* give four advantages of community development as being:

- that it allows development in response to felt needs of communities, thereby increasing their self-reliance, capability, confidence and awareness. . .
- that [community development activities] involve the poor in improving their living conditions . . .
- that [community development activities] complement government development efforts . . .
- that it stimulates local leadership and initiatives.[6]

The broad consensus deriving from this view is probably best illustrated by the definition of Dunham,[7] which views community development as the 'organised efforts to improve the conditions of community life and the capacity for community integration and self-direction'. At the same time, however, because the analysis of community development has failed to explore the full implications of the relationship between governments and communities this has provided the space for a totally different interpretation which has allowed communities to be manipulated by government and opened the way for the valid criticisms levelled by de Kadt and others and quoted in Chapter 2.[8] This is typified by the UN definition from 1956, which states that

> 'The term community development has come into international usage to connote the processes by which the efforts of the people themselves are united to those of government authorities to improve the economic, social and cultural conditions of communities, to integrate these communities into the life of the nation and to enable them to contribute fully to national progress'.[9]

A major reason for the increasing dominance of the second definition lies in the communities themselves. The target communities are by definition those facing serious problems. Thus they are often disempowered or disenfranchized, or alternatively they may be embittered or disillusioned. To be able to articulate their needs and direct them effectively they often need external assistance to identify, plan and organize remedial action. For

> 'while it can and does happen that autonomous groups within a community may decide on a project and carry it through independently, many factors mitigate against this succeeding and generally the process seems to require the help of employed initiators "to create sufficiently favourable conditions for successful group action without in any way infringing on group autonomy . . .".'[10]

Historically, this initiation has been the responsibility of the community development worker who, in turn, was an employee of government. There are many different types of support which can be offered to communities however. The view of needs and priority assessment adopted by the community development worker can differ significantly from person to person, depending on the discipline from which they originally come. Thus a sociologist will interpret a situation differently to an anthropologist, a planner or an economist.

It is this set of issues (the historical centrality of the community development worker; the internal conflict inherent in being a government employee; and the need to reconcile other professional perspectives and align these with community needs) which has provided the basis for community development theory. Thus the theoretical analysis is strongest when it leaves the conceptual issues and focuses on the practical relationship between the community development worker and the community.

The first important work in this regard was carried out by Batten, who drew a distinction between the directive and non-directive approaches to community development. The former approach is one where a community development agency adopts 'whatever it thinks people need . . . for their own good'.[11] The latter is one where a worker tries to get people 'to decide for themselves what their needs are . . . and how they can best organize, plan, and act to carry their project through'.[12] The aim here is the development and growth of the self. In drawing this distinction, Batten not only emphasized the central role of communities in the decision-making process; he also developed the concept which Moser was to describe 15 years later as the 'means and end approach'.[13] This was an important distinction which retains its relevance to current community development practice. However, it is written within a framework of non-directive community development, where the bulk of the work deals with the role of the community development worker in a non-directive situation. This approach is not always possible or even desirable. Even Batten acknowledged that 'a directive approach may be indicated in crisis situations where material needs predominate and the people are not in a position to help themselves'.[14] In many ways all that this distinction achieved was a widening of the distinction between community development as a support mechanism for 'self-help' and as part of a national development programme.

Sanders, in an attempt to cut through the variety of meanings and definitions which were proliferating by the end of the 1960s, argued that there are four ways in which those involved with community development appear to view it, namely as a process, a method, a programme, or a movement.[15] He then described these in the following way:

> 'Community Development as a Process.
>
> . . . a neutral scientific term subject to a fairly precise definition and measurement expressed chiefly in social relations: changes from a state where one or two people in a small elite within or without the local community make decisions for the rest of the people to a state where people themselves make these decisions about matters of common concern; change from a state of minimum to one of maximum cooperation; change from a state where a few participate to one where many participate; change from a state where all resources and specialists come from outside to one where local people devise methods for maximum use of their own resources.

Community Development as a Method.

... community development as a means to an end, a way of working so that some goal is attained ...The emphasis is on some (specific) end. Central planners, economic developers, and those representing one professional field may look on community development in terms of whether it will or will not help them achieve the concrete ... goals they have in mind.

Community Development as a Programme.

When one adds to the method, which is a set of procedures, some content – such as a list of activities – one moves towards community development as a programme. By carrying out the procedures the activities are supposedly accomplished. An illustration of what this means is the use of a number of small projects as the basis for a wider development programme.

Community Development as a Movement.

For some, community development becomes a crusade, a cause to which they become deeply committed. It is not neutral, like [community development as a] process, but carries an emotional charge. It is dedicated to progress as a philosophical, and not a scientific concept, since progress must be viewed with reference to values and goals that differ under different political and social systems'.[16]

Over the intervening period there has been the move towards project-based development described in Chapter 3. This has resulted in a decline in the potential for community development as a method and its almost total supersedence by community development as a programme. In addition, community development as a movement was never successful, primarily because of the inability of community development to address the wider issues raised by de Kadt[17] and discussed in Chapter 2. As a result, the number of ways of viewing community development was reduced to two, as a programme and as a process. Essentially, the former is goal-orientated, being founded in national development programmes,[18,19] whereas the latter

'is problem orientated at community level, the emphasis being on what happens to people psychologically and in their social relationships, i.e. the emphasis is primarily on human development. Resulting from this philosophy, the means employed in problem solving are considered to be of greater importance than the solution per se'.[20]

In the same way that directive and non-directive approaches both have their relevance in different situations, so it is with community development as a programme and as a process. Both approaches have evolved with time and are still functional and relevant today. A good example of the former is the Aga Khan Rural Support Programme (AKRSP) in northern Pakistan, which is explored in more detail in the following. Here there is a direct linkage to the ideas described by Sanders and the evolutionary path is clearly identifiable. The process approach has undergone a slightly different evolutionary cycle. Although it has been a major feature of many small schemes, it has not expanded in a clearly definable way. Instead it fused with the ideas emerging from the definition framework approach and re-emerged under the new name of community management. However, it will be shown later that both approaches retain strong similarities and have generally similar characteristics.

AGA KHAN RURAL SUPPORT PROGRAMME

The AKRSP was established in 1982 as a non-governmental organization 'to act as a catalyst for the development of the rural people living in the high mountain valleys of [northern Pakistan]'.[21] The experiment in rural development is based on a belief that rural people can improve their economic and social status through organization at a village level and that the key to sustainability in this regard is community participation.[22] One of the most interesting features of the AKRSP, which distinguishes it from earlier community participation programmes, is the degree of pre-planning involved, determining not only the objectives, but developing a clear and detailed strategy for implementation of the programme.

The objectives were fairly broad in themselves.[23] What makes this programme important was the way in which the achievement of these objectives was based on three factors. Firstly, it was linked to a strategic plan. The AKRSP emphasized organization, capital and skills as the essential elements of the strategy, but the attainment of these can be achieved in very different ways. The AKRSP programme chose a co-operative model of rural development as its base,[24] on the grounds that the existing stresses on land and production have already generated a tradition of collective behaviour, albeit for survival, and that this can be harnessed for growth.

Secondly, the AKRSP recognized the centrality of the socio-political surround in determining the success of their programme. This provided a strong element of pragmatism. And, finally, the third crucial factor in the development of the AKRSP programme was the structuring of the model for follow through to implementation. Korten argues that the organization model of rural development involves three basic components (a programme, participants and a support organization) and that the success of a model depends on 'a high degree of fit between programme design, beneficiary needs and the capacity of the assisting organisations'.[25] In their analysis of the AKRSP, Khan and Khan argue that this notion of fit is the central feature of successful projects. Ensuring the achievement of this fit became the basis of the structuring of the AKRSP programme.

The structure of the organizational model, with its emphasis on the key role of the support organization, is what defines this programme as community development. What makes it a success, and separates it from the manipulative model of community development, is the interpretation of community participation and the integration of the support organization into the wider fit with the programme and the organization. Thus

> 'The prospective beneficiaries - small landholders – must participate fully in each stage of the development of a specific program, starting from the articulation of their needs and assessment of their resources. The program has to address those needs of the beneficiaries that increase their capacity for sustainable development. It must offer to the participants outputs that use their resources and assist in making their organization viable. Organization is the vehicle through which the program provides inputs and services and outputs are realized by the participants on a sustainable basis. The program and beneficiary needs have to be welded together through a participatory organization'.[26]

The local organization in the AKRSP was identified as the village organization, which in turn needs to be both legitimate and credible, and two catalysts were identified as being central to the sustainability of a village organization: a village activist and the support organization social organizer. The critical factors in making the programme efficient and effective were considered to be the technical and social capabilities of the support organization. The role of the support organization was identified to include

> 'assessment of needs, identification of the entry point for social organiser and activist, speed and flexibility in management, cost-effectiveness of programme packages, and development and delivery of inputs and services directly related to the outputs the participants expect and need. The key to these capabilities is the learning by doing approach in which innovations are induced in response to and by the experiences and resources of participants'.[27]

The important features of the AKRSP from a community development perspective are given in the following list.

- It can be clearly defined as a programme, designed eventually to benefit almost one million people living in 1230 villages covering an area of 70,000 sq. km.[28]
- It rejects the World Bank economic or incentives model of development in favour of a co-operative model which recognizes the centrality of the socio-political surround.
- There is a clearly identifiable group of prospective beneficiaries.
- The acceptance of the support organization by the local communities clearly benefits from the religious base of the organization.
- The same benefit applies to the government. Because the Muslim religion is so dominant in society, this makes the support organization both more acceptable and less threatening to the government than would probably be so with a western secular development NGO.

CHARACTERISTICS OF COMMUNITY DEVELOPMENT

From this study, coupled with the analysis of theory and practice, a picture emerges of what constitutes successful community development in its broadest sense. A series of characteristics can be identified, which can be divided into different categories. The term characteristic is used here to mean a trait which can give a conceptual identity to community development, thereby allowing it to be compared with other approaches or forms of participation.

In using the word characteristic with respect to community development it should be noted that the term has a meaning which is different from other, more commonly used, indicators such as, for example, the six elements of community development defined by Cary, which provide a generally accepted definition of community development as a process.[29] The characteristics described in the following are broader indicators which have been developed in the course of carrying out this study of community participation.

Community Interaction with Government

In spite of the problems with government described in Chapter 2, many workers, with extensive experience of community development, but who come from very different backgrounds, argue strongly in favour of active involvement by government in community development. Thus, for example, Constantino-David[30] and Ekong and Sekoya[31] argue that certain forms of dependency on government are necessary for successful community development. In fact, Ekong and Sekoya go further than this and state that, for their own particular environment, 'the central government must intervene in the face of appalling conditions of poverty in many villages in Nigeria'.[32] They argue for joint action (between government and NGOs) in community development, as does Kalawole, who stresses the involvement and importance of traditional institutions as well.[33]

It is a reality that government cannot be ignored, if only because it defines the wider framework within which the community participation process operates. Thus it is virtually impossible to place any activity, but particularly those which are physical projects, totally outside the state system. Community development recognizes this, but in a very specific way. Thus it operates on the basis that civil society operates within a democratic state system which is, on balance, just and equitable. A problem arises when the regime is elitist, and this is the condition which has been highlighted by most workers critical of community development. Alternatively, it may simply be that the government is closed, ie it simply refuses to acknowledge any concerns or demands which come from below. There is also a third potential problem area. This arises when the government lacks the capacity to implement and administer its own policies. It is in this situation that the programme and process approaches differ and the distinction between community development and community management begins to emerge.

Community development, practised as a programme, accepts that the government controls the wider decision-making process. Where there is a lack of capacity, then the programme will build structures which are essentially supportive of the government role. This is clearly illustrated by the AKRSP, where

'The superstructure of the state rests on a nominal system of representation, in which the state bureaucracy exercised considerable power without accountability to the people. The decision-making power is now [ie after the implementation of the AKRSP] with the nominal representatives and bureaucrats. The development of Village Organisations (VOs), supported by the AKRSP, is an informal but an entirely participatory institutional arrangement to provide the missing link between the state and the rural poor'.[34]

With community management, on the other hand, the government is willing to see the management process as autonomous, with decisions being made at a local level. Thus the government has little, and sometimes no, direct involvement in the decision-making process surrounding the particular activity. However, it retains control of the political and legislative process, and community management functions within a government framework. The distinction between community development and community management in respect of the government's role is that, in the former situation, government involvement could be described as active, whereas in the latter situation it could be described as passive. In both instances, however, the success of the community participation process is dependent on the government being open to the involvement of people in the decision-making process.

Unfortunately, there are different degrees of openness to confuse the situation. In Pakistan, for example, the government is open to the extent that it allows the AKRSP to function. Yet Waseem, speaking of the same country, argues that 'government sponsored programmes contain in-built mechanisms which enhance the cooption of initiatives and further the interests of members of the bureaucracy who support them'.[35] He maintains that change only takes place if the centre of community action is located outside the state system. This viewpoint is supported by the situation in Karachi, where the urban context provides a different example and where meaningful participation in decision-making appears to be virtually impossible within the state system. In the former situation the government is comfortable with the participation process, whereas the same government is threatened by participation in an urban context. Such a situation was also encountered in South Africa (see Chapter 11). Thus a situation arises where the same government is open to participation in one context but not in another. A community development approach is succeeding in one situation, but empowerment is being promoted as the only effective form of participation in another situation within the same country.

The critical issue arising from the analysis of successful community development is not whether a government is democratic. Rather, it is whether the government is open to the involvement of communities. To be open and interactive with the community there does need to be a degree of responsiveness on the part of the government, but this is a separate issue to the government being representative or legitimate. This aspect of openness then is the first characteristic of both the community development and community management approaches to community participation. In both community development and community management, the degree of community involvement, which reflects the extent of openness, is effectively dictated by government.

Nature of the Decision-making

Historically, successful community development projects have been built around predominantly social issues to which people in a community relate easily. Biddle and Biddle summarized this clearly when they stated that 'Community development makes available to people the experiences that create the social skills needed to deal with each other, with neighbours, with experts, and with the powers that be'.[36] Arnstein also illustrates this when she describes it as 'the strategy by which the have-nots join in determining how information is shared, goals and policies set, tax resources are allocated, programs are operated . . .'.[37] Finally, in looking at community support through training, Srinivasan emphasizes the importance of training sessions being designed to simulate a community level process as closely as possible.[38] This is also supported by the AKRSP experience, where the emphasis is laid on the social and political framework.

Where other components are introduced into the decision-making process, eg the use of technology, these are introduced in such a way as to fit them to this framework. This is illustrated by an example from work on a community development programme in the Winterveld area of South Africa which dealt with a communal water supply.[39] In examining different water supply options the community rejected the notion of amortization, ie the repayment of the capital cost over a period of time using borrowed money, similar to a house loan. Instead they insisted on separating capital and running costs, representing the former as a lump sum and the latter as a monthly charge. In this way each family could be presented with a bill which represented their share of the water supply scheme and a repayment programme could be negotiated on this basis. This approach was possible in that particular situation, but may not have been in an urban environment where the community in question constituted only one part of the wider body being provided with water. Yet the ability to institute such a system of payment was critical to the success of the wider community development programme.

This particular project was one which spanned the divide between community development and community management. It began as part of a wider community development programme in the area, but because of its size became an autonomous project which later existed in its own right. This highlights the second distinction between the two forms. It is probably fair to say that the provision of welfare facilities has been regarded as the most important benefit of community development.[40] This leads back to the second characteristic of community development, namely it is built around predominantly social issues to which people in a community relate easily. With community management on the other hand there is a stronger economic and/or technical component. Nonetheless, the community management project remains clearly identifiable and self-contained.

Community Dynamic

Khan and Khan, discussing the AKRSP programme, make the statement that, generically, the rural poor are not a homogeneous group. Nonetheless they do have a high degree of economic homogeneity and the whole programme is based on the creation of homogeneity at a village level. In this respect the programme has the advantage of a small unit size for the villages. Thus, although the total population of the target area is in excess of 800,000 people, the average village size is only 666 people.[41] The programme is constructed around a village organization formed to take responsibility for the development process and to be eligible to join the programme three-quarters of the households in the same settlement must be members of the village organization.[42] The support of the AKRSP operates through a social organizer who operates in conjunction with a village activist appointed by the village organization committee. The AKRSP approach is a blend of directive and non-directive community development, although the latter predominates. Thus villagers identify and prioritize their programme (the first one of which is funded totally by a grant from the AKRSP), but at the same time the AKRSP has a clear definition of the support services which it can provide. Finally, the benefit of the religious base of the AKRSP should not be underestimated. Most people in the area covered by the programme are Muslim, divided roughly equally into three sects: Sunni, Shia and Ismaili.[43] As Ratcliffe mentions, 'religion plays a major role in the lives of people and pervades almost every facet of society'.[44] In addition, the Ismailis are followers of the Aga Khan, so the programme has resonance in the area. This is also useful in gaining the support of central government, which would be unlikely to allow the same degree of latitude to an external organization. So although there are obvious dangers, and care must be taken not to create the impression of favouritism, these are far outweighed by the advantages.

In a wider arena community development is synonymous with small group work. The basis of non-directive community development is to bring out people's needs and to encourage them to form groups capable of addressing these needs. With community development the process is designed to foster small groups with a shared interest which is strong enough to enable them to work together for the achievement of a specific goal. In this way small pools of homogeneity are created in what may be a larger heterogeneous community. Community management operates in a similar way, but often on a slightly larger scale. This was the case with the Ramogodi water supply, which involved 5000 people. In this situation, however, the risks of community fragmentation become significantly greater than for smaller, more clearly defined community development projects. Alternatively, the target of the community management programme may have a more clearly defined socio-economic classification, eg small farmers, which would provide a stronger form of communal bonding.

Thus the third characteristic, which applies to both community development and community management, is that although there may be a broader national framework defining the objectives of the project or programme, both the community development and community management projects themselves tend to be local, clearly identifiable undertakings operating within a fairly homogeneous base.

Primary Objective of the Community Participation Process

Community development is strongly focused on the needs of the community while functioning within a government framework. When other actors or interests are involved, it is assumed that they are (1) secondary and (2) subservient to either government or community. Thus they become an integral part of the community support programme managed by the community development worker. Again, this is well illustrated by the AKRSP. In addition to the one-time grant for the completion of the village organization's first identifiable project, the AKRSP provides all 'technical assistance in every aspect of the project',[45] together with technical and managerial support, all of which is channelled through the social organizer and the village activist. Thus the fourth characteristic of community development programmes, which also applies to community management projects, is that the satisfaction of community needs dominates the process.

Role of External Actors

The fifth characteristic of community development programmes reflects the very specific nature of the external intervention process, through what Paul calls the 'instrument of participation',[46] namely the community development worker. The dependence of community development on community development workers was illustrated earlier and is indicated by many of the early publications on community development,[47-49] as well as current writing on the subject.[50] In developed countries many community development workers are employed by the local authorities or, if independent, work closely with the local authority. Thus they are linked to the broader institutional framework. This is also often so in developing countries, eg India, except that here the government employer is the national government. Alternatively, they can be employed by the support agency, eg the AKRSP. In all instances, however, the community development workers, although supporting the community programme, see this as professional support and themselves as non-political.

There is a strong Anglo-American linkage to community development which has two implications. The first is the strong vocational element in the education of the community development workers, which extends through to graduate level. This is coupled with a strong antipathy towards any education which is seen as 'politically orientated'. The result is a focus at community level on training, rather than education in its own right. This applies regardless of the mode of training, ie whether didactic or growth-centred.[51] Community management is less rigid. People-centred development is playing a greater part, research is becoming more participatory in style (see Chapter 13) and there is an increasing recognition of the importance of tacit knowledge; all changes which have been brought about through the growth of independent NGOs (see Chapter 12). The fundamental approach remains the same, however. Thus the fifth characteristic of both community development and community management is the focus on training in a politically neutral surround or within a surround from which political debate has been excluded.

In summary, there are five characteristics of successful community development and community management projects.

1 They rely on governments being open to the involvement of communities in the decision-making process, but the degree of community involvement, which reflects the extent of openness, is effectively dictated by government.
2 Community development activities are built around predominantly social issues to which people in a community relate easily. With community management, on the other hand, there is a stronger economic and/or technical component. Nonetheless, the community management project remains clearly identifiable and self-contained.
3 They are predominantly local, clearly identifiable undertakings operating within a fairly homogeneous base.
4 The satisfaction of community needs dominates the process.
5 They focus on training in a politically neutral surround or within a surround from which political debate has been excluded.

These five characteristics put both community development and community management in context and define the parameters within which they can be shown to operate successfully. Thus both operate within national political, economic and social structures and form an integral part of those structures. Implicit in this is an acceptance of the structures on the part of the beneficiary group. It is this national social, political and economic surround, its acceptance and its implied values, which together define the successful working environment for both community development and community management.

The Characteristics of Empowerment/Conscientisacion

INTRODUCTION

Unlike community development, with its roots in the developed countries, *conscientisacion* has its roots very much in the developing world, specifically in Latin America. The term itself 'refers to learning to perceive social, political, and economic contradictions and to take action against the oppressive elements of reality'.[1] Freire believed that education provided the answer, on the basis that

> 'every human being, no matter how ignorant or submerged in the "culture of silence" he may be, is capable of looking critically at his world in a dialogical encounter with others [and that] provided with the proper tools for such an encounter, he can gradually perceive his personal and social reality as well as the contradictions in it, become conscious of his own perceptions of that reality, and deal critically with it'.[2]

The philosophy behind *conscientisacion* proposes a cultural, rather than a physical revolution, as cultural invasion is one of the major tools of oppression. This strong cultural focus leads Freire to describe the *conscientisacion* process as 'dialogical cultural action'[3] which in turn has four constituent elements: co-operation, organization, cultural synthesis and unity for liberation.[4] All four elements are essential to the success of *conscientisacion*.

Empowerment as an objective of community participation developed its conceptual form in the late 1970s, driven by world bodies such as the ILO, UNICEF, UNCHS and UNRISD, on the basis that such action would encourage meaningful change in society. Its approach differed to that of *conscientisacion* in that it was based more on direct involvement in programmes and projects, and was seen as more of an evolutionary process of change. This, it was envisaged, would take place through 'the organised efforts of dis-empowered groups to increase control over resources and regulative institutions'.[5] It was also assumed 'that the exercise of power by disadvantaged groups will enhance the satisfaction of basic needs . . . [since] the more they have direct influence, the more their real interests can be furthered'.[6] This approach to empowerment roots it very strongly in the development process.

Although *conscientisacion* and empowerment are very different in origin, philosophy and approach, they have often been confused or used interchangeably. This happened for several reasons. *Conscientisacion* was difficult to implement because it required changes which affected everyone in the society and was threatening to many of them. Empowerment, on the other hand, was far less explicit and could be applied locally without threatening the status quo. It was therefore easier to gain wide support, since the term could have a range of interpretations which made it more acceptable politically across a wider spectrum of interest groups. The outcome was a transition over time from one to the other. The way in which *conscientisacion* first merged with, and was then superseded by, empowerment can be traced through a three-stage process which began in Latin America, but which later extended to other parts of the world.

THE FIRST STAGE: *CONSCIENTISACION*

Robert Stephenson, the builder of the first commercial railway locomotive, suggested that better education of the drivers was the best way to improve the safety of the early trains. By understanding the process of operation of the engines they would limit the steam pressure and thereby prevent the engines from exploding. He was over-ruled by the owner of the railway and instead was told to design a mechanical device that would make it impossible for too great a head of steam to develop in the first place. A mechanical device would only need to be designed once, whereas education was an ongoing process which could prove expensive in terms of time and money. This debate took place over 150 years ago, but little has changed in the intervening period.

Education for change, driven from above, is rarely pursued as an end in itself. This is particularly so when the state has power which it is unwilling to relinquish. The only successful example of change through education occurs as a spin-off from education for a specific, quantifiable return. An example of this was the situation in South-East Asia during the 1980s, where improved productivity was linked to higher standards of education. Equally though, there is little incentive for poor people to adopt the *conscientisacion* approach. Because of the lack of direct correlation between cause (better education) and effect (the transformation in society), oppressed people find it easier to adopt more direct methods to bring about change. Education in South-East Asia gained support because its effect is rapidly translated into a higher standard of living. Thus to extend beyond its ideal into practical application, to change the entire educational structure of a society, in the way proposed by Freire, the process of *conscientisacion* has to be driven, or at least strongly supported, by third parties who are outside both the state and the oppressed group.

This third party can act in one of two ways. The first is to focus on individual sectors of society where they have a particular influence. This approach was illustrated by de Kadt, who describes the process in the following terms

'*Those who promoted the conscientisacion of the masses in Latin America . . . believed that the poor and exploited needed to be helped to become conscious of their situation, and [in the health sector] it was the doctors who took this task on themselves.*'[7]

This excessive dependence on a small professional group, who are themselves a natural part of the elite, is, however, unlikely to prove an effective vehicle for widespread change.

The second option is through a radical restructuring of society which occurs when the third party actually takes over the state and, in doing so, creates an opening which allows the growth and development of *conscientisacion*. There are examples of this. One is Chile between 1974 and 1980, where the country

'*saw such a mobilising use of community participation [when] the years of the Christian Democratic Government witness[ed] the widespread stimulation of community organizations among "marginal" groups in towns and among the peasantry in the country.*'[8]

Unfortunately, this experiment was terminated by a military coup. A second experiment, which also provides probably the best recorded example of participation through *conscientisacion*, was the case of Villa el Salvador in Peru. This case study is also useful in cataloguing the failure of this approach.

A detailed analysis of Villa el Salvador can be found in the work of Skinner[9,10] and Peattie.[11] The following is a summary of the key events. Villa el Salvador was founded in May 1971 and became an integral component of a national strategy of the revolutionary military government, aimed at restructuring the social, political and economic framework of Peru. Thus it was essentially part of an experiment into alternative forms of democracy. This was effected by the formation of two organizational structures.

The first organization, SINAMOS, was vertical, linking the development of Villa el Salvador directly with the President of Peru and intended to transform Peruvian institutions into structures characterized by participatory decision-making. The core of the linkage was development, with this vertical relationship having a specific role within the wider socio-political framework of the country. In the view of the government the democratic processes evolved for development could be de-linked from political and macroeconomic decision-making. The second structure was CUAVES, a co-operative seeing itself involved in all aspects and functions of local government. This structure could be described as horizontal and built up from a grassroots level.

'*Initially there were shared common views on development and it would appear that the need for community participation was shared by community leaders, SINAMOS, and government, embracing local development needs and national political and economic changes and therefore satisfying the aims both of the masses and of the state*'.[12]

The potential contradictions between these two systems of organization soon became apparent, however. The growth of a grassroots structure such as CUAVES, which covered all aspects of local government, could not be constrained within a narrow development framework as required by the government (which basically defined development as physical development of the environment). Thus 'with time a divergence in the military–community alliance later appeared which can be traced to latent differences in the perception of the purpose of participation, and the way in which decision making in development took place'.[13]

The point is made strongly in all the references to this project that the community was succeeding in developing Villa el Salvador, in mobilizing the community and in creating a coherent organizational structure. The fact that, in the long-term, the project was perceived to have failed to achieve meaningful, long-term change through *conscientisacion* is attributed primarily to this very success, which challenged government power over local decision-making, to the point where local institutions came to be viewed as a threat to central government. The government needed the *pueblo jovenes* (the residents of the informal settlements) initially to counter the loss in international and business support; this was no longer the case once they had consolidated their own power and modified their policies to win back international capital.

GROWTH OF URBAN MOVEMENTS AND THEIR IMPACT ON CONSCIENTISACION

Conscientisacion in its pure form might, and should, be an integral part of any meaningful attempt to restructure society; it is not, in itself, the primary vehicle for this change. This does not prevent the constituent elements of dialogical action, which form the basic of *conscientisacion*, being utilized in different ways and in different types of struggle. What happened in Latin America, in response to this failure, was a change of focus, with a greater emphasis being placed on organization and co-operation at a local level. The vehicle for this new form of struggle was the urban movement.

As Castells rightly points out, urban movements are not a new phenomenon, having a history going back several hundred years.[14] Nor are they limited to developing countries. It is in less developed countries, however, where, over the past 25 years, they have generated particular interest, partly through their influence on the international development process, but also because they are steadily becoming recognized as a legitimate vehicle for the expression of the needs felt by many impoverished and disenfranchized groups in society. This interest has focused primarily on Latin America, but there was also an important urban movement developing during that period in South Africa. This chapter will look at both in a comparative way as the differences between them have an important bearing on the wider community participation debate.

In the 1970s Castells argued that 'grassroots activity . . . is taking place against dictatorships which are based on increasingly narrow social support'.[15] Opposition to the state, the justness of the cause and the formation of an urban movement, no matter how great its support base, are not, of themselves, sufficient to enforce a change in the policy direction of national governments, however. Castells himself acknowledges that popular radicalism existed in many countries in Latin America and was clearly defeated all over the continent[16] and illustrates how Pinochet was able to crush the *poblodores* in Chile.[17]

This was also the case in South Africa, where there is a long and proud tradition of struggle against the apartheid state. However, as in Latin America, the impact on the state, before the rent boycott of the mid-1980s, was limited. This was in spite of the fact that the struggle took several different forms which drew people to its cause in different ways and for different reasons. First there were the mass demonstrations, such as the anti-pass demonstrations of 1919,[18] the Sharpeville anti-pass demonstration of 1960[19] and the Soweto uprising of 1976.[20] In each case the state responded with repressive measures of which the banning of 18 black consciousness movements and a large number of leaders in 1977 was typical.[21] This policy of banning and detention proved highly effective in preventing the spread of cohesive and effective opposition, to the extent that it was applied to all forms of dissent. Consumer boycotts collapsed because of a leadership vacuum and organizational weakness caused by banning and detention,[22] in spite of a very high level of public support. Boycotts of public transport, which workers 'frequently identified . . . as part of the cause of their exploitation',[23] also failed for similar reasons. Finally, the mass-based stayaway, another tactic of opposition to the state which re-emerged in the 1984–1985 period, was also effectively immobilized by the State of Emergency of June 1986.[24]

Nor did the struggle prove more successful when driven by an organizational goal. Thus early attempts to form a civic movement were inauspicious. PEBCO in Port Elizabeth began in 1979 and was soon considered to have the makings of a national body.[25] However, with the arrest and subsequent banning of the executive, the organization collapsed and, by late 1980, was largely ineffective.[26] In Soweto the Soweto Civic Association, formed in 1979, grew rapidly to a point where it had 33 branches by 1980. It was able to spearhead an effective campaign against rent increases, but was unable to make any significant impact on policy. Although 'state initiatives have afforded community organizations an opportunity to strengthen their position . . . none of [the community organizations] has succeeded in forcing the state to modify its structures fundamentally'.[27] This was the position at the beginning of the 1980s, when it appeared that the state had managed to suppress and contain the community-based organizations, in the same way as it had done with other organizations which opposed its authority.

Yet in the late 1970s (in Latin America) and early 1980s (in South Africa) the situation began to change. Suddenly the urban movements grew more successful, to the extent that they became a major force influencing policy, albeit generally at a local level. The question is why were these movements able to succeed at this time when they had failed previously? This is important, not only for the lessons which can be applied in other areas and sectors, but also because 'the provision of shelter and urban services by the state to a large proportion of the urban population is one of the major channels for political participation in community organization'.[28] Much may be known about what constitutes urban movements,[29] and how and why they arise[30], but this does not answer the question of why they succeed, or indeed what constitutes success. As social movements, Castells argues that they have failed, because they cannot provide a social alternative to society.[31] However, they clearly meet a need which is more than simply a form of political expression. The reason for this success is linked partly to a shift in the political environment. However, it also reflects the way in which community organizations applied the basic principles of *conscientisacion* to targeted objectives. This in turn resulted in a convergence of *conscientisacion* with empowerment. The end result of radical transformation remained an important factor and the mode of struggle had all four constituent elements of dialogical cultural action. At the same time, however, the result would be achieved through the attainment of a series of clearly defined goals, which would strengthen and build the community.

THE SECOND STAGE: THE TRANSITION FROM *CONSCIENTISACION* TO EMPOWERMENT

The first condition which needed to be in place before community organization achieved any noticeable success against the state was a change in the political environment to a less repressive state. The government needed to change to a position where it was no longer using the full extent of its coercive powers on ordinary people, ie those who were clearly not part of the organized leadership. There could be different reasons for this change in attitude which reduced the level of random (as opposed to targeted) state brutality. The government could be confident of its own power; it might have need of the broad support of the target group; it may be responding to external international pressure; or it could be changing from a policy of repression to one of manipulation. Whatever the cause, the result would be the same; the state would provide space for grassroots action.

This space could only be exploited if the communities used it correctly. Castells views the end-point (ie the degree of social change achieved) as important and, as a result, focuses on the negative aspect of the urban movement, namely that it

> 'can be an instrument of social integration and subordination to the existing order ...
> [and that] this subordination of the movement can be obtained by political parties
> representing the interests of different factions of the ruling class or by the state
> itself'.[32]

This was a valid conclusion for many of the mass movements of Latin America during the 1970s. However, it failed to address adequately the intermediate condition, during which the organizations used the space to achieve positive, quantifiable gains. Furthermore, it is limited geographically. Experience from South Africa indicates that the type of end-point defined by Castells is not the only outcome; instead these types of struggle can form the basis for more permanent social change.

The interesting feature of successful mobilization struggles is the continued success in the absence of clearly defined leadership. In many instances the leadership has been banned, detained or forced into hiding, which reduces its capacity to organize. Previously this had broken the mobilization. In this new form, however, the struggle to achieve the defined goals has continued. Although the nature of the protest may have been organized initially, its ongoing success depended more on the other dialogical elements of co-operation and unity. This could only be achieved if there was a very specific focus of activity. In Latin America this focus of activity was land; in South Africa it was rent and service charges.

Land invasions (collectively) constitute the majority of successful *conscientisacion*/empowerment struggles, particularly in Latin America, and their success was to show that empowerment was a viable and effective form of community participation. Although land invasions were not a new phenomenon (Lima's land invasion history, for example, goes back to 1900),[33] the growing urban crisis, the new form of interaction with the state and the integration of some of the wider principles of *conscientisacion* as objectives of the invasions all point to a new approach to the activity.

A good example of this is the case of land invasions in Buenos Aires, quoted by Cuenya *et al.*[34,35] This case study, and in fact most of these *conscientisacion*/empowerment 'events' are difficult to describe in development terminology, in that they are neither 'projects' as defined in the narrow sense of the word, nor programmes, but hybrids, one reason why they represent the intermediate stage between *conscientisacion* and empowerment. The Buenos Aires study is of a land invasion over a four year period from 1980 to 1984. Cuenya *et al* stress the importance of the changing political climate which characterized Argentina at that time, in which there was increasing, albeit limited, democratization which allowed both the settlement of the land and recognition of tenure by the government.

Cuenya *et al*[36] argue that the mass nature of popular demands for goods (such as land) requires that the dispossessed act through neighbourhood organizations, pressure on the public authorities and public mobilization. However, the paper also places this event within the context of de facto governments such as dictatorships. Hence the degree and pace of democratization is carefully controlled by the state. If this democratization changes too rapidly, the same approach can lead to 'the internal break-up and fragmentation in the settlers' organization'.[37] These workers go on to state that, under a democratic system, the direct channels of communication used for expressing demands 'under de facto governments (such as dictatorships) . . . become inadequate and break down as open political conflict is usually combined with the possibility of the return to conventional urban policies'.[38] This is confirmed by other research. Thus Ward and Gilbert (1983)[39] show how, although land invasions may be acceptable to many governments in providing land tenure to the poor, the ratification of such tenure, as well as the provision of services, is part of a complex system of patronage politics. This is part of a wider political structure in which key officials controlling the different sectors of local government are political appointees.

This case study shows both the strength and the weakness of this empowerment/*conscientisacion* approach. On the one hand the Buenos Aires project could be considered successful, in the sense that permanent tenure was granted to the squatters. On the other hand, however, the gains made by the community are difficult to convert into meaningful change in a wider arena, or even further gains of the same type. This appears to confirm the work of Castells, but he was studying urban movements 'from the point of view of the study of social movements, as opposed to that of local participation'.[40] Viewed from the latter perspective, a different conclusion emerges.

Conscientisacion/empowerment in this intermediate stage is an important form of participation, but it is also both complex and fragile. A deeper understanding of the nature of the relationship can be obtained from a study of the situation that developed in South Africa during the 1980s. Superficially the apartheid state became increasingly autocratic. There were two States of Emergency during this decade; banning and detention increased and there was also an increase in state-inspired assassinations. In other areas, however, there was an easing of restrictions. The policy of forced removals of Africans from urban areas was slowly abandoned and there was a tentative opening up of the debate on the future of urban areas. At the same time the state was being placed under increasing international pressure and its desire to give a favourable impression to its traditional trading partners meant that it was no longer as free to pursue draconian measures as openly as it had previously been. This in turn opened the way for new forms of struggle.

The critical transformation which changed the situation in South Africa was the rent boycott, which, over the seven years from 1983 to 1990, was able to successfully defy the state and give the civic organizations the base from which to build a powerful nationwide organization. The term rent in South Africa does not have the conventional meaning, as it has two components: a rental component made up of site and house rent for state housing tenants; and a service charge covering the cost of township capital development and the provision and maintenance of services. In practice, these components are indistinguishable to township residents as they are billed and paid together. Thus a rent boycott involves a refusal to pay both rent and service charges. The cost of housing historically has been very low, so that service charges actually constitute most of the rent in many townships. In Sebokeng, for example, service charges comprised 83% of the proposed total rent for 1984–1985.[41]

What distinguished the rent boycott from previous expressions of grassroots dissent and marked the watershed in the transition to political empowerment was the change from struggle as a form of organized protest to struggle as a participatory form. Based on historical evidence and the author's own research,[42] it appears that three conditions are necessary for this transition to occur successfully. The first condition is a strong urban movement within a geographically definable community. In this context,

Seekings places the urban 'unrest' which characterized the townships of South Africa in the period 1983–1985 within the context of the powerful Latin American 'urban social movements'.[43] The resulting movement in South Africa was the civic movement.

The second condition is the growth of a dominant single issue which can provide a focus for the community at large. In Latin America the most common successful issue has been land tenure.[44] In South Africa the expression of the struggle was the rent boycott, but the underlying issue was the level of physical infrastructure. An analysis of services in Soweto between 1969 and 1979 revealed that during this period capital works virtually stopped, while maintenance declined significantly and the quality of services deteriorated.[45] In addition, the period between 1960 and 1979 saw the population virtually doubled, while the number of sites increased by only 10 per cent.[46]

A survey carried out in 1989 as part of a study of Soweto confirmed the abysmally low level of services, but, more importantly, showed residents to have a clear understanding of the nature and extent of this deterioration.[47] In a second study in the eastern Transvaal the level of services was so poor, and posed such a health risk, that no payment for them could be justified.[48] Yet over the period 1982–1985, township rents to pay for these deteriorating services rose by up to 300 per cent.[49]

The third condition is that the dominant issue must provide the community organization with leverage for negotiation. In the case of land tenure, a group will invade land and then use the occupation of that land as a tool with which to negotiate with the state. In South Africa the bargaining tool was the rent boycott. People refused to pay until services had been improved.

The problem with this participatory form of empowerment is not simply that it is transitory, being difficult to maintain the collective momentum of the community, but that its outcome in terms of future direction is unpredictable.[50] There are four possible options. The first two were illustrated earlier. In the first, the community-based movement collapses, as illustrated by Cuenya *et al* in Argentina,[51] because it cannot adapt its tactics successfully to increasing democratization. In the second, the community-based movements are undermined by government, as illustrated in case studies from Mexico, Colombia and Venezuela.[52–54] Here the state manipulates the organizations through a system of patronage. Both of these are also compatible with Castells, interpretation. It is the two remaining options, however, which are of importance from a participation perspective, and neither of these is considered by other researchers. The third option represents the condition which developed in South Africa. There the state made a radical political shift which opened the way for wider political involvement in the structures of government. This also happened in Argentina, but in South Africa the movements were able to adapt to this change much more successfully. They were able to do this because of the way in which they modified their approach to the state, without damaging themselves, their cause or their credibility, as the confrontational form of participation evolved with the political transition of the early 1990s and changed into a new form of community–state interaction. The way in which this developed is discussed in Chapter 7.

THE THIRD STAGE: POLITICAL EMPOWERMENT IN A PROJECT-BASED ENVIRONMENT

There is then the fourth option. The government is not becoming more democratic. It remains autocratic, but still leaves some space for limited organization and mobilization. At the same time there is a change from an economic development surround to a project-based, sectoral surround. To take advantage of this space in this type of political climate, the community needs to be able to raise its own funds for development projects. Under these conditions, the state is caught in a cleft stick between encouraging the project, which it cannot afford to fund itself, and controlling the political repercussions of increased community awareness and self-confidence. This situation represents the third and final stage in the transition from *conscientisacion* to political empowerment.

A good example of this condition is the FUNDASAL-supported community housing project, which was constructed in San Salvador in the 1980s. The approach taken by this NGO, ie FUNDASAL, is used to justify the political empowerment approach to participation at a project level. This is illustrated by Stein's analysis, which argues that 'it is possible to achieve efficient and effective post-project maintenance if participation is conceived as a means to empower participants'.[55] This view defines the project as the vehicle through which to achieve social and political goals. However, Stein highlights four constraints to the process followed in San Salvador, which are important for an evaluation of the long-term sustainability of the empowerment approach to projects. These are: the national political crisis; the conditions of the loan; the internal administrative limitations; and the logic and philosophy of the model itself.[56] From an evaluation of the project and its constraints, four issues arise which provide an understanding of political empowerment as a form of community participation. These are: (1) the linkage with *conscientisacion*; (2) the relationship between the NGO and the community; (3) long-term sustainability and the interaction with the state; and (4) the issue of technical complexity. Each of these is discussed briefly in the following.

Project-based Empowerment and *conscientisacion*

From the beginning there was a

> 'debate within FUNDASAL about the nature of housing projects and the role of community participation. For some it was evident that it was possible to produce low-income housing on a scale that could help to decrease the housing deficit of the country. For others, the effectiveness of housing as a means to produce psycho-social change among the urban poor was evident'.[57]

It was agreed that there needed to be a balance between 'the short-run objective of improving the living conditions of the poor versus the long-run objective of empowering them'.[58] It did this through an education process which extended through the building programme and beyond. Thus it focused on satisfying the immediate need for housing, but at the same time 'attempted to contribute to promoting structural changes in the Salvadorean society through the articulation of a social force that could lobby for those changes, and through the generation of alternative models of community development'.[59] In doing this it merged the four elements of organization, co-operation, cultural synthesis and unity for liberation to be achieved through the dual medium of a project and an education process. This is a classic illustration of an empowerment project built on the principles of *conscientisacion.*

The Community and the NGO

The primary mechanism of interaction between the NGO and the communities was via social workers and 'to a large extent, through the social worker, FUNDASAL controlled, and was present, in almost any important decision the community took in terms of its consolidation'.[60] The problem of running social workers through an NGO in this way meant that

'The educational process which was meant to train project participants to acquire new skills and abilities at the material and organizational levels, and to raise their consciousness about the social reality, was not fully comprehended by [all] the social workers. On the one hand, education was understood as a process of transmitting mere information to participants about the administrative and bureaucratic steps necessary to obtain resources or other technical services from FUNDASAL. On the other hand, some social workers were more interested in responding to the necessities of the political process, and did not take into consideration the conditions, readiness and needs of the participants themselves. Some social workers were reluctant to conciliate elements of effectiveness and efficiency with broader socio-political goals. Others regarded the efforts of improving the housing and material conditions of the urban poor in the context of a civil war, as a demobilizing factor that impeded the radicalization of the participants' demands against the government or an element of integration to the status quo, rather than as a means for social change'.[61]

Compare this situation with that of the AKRSP project in Pakistan, where the role of the community workers is very clearly defined. This difference is a further indication of why the FUNDASAL programme does not fit the definition of community development. These contradictions, which Stein attributed to poor selection and training of the social workers, actually reflected the contradictions that existed within the NGO itself. However, they also raise the issue of the agenda and accountability of the NGO.
Thus Stein states that

'It is clear that housing was viewed by the majority of project participants as an end to be achieved by means of participation. Nevertheless, for FUNDASAL, housing was viewed as a means to achieve broader social goals that went beyond the mere provision of shelter ... [and that] the process of transforming the participants' ends into means [for long term empowerment] became the real challenge of the whole education process'.[62]

Given the clear socio-political agenda of the NGO, the question needs to be asked as to whether this is really any different from the government defining what constitutes successful community participation, an action which, if carried out by the latter, would be interpreted as manipulation. There is a belief, which is not limited to FUNDASAL but is common to many community participation projects supported by NGOs, that there is a beneficial symbiotic relationship between the NGO and the community. This contrasts sharply with the NGO's perceptions of the agendas of other parties concerned (this is discussed further in Chapter 12). Thus in the FUNDASAL project, Stein defines the agendas of the World Bank and the state as constraints which impede the project. There is a lack of recognition of the validity of other parties to hold and pursue their own agendas. The NGO's agenda is not questioned, for the reason described earlier. Yet on the basis of this analysis, the actions of the NGO itself could be interpreted as a form of manipulation of the community.

Long-term Sustainability and the Interaction with the State

When the FUNDASAL housing programme began, the state, although authoritarian, had provided some space for communal expression. With a coup d'etat in 1979 there was a closure of political space, and increased repression.

> 'The government and other powerful political and economical sectors saw with suspicion, and faced with hostility, the work of those NGOs who, through their methods and philosophy, attempted to go beyond the pure supply of a service (ie housing in the case of FUNDASAL) and were pressed to abandon their long-run objectives'.[63]

Coupled with the differing initial perceptions of the objectives of the project (between NGO and beneficiary group) raised earlier, this seriously affected long-term sustainability. Thus, of the 22 communities involved in FUNDASAL projects, only five were well consolidated (in 1986) and 17 showed regressive symptoms.[64] This is not atypical. In describing irregular settlement growth in Mexico, Colombia and Venezuela, studied over a four to five year period, Ward and Gilbert[65] return to the issue of organizations collapsing once their initial objectives have been met. This is the same problem that was raised with the Buenos Aires project in the previous section. In El Salvador Stein puts this down to an education problem, but overlooks the different needs of people in communities and the fact that these needs are not always synonymous, either temporally or spatially. The question raised is whether projects (such as housing) which are clearly defined and have a specific end-point are vehicles for long-term empowerment. The conventional argument, repeated by Stein, is that the post-project operation and maintenance phase should be seen as a continuation of the project. This is not an obvious perception for beneficiaries, however. The reality again is that long-term empowerment is extremely difficult to achieve in an environment where the government is antagonistic to the process.

Technical Complexity

This leads to the final issue, which is that of project complexity, in this instance the distinction between housing provision and infrastructure provision. In this project FUNDASAL identified sites, defined projects and used private construction companies for the initial stages. Finally, together with the families, participants were selected and formed groups for the mutual help stage of house construction. In other words, the participation process itself began with the shelter provision programme and did not enter the more technically complex stage of infrastructure provision.

By selecting a specific activity for the participation component, the capacity of the community to participate in a more technically complex component is questioned. It is not the capacity of communities per se which causes the difficulty, however. Rather, it reflects the difficulty of reconciling participation in a complex area of activity with the achievement of empowerment goals. For although control over the form of participation, by the NGO, is possible with the housing process, this would be more difficult to ensure if infrastructure were included, if only because of the increased number of actors involved and the greater leverage of the state in this area.

The FUNDASAL project illustrates the third stage in the evolution of the empowerment approach, namely its application to the implementation of specific projects. The case study was considered a successful example of empowerment.[66] However, this success is of a limited nature. The decisions were policy decisions related to the socio-political environment. There were important technical decisions to be made, illustrated by the three issues raised earlier, of which none was taken by the community.

CHARACTERISTICS OF EMPOWERMENT

The various studies outlined here, together with the work of de Kadt[67] and other workers who discuss the needs of the urban poor in Latin America, enable a set of characteristics to be identified which is different from that in which successful community development has been practised. Community development is clearly not a suitable vehicle for participation in an environment characterized by confrontation between the state and the community. Thus there is a strong case to be made for a different approach, and empowerment appears to fulfil this need. The characteristics themselves, although different, can be described in terms of the same sub-headings as were used in the previous chapter. For the purpose of defining these characteristics, two distinct forms of political empowerment have been merged. One uses projects, whereas the other uses non-project activities. In this sense there is a similarity with the relationship between community management and community development discussed in the previous chapter.

Role of Government

Having established the characteristics pertaining to successful community development projects in developed countries as well as in the (predominantly) rural areas of Africa and the Indian sub-continent, this can be compared with the appropriateness of community development in the urban environment in Latin America and South Africa. De Kadt argues that

> 'CD [community development] hardly ever faced up to the differences in interest that could exist between different members of "the community" that was to be "developed", notably in terms of their control over opportunities to make a living'.[68]

He further states that 'The community developers achieved little because they disregarded inequality, conflict and power relations'.[69]

Latin America in the period from 1960 to the mid-1980s is the primary case study arena used to support and debate the empowerment paradigm. De Kadt[70] is quoted earlier as linking inequality, conflict and power relations, and it is clear from the three case studies that development in these areas during that period was intimately bound up with the political process. Governments in the countries involved were, at that time, predominantly authoritarian and had little perceived legitimacy. There was neither an established democratic tradition nor a widely supported traditional base of the type found in Africa and India. Further, the strong relationships between political, social and economic issues already existed. There is much support for the concept that political struggle and power are at the centre of the community participation debate and hence the sole criterion for empowerment, in a Latin American context. Thus Gilbert and Ward, for example, state that land allocation 'is an integral part of the political process',[71] and that the allocation of land is most often used as a political bargaining point. This is a context-based statement. This is not necessarily true in other contexts, as the South African analysis indicates.

The lack of perceived legitimacy is reinforced by the political nature of the local authority structure. This follows the US model, where all key local government appointments are political. Thus there is very little distinction between government at different levels primarily because the latter were formed 'to assist state governments in carrying out their responsibilities'.[72] All are seen as part of the same monolithic structure. This close inter-relationship between national politics and local development at a *Barrio* level is a critical factor which runs through not just these case studies, but virtually all papers on development in Latin America. Thus Ward and Gilbert state that in Bogota 'The National Front and later administrations have continued to prescribe the terms on which they are prepared to negotiate with the poor',[73] whereas in Mexico City 'channels of community participation were *tailored to government needs*'.[74] It is interesting to note that, for the period when South Africa followed the empowerment approach to participation, the people were reacting against a form of local government which was operated along very similar lines to that of Latin America.[75] The outcome of this structure, when coupled with a totalitarian regime at the centre, means that the government is closed to the involvement of the community in the decision-making process.

Nature of the Project/Programme

In the above analysis the political situation dominates the debate, but this obscures other issues which are important and which define the other characteristics of successful empowerment projects. The first of these is that the successful empowerment approach addresses only one specific issue at a time. These issues are predominantly social, but also have a strong political component. They address what is collectively the single most important need of the community at that point in time by the use of direct action. They operate primarily within the context of an urban struggle, with typical issues being land tenure (often by land invasion) and shelter. *Conscientisacion* was primarily a programme-based approach, in the same way that community development was originally. Empowerment can operate in a hybrid environment, but has also adapted to a project-based environment. In the latter case the application may have a technical component, eg housing, but this is of limited complexity and the dominant issue which is driving the community group is still predominantly social; it is the issue of shelter, rather than the construction process, which is critical. The South African case study, which dealt with the level and quality of services, is probably the most complex example of successful empowerment which exists, and indicates a wider potential for this form of participation. As with community development there is also a specific type of linkage with technology which operates within the empowerment approach, which is discussed in greater detail in the next chapter.

Community Dynamic

Within empowerment struggles the issue of community cohesion is central. De Kadt criticizes the community development approach for its inability to handle heterogeneity in communities.[76] However, community development was never intended to function in this type of environment, as the previous chapter indicated. Interestingly, the detailed analysis of the empowerment struggles summarized here indicates that the wider question of community homogeneity was not addressed by empowerment in an effective way either.[77] What the empowerment approach does is to mobilize people around specific issues. This generates a very strong commonality of purpose around these issues, which is the third characteristic of empowerment. This commonality of purpose is not the same as community homogeneity, however. When successful, the empowerment approach is capable of developing a powerful sense of community cohesion. However, as was mentioned earlier, once this specific issue has been addressed, this community cohesion often collapses, either through manipulation by the state or because, with the achievement of the specified goal, the natural heterogeneity of the community re-asserts itself.

Primary Objective of the Community Participation Process

The central feature of the empowerment approach is the confrontation between the community and the state, which creates the classic duality which many researchers continue to see as extant in all participation projects. This duality has an effect on external actors, who are then classified either as supportive of the community or opposed to the community. This is illustrated by the FUNDASAL project where the World Bank is seen as impeding the project (ie opposing the community), whereas the NGO is seen as supporting the community. This duality represents the fourth characteristic of the empowerment approach. This makes it difficult to bring in other actors (eg development professionals) unless they also align with one side or the other. This duality is integral to the nature of the empowerment struggle. The primary objective of the community leadership is to achieve a fundamental change in the society.

Role of External Actors

Empowerment has its roots in *conscientisacion*. There remains, therefore, a recognition of the importance of both the individual elements of dialogical action, particularly the importance of cohesion and unity of action, as well as the centrality of education in its social context (as opposed to its training role). This means that helping people to place themselves in a social, political and economic context is an integral part of the empowerment process. This view of education is rejected in many societies, including Anglo-Saxon societies, and is an anathema to most donor agencies. This is the main reason why there are two basic interpretations of empowerment, that of the UN, summed up by UNRISD in its definition of community participation, and that of the World Bank, which is described by Paul.[78] The latter seeks to give people a share of power and responsibility without providing the social context which explains why they need to be supported in their struggle to achieve this power and responsibility. This is a contradiction in terms.

The empowerment approach also influences the structure of support organizations. Because of its political implications and its form as a community/government duality, this necessitates the political alignment of support organizations. This has transformed the support organizations from the perceived non-political support of community development to one in which the support was clearly aligned, politically or ideologically depending on the nature of the target goal, with the community. This has major implications for NGOs, who provide the bulk of the support base to community organizations, which has not been fully recognized. The support organizations need to be politically and ideologically aligned with the community organizations they are supporting and therefore education and training will always have a political component.

In summary, the equivalent characteristics of successful empowerment projects may be defined as:

1 They operate outside government structures in an environment where the government is closed to the involvement of the community in the wider decision-making process.
2 They concern themselves with specific issues with a strong political connotation.
3 Although the community itself might represent a heterogeneous base, the projects are such that they generate a strong commonality of purpose among the group.

4   The participation system in empowerment operates as a duality between the community and the state, with the primary objective being to achieve a fundamental change in the society.

5   The support organizations need to be politically and ideologically aligned with the community organizations they are supporting. Education and training will always have a political component.

From this description of characteristics it is clear that the whole structure of the empowerment approach is different to that of community development. Empowerment has not superseded community development. Each is suited to a specific arena and to the associated problems that lie within it.

Characteristics of Community Participation in Negotiated Development

NEW FORMS OF COMMUNITY PARTICIPATION

There had been a general assumption in published work, which persisted well into the 1980s, that community development and political empowerment were the only two approaches to community participation which existed. The first sign of change came in 1983 when Oakley and Marsden attempted to describe community participation in terms of broad categories. As was illustrated in Chapter 3, these could be consolidated back to the above two approaches, but the thinking behind this analysis is indicative of a vague unease with the constraints imposed by this limitation. Eventually, with the project-dominated development environment of the late 1980s, this limited interpretation became unsustainable. From the work of Korten and others in Asia a new approach, that of community management, began to emerge. This has now become the dominant approach to community participation in many developing countries.

Community management stems from a rural base and, like empowerment before it, was seen as more appropriate than community development, which had retained an extensive following in Asia. However, there was also a demand for a new approach emerging in the urban sector. Because of the dominance of dependency theory and the empowerment approach in development thinking around urbanization issues, community participation in various urbanization activities, including infrastructure provision, has been judged in terms of the degree to which people have been empowered in the political sense, ie the empowerment approach. This is apparent in the evaluation of the Lusaka upgrade, as well as from a growing number of publications on developments in South Africa. As was shown earlier, this was a valid criterion on which to judge the success of community participation in South Africa during the 1970s and early 1980s, but it was less valid elsewhere in Africa, and no longer applied in South Africa from 1990 onwards. The reason for this is that the crisis of urbanization in Africa is creating a new situation, which differs significantly from that in Latin America.

The dissimilarity revolves around the different levels of institutional and technological capacity within the countries concerned and the ways in which this capacity is controlled. This capacity exists in Latin America to a far greater extent than in Africa, and even parts of Asia. Gilbert described the situation thus:

> 'the positive correlation that exists between the level of national wealth and the quality of housing means that there are higher proportions of poor urban dwellers in Asia or Africa than in Latin America. In addition it is probable that the African and Asian urban poor live in worse conditions than do their Latin American counterparts. Standards of servicing, for example, are superior in Latin America to those of Africa or Asia. In Latin American cities the poor must wait several years for electricity or running water to be installed, but services normally arrive. By contrast, the poor of most Asian or African cities may never receive services. . . . While these superior services and resources may be disproportionately concentrated in middle- and upper-income housing areas, even the Latin American poor benefit to some degree from the higher levels of national and urban resources'.[1]

The outcome has been to place a greater emphasis on community participation in the actual provision of services than has been the case in Latin America, and it is the attempt to achieve this which has highlighted the shortcomings of existing systems and the need for an alternative approach to community participation. The evolution of this new approach has been the most rapid, and effective, in South Africa, although it is not limited to that country. The approach itself can be described as negotiated development.

THE NEED FOR AN ALTERNATIVE APPROACH TO COMMUNITY PARTICIPATION

Economic growth and transformation of the economy involves a permanent re-allocation of resources.[2] In developing countries an increasing percentage of this allocation is being made to physical urban infrastructure provision,[3] which by its nature has a high technological component. As Chapter 4 indicated, the management of this infrastructure has proved to be a challenge which is placing an unbearable strain on local authorities in many parts of the developing world. In addressing the resultant problems, the primary focus, which is that taken by the World Bank and most bilateral aid agencies, is to concentrate on building institutional capacity. Simply addressing this issue on its own is not the solution, however. The root cause of the problem has to be addressed, which is the relationship between people and the urban environment. The spatial component of this relationship is a widely explored topic. This chapter will address a different aspect of the problem, which is equally important but less well understood, namely the relationship between technology and community participation.

There are several ways of dealing with technology from a community participation perspective. Community development and community management adopt the appropriate technology approach, but this is not possible in a large urban conurbation. To many professionals concerned with the spatial aspects of the urban environment it is not even discussed as an issue, but simply ignored. In this situation it is seen purely as a support service which does not influence the main debate. However, this view is only possible if there is adequate management and financial capacity, a point which is overlooked by many social researchers.[4] A third way is the current technocratic solution, which is becoming widespread. This is to impose a level of service on communities based solely on the criteria of affordability, but judged purely in financial terms with no social cost attached. This view was discussed in Chapter 4 and was the basis for the Lusaka upgrade discussed in the next section. This standpoint is being increasingly rejected by urban communities.

What is needed is a new means of integrating community participation into the process of management of urban infrastructure. The question is, how is this to be done? For although urban infrastructure spending in developing countries is increasing rapidly, the evaluation of these projects, particularly with respect to community participation, is extremely limited. One early evaluation was the Lusaka upgrade and this will be examined briefly. The major body of work on this subject has taken place in South Africa, most during the period immediately before, and during, the political transition to democracy which began in 1990. It is this work which will be the primary source for the development of a new approach. Because this is new work, it is interwoven into different chapters of the book. This chapter will focus on the historical development which created the new approach in South Africa and will draw on work in other chapters when it comes to developing the characteristics of this new form of participation.

THE LUSAKA UPGRADE (1974–1981)

As with the case studies quoted in the previous chapter, the Lusaka upgrade is well documented.[5] This section highlights the key issues.

Community participation was always intended to be a key component of this upgrading project. The project appraisal report envisaged infrastructure installation as being preceded by

> 'a programme to promote an understanding of upgrading and to mobilise community support and participation essential to progressive improvement, with the intent of consulting residents regarding servicing layouts and assisting them in organising self-help labour for water pipe excavation and standpipe construction'.[6]

The plan envisaged local development committees, comprising community representatives chaired by a local councillor, which would participate in overspill plot allocation, mobilize self-help labour and be responsible for promoting long-term development programmes promoting continuous improvements to dwellings, infrastructure and community services.

The evaluation described by Rakodi makes clear the contradictions inherent in this approach. Thus the goals (of participation) could be divided into two parts. The first part comprised a series of general statements of principle regarding the role of, and the benefits to, the community. Although they sound encouraging and supportive, they are without value or meaning unless translated into action, the purpose of the second part. The second set of goals defines specific target objectives. These include the facilitation of speedy implementation and the achievement of lower costs; increased user satisfaction; the inculcation of a sense of responsibility for the maintenance of services and facilities; strengthened self-reliance; and the involvement of local residents in local decision-making.[7] The defined targets, as laid out, are not only contradictory, in trying to satisfy such a multiplicity of objectives, but also conflict with the financial objectives of the World Bank and the political objectives of the ruling party. The reality was that participation could only focus on concrete goals related to physical involvement. What was required was community involvement in the early stages of the project cycle (which centred upon decision-making), but this did not happen (with the exception of two minor areas) for a variety of reasons, not all related to the constraints outlined here. Instead there was involvement in the later part of the cycle, where the community was expected to contribute materially. This proved unsatisfactory from all points of view as it did not achieve any of the objectives.

It was not only the practical problems of community participation which constrained the project, however. There was also a fundamental difference in the perception of the meaning of participation. In terms of achieving wider social goals (of enhancing community involvement in local level decision-making), Rakodi cites the UN[8] concept of information giving, which is 'intended to be either a persuasive activity, aiming to influence attitudes, or an open activity, aimed at achieving participation or interaction between the citizens and the authorities'.[9] Rakodi claims that in the Lusaka case the information giving was persuasive in nature, aimed at creating awareness (of proposals, options and financial responsibilities) counteracting potential opposition and ensuring active co-operation with, and the support of, the implementing agency. It could be argued that this exercise was partially successful, in that the overall scheme was generally accepted. But it could equally be derided as an exercise in manipulation which was recognized by the community and dismissed, a viewpoint supported by the failure of the project in certain key areas such as the collection of service fees.

Regarding the benefits of the participation exercise for the community, these actually involved an additional burden being placed on the community in areas such as maintenance, service charge collection and ongoing development initiatives. At no point, however, were the residents given the opportunity to take responsibility for the underlying decisions. This need for building up experience in decision-making, starting first at a local level, is strongly made both by Rakodi and also by Skinner in the Villa el Salvador project. From a political perspective Rakodi notes that there is only limited scope for participation at a level beyond the immediate project, yet this did not, per se, prevent community participation at the project level. This indicates that the two levels operate independently. In fact, this is not the case and the inability to recognize this was one of the underlying reasons for the failure of the participation process at Lusaka. This interaction between decisions at local and national level is a central issue which distinguishes participation in these activities from community development and community management programmes. Working with this type of project the two are inter-dependent.

The nature of this inter-dependence has been prevented, to a large degree, by the apparent linkage between community participation in projects and the project cycle. Within this context (of the project cycle) all community participation, whatever its type, will be subservient to the needs of the project. This subservient relationship formed the basis of what Moser described as a means[10] approach to participation and its inequity led to the evolution of the ends approach, in which the answer was to be found in empowerment. However, both of these views (of separate means and ends) are invalid. The notion of degrees of participation is a myth, which reflects the conventional development professional's specific view of community participation. In practice, most of the community inputs are manipulative. The key question is that raised first in Chapter 3; namely, who decides the type and degree of community input? Not the community. Even where the community might agree to partake in one specific type of input, someone outside has already made a decision on the structure of the community involvement in the discussion. The only meaningful type of participation is that which involves the central decision-making process.

The assumption that this justifies the empowerment approach (which is the basis for community management) is not the solution, however. The interaction between community participation and the project cycle is complex and it is simplistic to argue that the answer is simply community control. This raises numerous questions. What is the local authority for? What if the community lacks the skill and capacity? How can loan finance be guaranteed? The most important question, however, is: does community control really mean active community participation in the decision-making process? The answer is that the two are not necessarily synonymous because community management can also be used manipulatively.

An opportunity to explore these issues further, and at the same time develop a new understanding of the relationship between community participation and urban upgrading, was provided by the political transition in South Africa. This was made possible because, by the late 1980s, upgrading had become the dominant issue in the debate between the state and community organizations. To understand how this developed and why it had such a major impact on the community participation process, to the extent that it led to the development of a new form of participation, it is necessary to go back to that point in time where community leaders were being banned and the state was seeking to regain the political initiative in the face of increasing rent boycotts.

SOUTH AFRICA, 1985–1990

In the early stages of the rent boycott described in the previous chapter, the government may have been able to defuse the situation by writing off arrears or changing the whole payment system. Had they done this, a situation could have developed in which the state kept the initiative and a new era of rule by patronage, similar to the situation in Latin America, evolved. However, the racist nature of the apartheid regime ideologically prevented this type of 'compromise' and a very different situation developed. Because they were totally out of touch with the feelings of African people, the government refused to accept that there was majority support for the boycott, preferring to believe that it was the work of agitators and intimidators.[11] As a result, the government created a three-pronged strategic response to the boycott, which comprised (1) the elimination of opposition by arresting township leaders, (2) turning black local councillors into political representatives of the state by incorporating them into regional and national councils, and (3) addressing the issue of the upgrading of the physical infrastructure. The decision to upgrade the townships was considered such a key element of the government strategy that the defence minister took personal responsibility for its rapid implementation.[12] With several hundred townships, and upgrading needs running into billions of rands, the government began by choosing the most volatile areas first, but even this task proved impossible in the short term.[13] What had been defined by communities as a straightforward issue (ie refusing to pay rent) became an extremely complex task (ie upgrading on a major scale). Nonetheless, by using its considerable power in this way and making upgrading of services the central focus of the ideological struggle that was taking place, the government dictated the agenda for the period which followed, when the civics re-emerged and began to regroup in 1989. As Collinge states, it was 'the pressures to negotiate on service provision to entire communities . . .[that] shaped thinking on the long term nature of civics'.[14]

The final move which confirmed this agenda into the changing 1990s was the decision taken by the South African National Civic Association (SANCO) on its future structure. In the run up to a national consultative conference of between 600 and 700 civic organizations in May 1991, three possible directions were considered for the future of the civic movement.[15] The first was to be replaced by African National Congress (ANC) branches or to become ANC residents' associations. The second was to attempt to take over the administration of towns and cities. The third possibility was that 'the civic movement must remain autonomous, a broad mass-based structure, which will not attempt to take over local government'.[16] At the May 1991 conference to form a national civic organization, delegates voted for the third option. This decision was supported by the ANC, stating that

'there is a need for grassroots democratic organization in all societies, that social movements – because they relate directly to social issues that shape people's lives, and are not mediated by the necessity of holding or attaining power – are best placed to answer this need'.[17]

With this decision, the major actors in South Africa had placed at the centre of the community participation debate an issue in which technical and economic components would be as important as social and political issues. These were the factors underlying the need to adopt a new approach to community participation in South Africa during the years of political transition.

SOUTH AFRICA, 1990–1994

The unbanning of political organizations in February 1990 was followed by other changes, including the acceptance by the government of the principle of single non-racial local authorities. Large sums of money were allocated to upgrading, eg R750M through the Independent Development Trust (IDT), and R1000M from the oil reserve fund, to be administered by provincial administrations. Effectively, the state withdrew from its central role in service provision on the grounds that it had insufficient resources and a wider resource base was needed which devolved some responsibility for service provision onto other actors. This decision changed the nature of the participation process significantly. No longer was there one dominant issue with two major actors (the government and community organizations). Once the civic movement accepted this new situation, it found itself in a completely different type of participatory environment, in which the duality of a government–CBO confrontation gives way to a wider forum where multi-objective decision-making is achieved by consensus.[18]

The first major test of operating in this new environment was the formation of the Metropolitan Chamber, in which a group of actors mapped out a common future for the Johannesburg–Soweto conurbation. The Chamber agreed a high level of services for Soweto as a matter of principle, without discussing where the money to pay for services would be drawn from. It is possible that this could be achievable, given that (1) the high political profile of Soweto will give it a priority in subsidy allocation by central government, (2) Johannesburg runs a major surplus on its electricity account which allows room for an internal subsidy and (3) that the boundaries of the new Johannesburg–Soweto conurbation do not incorporate any of the major informal settlements of the PWV, where the infrastructure needs are greatest.[19] This was a successful negotiating process from Soweto's perspective. However, to extend this level of service on a national basis would cost in excess of R3.6 billion per annum,[20] a sum which is not available from current funding sources. Thus this particular negotiation was unique and unlikely to be replicable.

The type of negotiation which civic organizations now had to face had two distinct components. The first component involves the distribution of existing capital assets, and in this respect the experience of the East Rand negotiating forum is likely to prove typical.

The Greater Benoni Forum was established as a body which would pave the way for the merging of the currently segregated areas of

Benoni/Actonville, Wattville and Daveyton. In the negotiations the Wattville Civic Association is supported in its negotiations by the service organization Planact.

The major part of the discussions have been taken up with the issue of physical infrastructure, and in this area Benoni is represented by its town engineer's department. There is no doubt that its technical knowledge and capacity are far in excess of that of either Daveyton or Wattville. The basic premise used by Benoni to determine guidelines for the future is that Benoni should be the norm in terms of conceptualizing how a new unified town might function. Unfortunately, this does not mean the creation of a unified standard, similar to that of Benoni. Instead, it means that: (1) the existing residents of Benoni own the services; (2) each area should have a level of service which reflects the income level of that area; and (3) it is unreasonable to expect residents of Benoni to subsidize the other areas.

All this is presented with extensive supporting evidence giving breakdowns of cost, staffing needs, etc. Clearly these arguments are fallacious. In reality, there has been a subsidy for many years, but it is the reverse of that described here, with Benoni residents being subsidized by those living in the townships. The latter were the mainstay of the industrial and commercial base, but were excluded from all social amenities and benefits. As a result, a select minority of residents, ie those living in Benoni, have been able to accumulate a capital base of physical infrastructure worth hundreds of millions of rands.

The basis of the Benoni argument is being disputed because the Wattville civic has access to its own technical expertise. Thus the fallacy of the argument has been highlighted and the residents of Wattville and Daveyton should achieve a significantly more equitable allocation of the local authority's capital base.

This experience showed that most civic organizations were likely to find themselves negotiating under much less favourable conditions than those existing in Soweto. Equitable resource allocation of the municipal capital asset base would still be insufficient to meet the needs of all sectors of the population within municipal boundaries. The prospects for meeting the needs of the growing population living in informal settlements outside existing municipal boundaries under these conditions meant that there would have to be negotiations about the actual nature, and the levels, of the physical services to be provided. These would take place both at a national level and in individual communities. Thus upgrading can be seen to have elements of both a national programme and (a multiplicity of) individual projects.

This was the environment that community organizations faced in early 1990 and will continue to face under an ANC-dominated government. Drawing on over a dozen case studies of upgrading during the political transition, the characteristics of negotiated development began to emerge. These are discussed in the following together with some of the case study material. The remainder of the material will be discussed in greater detail in later chapters which deal with project implementation.

CHARACTERISTICS OF NEGOTIATED DEVELOPMENT

Community Interaction with Government

The new form of negotiation which took place in South Africa during the early 1990s was possible because the government was open to the involvement of communities in the decision-making process. However, the nature of this involvement was different to that of community development. The nature of the involvement was more widespread, took into account the political as well as the social and economic conditions, and eventually extended to an input on legislation.

The basis for such an extended form of community involvement was two-fold. Firstly, the attitude of the state was dictated largely out of necessity rather than choice. The government was becoming weaker nationally, whereas in the urban areas it was simply unable to develop the programme of urban upgrading without the support and involvement of community organizations. The government could not therefore impose a technocratic solution based on affordability. Equally, the community organizations recognized, with great reluctance, that financial and technical constraints would not allow the provision of full services. Even so, the approach need not have developed the way that it did. There could equally well have been an impasse. This is where the second facet was important.

The two major groups in the political struggle were the ANC and the Afrikaaner National Party (NP). To outsiders both groups, but particularly the latter, presented an intransigent and uncompromising facade. Within their own ranks, however, both operated a decision-making process which was driven by consensus. The British system of government which nominally formed the basis of governance was imposed on the Boer Republics after their defeat by the British during the Boer War, although it was never fully accepted. The Afrikaaners used it to achieve power, but never believed in it. Policy continued to be set by a secret society termed the Broederbond, which represented the collective interests of political, church and business leaders within the Afrikaaner community. The African people had never been part of that system in the first place, having been excluded from it by legislation. This meant that internally they continued to practise a system of consensual decision-making based loosely on tribal law.

Once a political impasse was reached and the NP was no longer able to suppress the opposition, the inherent and shared consensual traits enabled a two-tier system of decision-making to emerge. The upper tier of the *de jure* government retained legislative power, but the real decisions about fundamental issues regarding the management of different economic and social sectors were made at the lower level, which included both parties. The result was the development of new forms of power-sharing in the decision-making process.

Nature of the Decision-making

The struggle which formed the basis of the South African rent boycott was a political issue about the unacceptable quality of physical infrastructure.

With the political transition two fundamental changes occurred. On the one hand the state recognized the validity of this demand and agreed to address the issue. On the other hand, there was a recognition by community organizations that there was insufficient money to provide a high level of service to every family in South Africa, and therefore compromises would need to be made. This placed the role of technology at the centre of the debate. There were several different services involved and each had associated with it several different levels (water, for example, may be collected from a communal tank, delivered to communal or individual standpipes, or supplied to a house and fully plumbed internally. It can also be cold only or heated). This multiplicity of options carries with it the notion of multi-variable decision-making. If communities were to be an integral part of the decision-making process, they needed to take these types of decisions. To achieve this they had to question the role and structure of their own organizations and to develop new approaches to decision-making within the community structures. They also had to re-examine the nature of the relationship between themselves and support organizations such as development NGOs. In summary, the community had to deal with broad issues with multiple levels of decision-making and a strong economic and technical component.

Community Dynamic

Participation in a confrontational situation requires a strong, monolithic community organization. On the other hand, this type of structure suffers serious problems in a complex environment such as that just described. The widening debate about different levels of service increases the complexity, and the nature, of the decision-making process. The conditions which require multi-objective decision-making and priority setting also affect the internal dynamic of the community. Different interest groups form and the community organization, if it is to survive, needs to recognize these changes and adapt its structure accordingly. A failure to do this can have serious consequences, in terms of internal conflicts, for both the civic and the community.

This is illustrated by the example of Alexandra, discussed later, and was an important feature which shaped the national civic movement during the political transition. Chapter 11 focuses on this issue in depth, as it is central to the creation of new and effective participatory strategies in this type of environment. The chapter provides three case studies of upgrading projects in South Africa which focus on both the internal and external relationship problems faced by community organizations when participating in urban upgrading programmes. One of these in particular, namely Luganda in Natal, provides a good illustration of how one such community organiza-tion dealt with this type of internal change. Although benefiting from the community being small and closely knit, the process which is described here could equally be applied to larger, more diverse communities.

The project application for Luganda was submitted to the IDT jointly by a non-governmental development organization and the Luganda Residents Association (LRA). The application was for the servicing of 1861 sites. The LRA had unanimous support among residents in Luganda and maintained a high degree of community involvement in the project, with community meetings held regularly every second or third Sunday for report back and discussion.

With the approval of the project, Luganda residents became responsible for a R13 million project, and this necessitated a review of community structures. During the period between the application and approval of the project a civic was formed which took over responsibility from the LRA. This body was also responsible for negotiating, at a policy level, issues such as service charges and the future of local government. During this intervening period, the Borough of Pinetown had also taken over the responsibility for the ongoing maintenance of services and the future administration of Luganda. Resulting from these changes, the Borough proposed a closer relationship with the civic on the IDT project.

The initial relational structure envisaged by the community organization is shown in Figure 11.5 in Chapter 11. With hindsight this proved to be idealistic. The various external actors were too powerful to accept a supportive role. More importantly, however, the notion of a monolithic civic structure also proved inadequate for dealing with this type of project. The civic felt that they could be compromised in the wider political negotiating process if they were to become too closely involved with the Borough (Luganda was just one of a dozen African settlements in the southern Pinetown area and major negotiations were anticipated in the coming months on a variety of sensitive issues). Hence another body was needed as a vehicle to manage the IDT project. There was already a working committee in Luganda, at which the civic and various community groups (eg women, youth, sport and religious bodies) met to discuss the wider needs of the community, but this was also considered inappropriate. As a result, a third body was formed, namely the Luganda Development Trust (LDT).

The management structure which emerged from the Luganda negotiation process is shown in Figure 11.6. It may appear initially to be awkward and unwieldy. In fact, and in practice, it reflects a deep understanding on the part of the community of the complexities of the participation process. The Luganda project evolved naturally into three community participation components: a civic, representing the political demands of the community; a trust, taking technical and financial responsibility for a specific project; and the working committee, which, in conjunction with mass meetings, was the vehicle for expressing people's needs and concerns on local issues. In essence, what the evolution of the different groupings in Luganda represented was a specific approach to dealing with a heterogeneous community which, because of the complex nature of the decision-making process and the involvement of external actors, has different internal objectives and priorities which need to be reconciled.

The Primary Objective of the Community Participation Process

The relationship between urban upgrading and the wider environment can be explained most easily through a case study, in this case the upgrading of the Alexandra township which was discussed in Chapter 4. This section described the growth of Alexandra over a long period and the way in which residents were continually manipulated for ideological reasons. It would therefore be logical to assume that any improvements which took place would be directed towards benefiting the community. In reality this was, and could only be, partially true.

The discussion in Chapter 4 listed 12 groups of actors. The impact of such a proliferation of parties was to fragment the process of decision making. The irony was that this fragmentation was caused because the sole focus was stated to be the upgrading of the community. In practice, the different actors focused on very different needs and had different agendas. However, because the objective was supposedly a common one, these needs were suppressed, and agendas became hidden. The reality was that the physical improvement of services could not be treated in isolation, but needed to be addressed within the context of alternative political structures and appropriate financial mechanisms for long-term operation. Metropolitan planning needs should have been taken into account. Alternative land tenure systems should have been evaluated, which would in turn have required new policy initiatives from central government. By focusing solely on the community, the development professionals were evading their responsibilities. Engineers were designing and building infrastructure systems which were not sustainable. Planners were accepting a structure plan which benefited 15 per cent of the population at the expense of the remaining 85 per cent, and which created a recipe for civil strife.

The primary objective, in this kind of situation, has to be the achievement of balanced development which takes into account several different needs and recognizes the large number of variables. The community needs have to be integrated with the needs of other geographical areas. Development professionals have to recognize their wider responsibilities. In urban development, it is virtually impossible to identify a situation wherein the needs of the community can be considered in isolation. The community is part of a wider physical environment, and it is essential that the interaction between the community and this wider environment is taken into account,

Role of External Actors

The types of external inputs which were required to support the new circumstances described here had as great an impact on the NGOs as they did on the community organizations themselves (see Chapter 12 for a wider discussion of this issue). During the apartheid era NGOs had a clearly defined role and were required by circumstance to be partisan, supporting communities totally in their struggle against the state. During the transition this changed. On one level there remained a need for partisan support, in training community organizations to deal with technically complex subjects, for example. However, even this needed to be less politically driven than it had previously been. For those NGOs had to debate with engineers and other development professionals who did not understand, and were extremely wary of, what they perceived to be the NGOs' political agenda. At the same time there was a co-ordination/mediation role developing which was necessary to manage the multi-variable decision-making process. The same development NGOs wanted to play this crucial part, but found it conflicting ideologically with their strong pro-community stance. This resulted in a change of alignment and emphasis, not only among the NGOs, but among development professionals generally, as they sought to redefine their historical roles. The resulting intervention needed to be multi-faceted and serve a variety of different needs, some of which will be politically aligned and some politically neutral.

In summary, the characteristics of urban upgrading projects can be classified under the same broad headings as for previously described forms of participation.

1 They operate within a strongly interactive relationship between the community and the state, in which the government is open to the involvement of the community.
2 They deal with broad issues with multiple levels of decision-making and a strong economic, and often technical, component.
3 They have to be able to deal with a heterogeneous community which will have different objectives and priorities which need to be reconciled.
4 The participation system process should lead to the achievement of balanced development which takes into account several different needs and recognizes a large number of variables.
5 The type of intervention required is multi-faceted and serves a variety of different needs, some of which will be politically aligned and some politically neutral.

The involvement of communities in complex urban upgrading marks a partial return to the original notion of development, wherein there was a national programme which was carried out through a series of localized projects. The involvement of communities in the provision of infrastructure for their own areas cannot be separated from the wider policy debate. This is because it is at the national (or regional) level where the discussion on the balance between needs and affordability, the social cost of different levels of service, operational policy and subsidy policy takes place. There is also a major difference. Now the social cost and the social impact of different levels of service are an integral part of the agenda. The result is a move away from the current project-based participation towards a multi-sectoral programme with a project component.

This provides the basis for the detailed development of this new form of community participation which is carried through in the following chapters. At the same time, this exploration of the characteristics of urban upgrading completes the set of analyses of the different approaches. The next chapter will draw together the different characteristics which have been identified in the last three chapters and use these to provide a basis for a unified theory of community participation.

The Community Participation Surround

INTRODUCTION

Two conclusions were drawn from the early historical analysis of community participation which have since become fundamental principles. The first is the notion that there is a single dominant form of participation and the real problem of research into participation is to define and quantify that form. The second is that community participation is essentially a struggle between those governed and those governing, which can be described in the form of a duality. Neither of these 'principles' has been seriously questioned in the intervening period, with the result that they form the foundation of virtually all major research work on the topic.

Both of these assumptions are invalid. In respect of the first, different approaches to community participation continue to flourish. This is clearly illustrated by the continued success of community development, albeit in specific circumstances. With respect to the second, there are times when a duality between community and state does form the basis of the participation process, but this is far from being a universal condition. So neither of the two facets constitutes a basic principle of participation. Earlier researchers, influenced by the ideological struggles taking place at the time, misinterpreted the paradigm approach model. Essentially, this model of community participation was an extremely good hypothesis, given the knowledge and the political economic climate of the time. Its major importance simply lies in a different area.

Because it was so closely allied to the political and economic debate of the time, community participation was interpreted as a linear model, wherein one form of participation supersedes another. An alternative interpretation of the paradigm approach model is to view it as the first phase in the development of a multi-faceted and complex model of community participation in the decision-making process. Seen in this light two very different principles emerge. The first of these is that there are different approaches to participation, and the model defined two, community development and empowerment, which have both stood the test of time, although there are also others. Community management is one of these, as is the form of negotiated development currently evolving in South Africa to deal with the problems of urban upgrading.

The second, and possibly more important, principle is that all forms of participation operate within some type of surround and are influenced by that surround. Unfortunately, the specific surround chosen for the paradigm approach model, namely the economic development paradigm, was too restricted and there was insufficient attention paid to the relationship between the form of participation and its surround.

These two principles form the basis of a new approach to community participation. The purpose of this chapter is to explore them in greater detail; to define a new type of relationship between the various different forms; to create a universal surround; and then, finally, to place urban management within this surround. The basis for achieving this is the integration of the different sets of characteristics of community participation which have been defined in the three previous chapters.

POWER AND COMMUNITY PARTICIPATION

What is power? In a paper in 1983, Shepherd stated that the ILO encouraged the use of the term to allow it to confront questions of power both ideologically and in its dealings with governments, following which he argued that

> '*decision making processes are the most obvious instances of the exercise of power. Therefore if participation in decisions can be broadened or made effectively representative, this means that power is being shared and that groups formerly excluded from the exercise of power are included'.*[1]

This remains a valid starting point for the debate on power. But what of community participation, and how do the two concepts merge and integrate?

The quotation talks of broadening participation in decision-making. This leads to the widely accepted concept that this broadening involvement can be represented on a continuum. Arnstein was the first person to develop this concept in 1969. She described participation in terms of a series of increasingly meaningful inputs into the decision-making process, with each rung corresponding to the extent of citizens' power in determining what she called the 'end product'.[2] This ladder had eight steps, an acknowledged simplification, as 'in the real world of people and programs, there might be 150 rungs with less sharp and "pure" distinctions among them'.[3] This is the continuum which is illustrated in Figure 8.1a. As discussed earlier, Arnstein was not challenging the state; instead, she was exploring ways in which citizens could increase their involvement in decision-making within a political structure which was broadly acceptable.

This is very different from the intepretation of power in a Latin American context. Figure 8.1b illustrates a second continuum, derived this time from the work of Moser. This is project-based and moves from project objectives, through capacity building to political empowerment. Such empowerment may be an idealistic objective, but the way in which the continuum is structured to achieve this objective is fundamentally flawed. To understand why this is so it is necessary to return to the first category

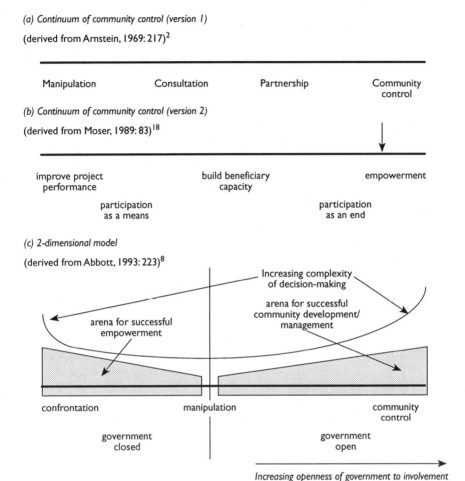

Figure 8.1 *Comparison of different interpretations of the relationship between power and community participation*

of characteristics derived from the evaluation of the different approaches, namely the openness of goverment.

ATTITUDE OF GOVERNMENT TO THE INCLUSION OF THE COMMUNITY IN THE DECISION-MAKING PROCESS

The dominant view of government in the participation process is derived from the analysis of participation in the early 1980s. This saw government either as manipulative of communities or controlling communities to meet the ends of a minority. The result has been a drive to reduce government to a supportive role in a process of empowering local communities. The resultant trend towards a focus on local communities prevents a realistic assessment of the relationship which is essential to a real understanding of community participation.

The problem with this world view is that it simplifies what is a very complex relationship between government and people. The reality, which is very different, is that it is simply impossible to define any aspect of communal life from which the government is totally absent. Having said that, it is necessary to recognize that there are different sectors within government as well as different types of involvement. Thus a distinction needs to be drawn between the legislative, executive and judicial arms of government, as well as between national, regional/provincial and local government. Within all of these there is a second, equally important, distinction to be drawn, namely that between active and passive involvement.

Failure to recognize this fundamental truth is one of the primary causes of misunderstanding in the debate on community participation, as illustrated by the differing viewpoints discussed in Chapter 5. The reality is that the government defines the wider framework within which the focus of the community participation process operates and, because the legislation affects every aspect of people's lives, it is virtually impossible to place projects totally outside the state system. Community development recognized this, accepted it and was designed to operate within the system. Its problem was with the specificity of its interpretation of government involvement, which made it dependent on the government playing an active and supportive part in the process. As a result it is a form of partic「-ipation which is easy to manipulate by an unscrupulous government.

This problem can be treated in several different ways. The first is the one adopted by the new community management programmes. This seeks to convert active support, on the part of the government, into a more passive type of support. Thus instead of controlling the process, the government's primary role changes to one of providing enabling legislation, approval of donor agency funding, etc. However, this still requires the government to be supportive of the focus of the community participation activity. This is more easily done within the context of a clearly defined project. Hence community management tends to be project-based.

There is a second response to the problem which is very different. When the government fails to be responsive to local needs, for whatever reason, then conventional participation, using either of the two described approaches, does not function effectively. Often, in this situation, the governments involved are authoritarian and, further, have little perceived legitimacy, coming neither from a democratic base nor a widely supported traditional base. As a result the government is threatened by local demands which are perceived to challenge its authority. This makes it closed to any community involvement in the decision-making process. Under these circumstances, the confrontational stance of the empowerment approach is ideally suited to forcing concessions from the state and it is in this type of situation that the empowerment approach has achieved its greatest success.

Successful participation in urban upgrading raises a new set of issues which is not covered by either of the two solutions just described. The government again needs to be supportive of the involvement of the community in the decision-making process, as with community development and community management. However, the type of support required by government is very different. The decisions to be made extend in their influence beyond the individual communities, so cannot be delegated. Equally, however, there is a need for local communities to be involved in this wider decision-making process. This requires more of a direct sharing of decision-making responsibility. This aspect of government–community relationships is governed directly by factors arising from the categories listed in the following pages.

This concept of government support/rejection can best be described by the use of the terms open and closed. In one situation the government is open to the involvement of communities in the decision-making process, whereas in the other situation it is closed. Clearly, there will be differing degrees of openness, thereby returning to the concept of a continuum, but it is not the conventionally perceived continuum which sees a steady transfer of power from the state to the community. Instead, it reflects the degree to which the state is prepared to delegate responsibility for aspects of the decision-making.

The result is illustrated in Figure 8.1c. Where the government is totally closed to community involvement and prepared to support this stance by the use of physical violence, then none of the approaches can work. As the government relaxes and creates windows of opportunity, then the way becomes open for political empowerment in specific areas. Ironically, this is the area in which communities can have the maximum power. However, it is also the area where the state will attempt to control by manipulation. As the state becomes increasingly open to community involvement, then community development becomes the most appropriate approach. Here, however, the state is still controlling the process. With further openness the state's role moves from active control to passive support through, for example, the passing of enabling legislation, and the way is open for community management.

This new interpretation illustrates how the form of political empowerment described and advocated by Moser and others does not lie at the end of the continuum. Instead, it is to the left of the manipulation/state-controlled zone. This is compatible with the realities of confrontation and political empowerment in the context of Latin America in the 1970s and 1980s. What lies at the extreme right of the continuum is much more akin to the type of community power described by Arnstein. In fact, Arnstein's continuum is identical to the right-hand side of Figure 8.1c. At this point on the extreme right there may in fact be real power, but this is not a natural progression. If it exists at all, it exists because the state chooses to delegate. So the one-dimensional continuum does not in fact address the issue of power at all in any meaningful way. It describes one component of power (albeit an important component), namely the openness of government to the inclusion of the community in the decision-making process. To explore power fully requires a knowledge of other facets which constitute power. This is where the other characteristics of different community participation approaches become relevant.

COMMUNITY PARTICIPATION AND THE FACETS OF POWER

Chapters 5, 6 and 7 examined different approaches to participation and identified their dominant characteristics. The hypothesis behind doing this was that there has to be some linkage between the different approaches; that they cannot operate totally in isolation. This proved to be the case.[4] At the same time, by classifying the approaches in some way, it was anticipated that this would provide an understanding of the wider aspects of community participation, in particular the relationship between power and decision-making. The characteristics of the four different approaches to community participation (community development, community management, political empowerment and negotiated development), can all be defined in terms of five broad categories, which are summarized in Table 8.1. Each of these deals with a specific aspect of this process. The issue of openness of government has already been addressed. The remaining four categories (the nature of the decisions to be made; the community dynamic, ie the interaction between different sectors of the community; the nature of the interaction between the community and the activity, be it a project or a programme; and the external facilitation process) are discussed in greater detail in the following pages.

Nature of the Decisions to be Made

This is the most complex characteristic after openness, as it has several different dimensions of its own. It is dealing with decisions which need to be made about an external activity with which the community is involved. One dimension reflects the basic type of decision, ie whether it is predominantly social, political or economic/financial. Increasingly, many decisions relating to development activities will also have a technical component. Some of the problems requiring decisions will relate more directly to social need, affecting the way in which people live in their everyday lives, and these are more easily processed by communities as they rely strongly on the use of tacit knowledge. This is often the case in community development related activities. However, these problems can also be translated into political demands, as in land invasion, for example, and in this form it is a characteristic of empowerment-driven participation. Where economic and technical issues dominate the debate around the problem, then this becomes significantly more complicated in terms of community decision-making. This is typical of the situation in participation on urban upgrading.

The second dimension relates to the number of variables which are generated by the problem and for which decisions have to be taken. The number of variables may not itself be inhibiting. For example, agricultural projects can demand multiple choices, but this can be dealt with at the

Table 8.1 *A summary of the characteristics of community development projects, empowerment projects and projects in urban upgrading*

Characteristic	Community Development	Empowerment	Negotiated Development
Role of government	Open	Closed	Open
Nature of the decision-making	Social/economic Small programmes, clearly defined outputs	Political/economic Single target programmes, clearly defined outputs	Economic/technical/social Multi-variable objectives, multi-faceted programmes
Community dynamic	Focused, through project selection	Focused through strength of communal need	Diffuse and heterogeneous
Primary purpose of the community participation process	Limited. The project/programme is community centred and can be managed without reference to the wider environment	Centred around the dispute between community and government. All other actions are subservient to this end	Integrated systems management Very open interaction with the wider environment. Cannot be dealt with in isolation
Role of external actors	Training focus	Educational focus	Integrated training and education

community level where it draws on local expertise, another example of the use of tacit knowledge. It is more complex when the subject is predominantly technical in nature, but again this depends on the interactions within the first dimension. For example, the decisions involved with building a creche are limited; and so is the decision about siting a well. Where five different water supply options are available, each of which has different financial and social implications, the level of complexity increases significantly. The role of technology is an increasingly important aspect of this particular category of decision-making and each of the three forms of participation has derived its own method of dealing with the problem. So, for example, where technology plays a part in community development programmes and community management projects, the technical capacity often does not exist to operate complex systems. In this situation ways are sought of identifying and supplying simplified technology which can be matched to the management capacity of local communities. This is the basis of intermediate or appropriate technology. The rationale behind this is to reduce the number of decision-making variables.

In empowerment struggles, on the other hand, technology is handled in a very different way. There is generally a much greater level of institutional and technological capacity within the countries concerned (ie those of Latin America), as was highlighted by Gilbert and Ward[5] in Chapter 6. From a government perspective, control over the physical infrastructure is seen as a valuable asset which can be used for leverage and patronage. Viewed from a community perspective, on the other hand, the infrastructure is seen as part of the operational urban management system and is something which the empowered will be able to take control over should their struggle be successful. What has happened in this case is a different form of simplification to that of community development. The decisions which should be operating in two dimensions have, in effect, been concatenated and reduced to a single issue, ie control.

In the situation where the infrastructure itself is the focus of the participation process, and particularly in Africa, where the management capacity is inadequate for the operation of complex services,[6] then neither of these routes is appropriate. There is a limit to the degree of simplification which can be provided to urban infrastructure. If communities are not going to have basic low level services imposed on them, then they must be able to take part in the debate on the level, cost and maintenance of infrastructure from the beginning and at a high level of technical debate. This takes the decision-making process into a new and relatively uncharted area of complexity.

Finally, and increasingly of greatest importance, is the degree of interaction with the different levels of decision-making. With the growing recognition of the importance of environmental sustainability, the freedom to take local decisions without reference to the wider physical environment is being reduced. Decisions will increasingly span different sectors. In addition, there will be an increasing interaction between decisions at local, regional, national and international levels. As this occurs so the boundaries between policy and implementation will become more blurred. What may have been perceived until recently as the preserve of national government, in the area of policy-making, for example, will increasingly be influenced by local level needs.

Community Dynamic

All activities have some impact on the community and modify the community dynamic in some way. Again, the different approaches deal with this issue in different ways. The whole basis of community development is that it seeks to assist groups who share a common problem, and this in turn creates its own form of homogeneity. This was clearly illustrated by the Aga Khan programme, where a pre-requisite to involvement by the AKRSP in a village was the support of 70% of the families in the village. This was made possible by the small size of the villages (averaging approximately 650 people).[7] Increasing the size by an order of magnitude, as experienced on some South African projects,[8,9] still allows a degree of consensus to be reached, but the likelihood is that smaller neighbourhood projects will become more common. Where the problem of size is compounded by government intransigence or opposition, then this type of project becomes almost impossible and this, of course, was the basis for the early criticism of community development.[10]

The empowerment approach itself never really tackled the problem of homogeneity. As Chapter 6 illustrated, it simply developed a new form of homogeneity. Thus it operated most successfully in situations where the needs of the community were greatest, and could be focused on a single dominant issue, so that a very strong sense of community cohesion could be generated. This type of cohesion was found in many communities in South Africa during the apartheid era. The problem is that this type of community cohesion is not sustainable, as was clearly demonstrated in the earlier discussion. When the specific objective is achieved, the reason for the cohesion is removed. The community may then fragment or become open to manipulation and destabilization.

The problem which needs to be faced by urban upgrading, and similar programmes being dealt with through negotiated development, is that they cannot escape the issue of community heterogeneity through either of the routes just described. As a result, they have to devise ways of dealing with it. The South African experience indicates that this issue of heterogeneity needs to be addressed on two levels. The first level is that which explores the nature of homogeneity within the community at a grassroots level. It is looking at groups from the perspective of their common interests. Thus it explores the needs of people as socially integrated neighbourhoods, as families, or even as individuals.

The forces of attraction operating at this level are weak in western society when faced with conflicts which negatively affect their homogeneity. This has led Smit to argue that

'the notion of a community is always something of a myth. A community implies a coherent entity with a clear identity and a commonality of purpose. The reality is that communities, more often than not, are made up of an agglomeration of factions and

> *interest groups often locked in competitive relationships. Development projects often have the effect of accentuating differences ...'.*[11]

He then lists, as an example, 12 axes of potential conflict, based on experiences in South Africa. These axes are:

- conflict between political organizations;
- conflict between different organizations claiming to represent the community;
- conflict between landowners and tenants;
- conflict between tenants of rental housing schemes and backyard shack people;
- conflict between hostel dwellers and local residents;
- ethnic tensions;
- conflict between youth and parents;
- conflict between local business people and residents;
- conflict between shack dwellers and those in formal housing;
- conflict between groups and individuals competing in the same terrain (eg taxi wars);
- conflict between traditional leaders and modernists;
- conflict between men and women'.[12]

What is being witnessed in this situation is a second level which is superimposing itself on the first and dominating it. It is a level which is dominated by power groupings and it is a condition which an unscrupulous state seeks to exploit, either to maipulate the wider community or to install a system of patronage. In dealing with community homogeneity, both levels need to be recognized and addressed. Having said that, it is the degree to which the second predominates which determines how close the participation is to dealing with the issue of power in any meaningful way.

PRIMARY PURPOSE OF THE COMMUNITY PARTICIPATION PROCESS

The means and end debate saw the purpose of community participation starkly in terms of a duality of community growth versus project success, although both were defined in several ways. In community management projects this view has some validity. Generally, however, with both these and community development projects the primary aim of the participation process can be seen to be the satisfaction of a clearly defined community need, carried out in such a way as to contribute to the long-term growth of the beneficiary group. In empowerment projects there may be an immediate goal, which is the focus of the struggle, but the primary aim is to improve the condition of the beneficiary group by causing a shift in the attitude of the state. Although different from the first, both of these share a primary focus on the needs of the community defined in terms of a beneficiary group.

The situation in negotiated development is different. Where the importance of economic and technical factors increases, and the number of variables in the decision-making process grows, this increases the number of actors who are involved directly and changes the process of interaction between them. However, it goes further than simply involving more actors. It exposes the interactive nature of the web which binds local development to changes in the wider environment.

Decisions around the former affect the latter and vice versa. In this situation, for the participation process to work effectively, the focus needs to be widened. Community need is still of major importance, but it has to be viewed in a wider context. The specific project has to be seen as interactive with the higher level policy decisions which affect that project.

Role of External Actors

There are substantial differences between the forms of external facilitation processes which are appropriate to different forms of community participation. This is illustrated by Srinivasan[13] in her description of behavioural concerns. Unlike Freire, who saw education a providing the basis for the cultural transformation of society, Srinivasan identified three different types of behavioural concerns which might be relevant to different people in different situations. These she defines as coping, transforming and transcending. She then argues that these three behavioural concerns

> 'correspond to three distinct (though not mutually exclusive) educational strategies that are currently in use at the micro level: Didactic . . .; Conscientization or Consciousness-raising . . ; and The Growth-Centred approach'.[14]

Srinivasan looks at these different strategies in relationship to people-centred development. It is worth examining what she says about this subject because of the way in which it reflects support for a specific type of external facilitation process. Thus she states that:

> 'The term "people-centred development", as applied in the 1989 Manila Inter-regional Consultation on Environmental Sustainable Development, reflected a loss of faith in the prevailing modes of development controlled by State-dominated policies and foreign-assisted institutions. This model was faulted for imposing external agendas on the poor, for weakening government accountability to its own citizens, for escalating the national debt burden, for depriving the poor of access to productive assets essential to their livelihood, and for divesting people of their sense of community and control over their own lives. Transformation of this system to one authentically centred on people was thus seen as a priority concern. Such a change would restore control over resources to the people and their communities to use in meeting their own needs; would broaden political participation and official accountability through people's organizations and participatory local governments; would safeguard freedom of association and open access to information as a civic right; and would assess the success of the development efforts in relation to people's enhanced capacity to determine their own future'.[15]

Although this describes the philosophy which underpins community management, its relevance here is the way in which Srinivasan returns to Freire's belief that the type and form of external intervention is the key to achieving this social transformation. However, whereas Freire's route was via *conscientisacion*, Srinivasan uses the growth-centred approach, which is based on the notion of trainers as facilitators.

Both Freire and Srinivasan develop strong, valid arguments in support of their approach, but both suffer from the same weakness. Both relate their approaches to specific conditions which they see as the central issue to be addressed. With Freire it was freeing of the oppressed; in Srinivasan's case it is the breaking out of the poor from the poverty trap. The external facilitation role in negotiated development will be different yet again. The important point to make is that all are specific to particular approaches of community participation. They are not necessarily appropriate or feasible in other situations. It is therefore necessary to know which form of participation is correct for a given situation before an appropriate intervention strategy can be determined. This also means that there is a need for the organizations providing the external support to recognize these differences and to structure their own organizations accordingly. For this reason, the nature of the external facilitation process can be described as a secondary, rather than a primary, category. It is not of itself a determinant which relates directly to power (for the community), although it can be used as a way of obtaining power for those doing the facilitation. This question is dealt with in some detail in Part 3 of the book.

COMMUNITY PARTICIPATION SURROUND

Listed separately, the characteristics of decision-making just outlined provide a useful explanation of why different approaches to community participation might be required in different situations. They also give some indication about which approach might be the most appropriate in a specific situation. In their descriptive and tabular forms, however, they are at best a guide and a tool for evaluation. They do not provide either a particularly useful or an easily accessible planning tool. What is now required is to restructure them into a form which is more specific and appropriate to the wider understanding of the community participation process.

The three categories, comprising the nature of the decisions to be made, the community dynamic and the primary purpose of the decision-making, all influence the achievement of real power through the community participation process. But they also go further than that as each one represents a different facet of what may be termed the complexity of the decision-making process. This in turn is an indicator of the complexity of the external surround within which the decision-making is taking place. It reflects a shift from a condition where single issues dominate the decision-making (the lowest point on the axis), through to a condition of multi-faceted and interactive decision-making. At a certain point between these two a transition occurs. Beyond this transition it is no longer possible to address community needs in isolation. At this point the essence of the participatory process changes from one which is community dominated to one which seeks to ensure the active and meaningful involvement of the community in a much broader decision-making process. The community is no longer the primary focus, but instead exists as part of a system.

By placing this integrated facet of complexity on a second axis with openness of government, a two-dimensional structure emerges which gives a more detailed understanding of the relationship between power and the participation process and describes the shift outlined earlier. Furthermore, because it has addressed the issue of power in totality, the relationship between openness of government and complexity of decision-making exposes the limitations of the duality paradigm of community versus state and provides a holistic surround in which to place community participation.

This surround can explain how the approaches of community development and empowerment, as well as community participation in negotiated development, operate successfully in different situations. It also goes much further. By breaking the surround down into sectors, which reflect different relationships between the two variables, it becomes possible to predict, for any given situation, the most appropriate form of community participation. This is an extremely useful planning tool, as it can show how the appropriate form of participation is in fact dictated by the wider surround. To provide optimum benefit in this regard, however, the sectors need to be broken down and their relationship defined. To describe the role of the different sectors of the surround within which the different participation approaches are appropriate, they were defined as 'arenas of community participation'.[16]

ARENAS OF COMMUNITY PARTICIPATION

The community participation surround is illustrated graphically in Figure 8.2. The wider surround itself is defined in terms of the two determinant factors placed on axes. The horizontal axis represents the degree of openness of government towards the community participation process, starting on the left with a closed system. The vertical axis represents the increasing complexity of the decision-making process. This two-dimensional surround then generates four sectors.

The first sector is sited on the left-hand side of the surround, where the government is closed to the involvement of the community in the decision-making process. The boundary of this sector moves to the right as the complexity increases. The reason for this is that it becomes easier for governments to maintain a non-participatory stance when there is a high degree of project complexity, as this makes community cohesion difficult. The government is in a very strong position to control the flow of information, which is an essential part of decision-making on complex issues. This sector is defined as the arena of exclusion, where community participation is extremely difficult, if not impossible.

The response of community organizations in this situation is to exploit specific windows of opportunity. The state may be oppressive, but it will often encounter difficulties in maintaining hegemony in all spheres of activity. Hence it remains closed to community involvement generally, but

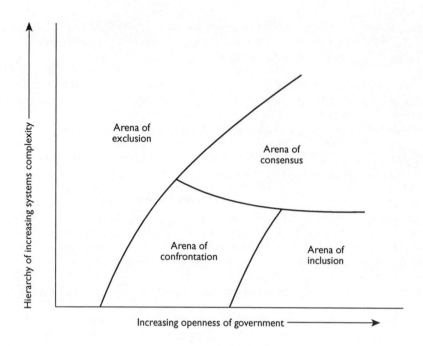

Figure 8.2 *Community participation surround and the different arenas of participation*

there are specific sectors or activities where some engagement is possible. This is the sector into which the political empowerment approach falls. However, community participation is possible in spite of government opposition only because the issue is a simple, straightforward one around which community cohesion and mobilization can occur. In terms of community participation this sector is defined as the arena of confrontation.

Further to the right lies a sector in which the project is simple, but where the government is now open to a degree of involvement by the community in the decision-making process. The community development approach falls into this sector. Here the government supports community involvement, but it takes place within a government-defined framework. In terms of community participation, this sector is defined as the arena of inclusion.

Moving upwards and further to the right leads to the fourth and final sector, in which the project is complex, but where the government remains open to the involvement of the community in the decision-making process. Negotiated development as a form of community participation falls within this sector, which is defined as the arena of consensus. Because the decision-making is more complex and part of a wider system, the outcome here is different to that which operates in the arena of inclusion. Essentially neither party is able to take complete control. At the same time, however, they cannot always make the decisions together because there are other factors involved which bring in other actors. There may also be deep-rooted differences between them. The result is a move towards new forms of decision-making which revolve around different forms of consensus, of which the negotiated development approach is just one. The arena of consensus abuts both the arena of inclusion and the arena of confrontation. Generally the shift away from confrontation on the part of the government will incline towards the arena of inclusion, as this still leaves the state in the position of power. In the South African situation, however, this did not happen. Instead there was a transition to the arena of consensus, although the transition occurred around the junction of the three.

The siting of activities in different sectors of the surround makes it possible to view community participation as a dynamic process. The political, social and economic conditions surrounding an activity may be examined to see the way in which changing conditions of government openness and changing complexity might push the activity in the direction of another sector and thereby change the arena of community participation. For example, with the Buenos Aires project (Chapter 3), Cuenya *et al*[17] argue that the return to a democratic system of government means that the previous channels by which participation was practised (which were confrontational) become inadequate. In other words, there is a force pushing the project from the arena of confrontation into the arena of inclusion. If allowed to proceed this would lead to what Cuenya *et al* call conventional urban politics. However, if a need then arose for greater community involvement in discussions around wider urban issues, including technical issues, this would create a new force. The community would become involved in a much wider system, as happened in South Africa, and this would create a force pushing in the direction of the arena of consensus. If this were to happen, a different type of community participation would then become necessary.

This recognition that community participation takes place within a dynamic surround, and that conditions can therefore change in a variety of ways (including reversibility), is critical to an understanding of community participation. It is also a factor which is not dealt with in existing publications. Although Moser accepted that projects might require a time period to change to participation as an end,[18] this was an idealized one-way movement along a one-dimensional continuum. In the surround shown in Figure 8.2, the forces which induce change can be identified for different scenarios and can influence change in any direction. The probable impact on the participation process, which may even necessitate a change to the appropriate participation approach, may thus be deduced.

What becomes important in this situation is the surround itself. The notion of power as expressed through decision-making is broken down into its constituent parts. The surround with its different arenas becomes a predictive tool which increases understanding and improves the chances of success in community participation. Finally, the surround provides the conceptual framework which forms the basis for more appropriate implementation of community participation (Chapter 9).

DELINKING APPROACHES FROM THE WIDER SURROUND

The generation of this surround constitutes a radical departure from the existing interpretations of community participation. The notion that participation is structured to match a definition is superseded. Existing approaches can be seen for what they really are, ie responses to a specific activity which is situated at a specific point in the surround. This is distinct from the surround itself. Hence an approach cannot change when the nature of the activity and its position in that wider surround changes.

This can now be demonstrated by summarizing the findings of the historical analysis in Chapters 2 and 3. In the first instance, the paradigm approach model recognized that there was a link between a specific approach to community participation and a specific surround. In that instance, however, it did not define the term broadly enough. Instead it chose an economic paradigm, which was itself subject to change. This left the associated approach in a difficult position conceptually. The approach was then linked to a project. This was totally unsuitable as a surround, however, as every project was different. The way out of this dilemma was to abandon the notion of a surround. In its place the approach was linked to something which was considered universal, namely the definition. However, a definition is an abstract ideal which does not recognize the validity of other

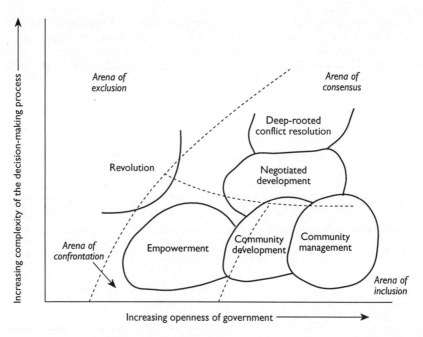

Figure 8.3 *Different approaches as appropriate responses in the four arenas of community participation*

factors to modify the participation process. The world is not an ideal and there is a myriad of practicalities to be dealt with. There is no approach which, when matched against an ideal, can cope with these realities. The result was a condition which was the opposite of that of the paradigm approach model. Instead of being superseded, the approach becomes fixed and immutable. It may be refined, but that is the limit of the allowed change. To take this change further would be to invalidate the definition. Faced with this conundrum, the different actors, with their different needs and agendas, will seek to interpret the approach in a way which is compatible with these agendas, ie each will interpret the term community participation in the light of their own rationality.

The only viable alternative is a universal surround, with many different approaches. In this way the approach is matched to the condition pertaining to a specific point within the surround, rather than being mistaken for the condition. The result is shown in Figure 8.3. Here different approaches have been superimposed on the surround in terms of their relationship with different arenas. This shows clearly how they are responses to a specific condition, why they are appropriate in specific situations and why they are superseded when conditions change. And conditions do change, continuously and, sometimes, rapidly.

COMMUNITY PARTICIPATION AND SYSTEMS THINKING

Successful community participation will lead eventually to the arena of consensus. This will arise either because communities find themselves already operating within complex systems, as with the South African transition, or because the success of programmes in the arena of inclusion will lead to a broadening of the base of activities with which communities are involved.

The axis of increasing complexity differs from the axis of openness in that it is not an obvious continuum. Instead it appears to involve a step change from issue-based decision-making to systems-based decision-making. These two forms of decision-making require actors, including community-based actors, to perform in different ways. The nature of this difference and its effect on different actors is discussed in Part 3. This section will limit itself to a discussion of the nature of the transition as this is central to an understanding of community participation in all complex activities, including urban management.

Analysis and decision-making may be explored in two different paradigms. The first is scientific reductionism, the breaking down of a problem or difficulty 'into as many parts as might be possible and necessary in order best to solve it'.[19] The apparent discontinuity of the axis of complexity indicates that this is not the appropriate paradigm in which to understand community participation in complex decision-making processes.

The second paradigm is that of systems thinking, a 'concept of organized complexity'.[20] This holistic thinking is built around two characteristics, hierarchy and emergence. In the first, there is a hierarchical type of organization, with a hierarchical theory concerned with the fundamental differences between one level of complexity and another,[21] wherein emergent properties denote the levels.[22]

Viewed in this light, the transition along the axis of complexity begins to make sense. There is no longer a need to assume a discontinuity in the transition. Instead there is a move along a systems hierarchy from one level of complexity to the next. Viewed in this light it becomes clear that participation may take place effectively at any point on the axis, provided that the type of participation used is appropriate to that level of complexity. In other words there is a continuum along this axis, based on a hierarchy of increasing systems complexity, of which community participation forms an integral part. This provides the final definition of the second axis.

URBAN MANAGEMENT AND THE ARENAS OF COMMUNITY PARTICIPATION

The recognition that community participation operates within a human activity system finally eliminates the idea of a single participatory process. It also brings with it new problems, for it means that there could more than one participatory process operating at any one time. This can only succeed if there is a clear understanding of where each of these different processes interlink, and what their relationship is with the hierarchy of complexity. This can be illustrated by a case study of urban management as it applies to South Africa at the present time.

Chapters 4 and 7 discussed the variables present in urban infrastructure provision. When these are translated into real situations in a South African context, three levels of complexity begin to emerge. The highest is at the level of the urban centre and is particularly relevant to metropolitan centres. Apartheid has created separate geographical areas based on racial classification, but these areas also have highly variable levels of infrastructure and amenities. The highest level of complexity of participation will involve the redistribution of wealth and assets between the various areas. This involves all residents equally. The second level will deal with the future nature of particular suburbs, their levels of densification, amenities, etc. Here the views of the residents of the particular suburb will carry a greater weighting. However, because there will be a tendency, particularly in more well-endowed suburbs, to retain the status quo, other areas will have a right to be involved in this decision-making process. The third level is that of management of the services and amenities within the individual suburbs. Here the participatory process will limit itself almost exclusively to the residents of that particular suburb. This level is now moving towards the area of local community management.

In other words, lowest level systems may operate within higher level systems. There may be participation taking place within the arena of inclusion, but this will be part of a wider participatory process which is operating in the arena of consensus. These different processes must work together. At the same time, however, they must avoid mixing issues. So the participatory process around the issue of local area management must not become directly involved in the debate about redistribution of resources. If it does, then there is a strong possibility that both processes will fail. To achieve successful community participation under these conditions there needs to be a clear understanding of the key issues which govern the process in the different arenas, ie the implementation of community participation.

Building a Practical Model of the Community Participation Process

INTRODUCTION

The wider surround, with its associated arenas, forms the basis of the community participation process. As such it can also be described as the conceptual framework for community participation. Clearly this is much wider than previous uses of this term.[1] It is a more accurate interpretation, however, as it determines the most appropriate form of participation necessary for the decision-making process to function optimally in respect of any given activity. The conceptual framework of surround and arenas provides the foundation for the participation process which follows. It is, of itself, incomplete, however, as it does not indicate how the participation process will operate in practice. For this, an effective strategy of implementation is required. Although the conceptual framework provides the first component of the participation process, it is the implementation strategy which provides the second, complimentary, component. Together these two components comprise the structure of the participation process.

It was the lack of a logical and cohesive relationship between concept and implementation which was a major shortcoming of previous models of community participation. The paradigm approach model focused on the relationship between the approach and the wider surround (the paradigm) and, consequently, never successfully addressed the issue of detailed implementation. The project-based model, on the other hand, focused almost exclusively on implementation, without giving adequate consideration to the wider surround. The latter, of course, has had some success with the use of community management, because it has been operating almost exclusively within the arena of inclusion, for which it is well suited. But why is it so well suited to this arena, and what type of implementation is suited to other arenas?

There is still something missing. The conceptual framework provides the basis for choosing the appropriate arena, but it does not detail how the transition to an effective implementation strategy will happen. Nor does it describe that strategy, which will be different for different arenas. This is a separate exercise. Fortunately, much of the earlier discussion on the historical development of community participation provides the information necessary to construct appropriate implementation strategies. This is the purpose of the chapter.

IMPLEMENTATION AND THE ELEMENTS OF COMMUNITY PARTICIPATION

By definition, community participation can only be expressed through an activity of some kind. Hence there is always an interaction between the activity itself and the community group involved with that activity. This interaction then generates its own dynamic. Moser recognized that, historically, where the activity is a project, then the project has tended to dominate and determine the nature of the participation process.[2] Thus she perceived the relationship between the two as one of dominance/ subservience. The basis of the end approach to participation was the dominance of the participation process over the project. Recognizing the problems this entails in practice she argued, as quoted earlier in Chapter 3, that 'In reality it is not the evaluation of participation either as a means or as an end which is important, but the identification of the process whereby participation as a means has the capacity to develop into participation as an end'.[3] Thus there is a transition from dominance of the project to dominance of the participation process. This seems logical in theory, but it has serious practical difficulties.

The fundamental flaw from which most research, including that quoted here, suffers, is that it is reductionist in its approach, rather than analytical. Thus it seeks to explain community participation in terms of a single, clearly defined ideal. To achieve this goal, key phrases have been developed which aim to encapsulate the essence of the community participation process and develop a single form of participation which is applicable to all situations in all parts of the world. The interaction between the activity and the beneficiary community does not operate in that way and should be seen rather as a symbiotic relationship between two complex processes. Depending on the nature of the activity this interaction can operate in two ways. The first is limited to the beneficiary group and the activity, whereas the second is wider, embracing a range of outside actors, as described in the previous chapter. The elements of community participation are the products of these interactions and it is these elements which translate the conceptual framework from a theoretical concept to a practical vehicle applicable to real situations.

There have been several researchers who, while not producing alternative models of the participation process themselves, did identify certain elements which appeared to influence the participation process. A limited number were also used by researchers linked to the project-based model.[4-6] In all cases, however, the effective use of these diverse elements was hindered by constraints of existing models, as well as by problems of terminology. Thus the same term, used by different workers, might have different meanings, depending on the context within which they are situated. When these diverse terms are rationalized, grouped and compared, they generate a total of 11 elements which appear to be important and need to be accounted for in the community participation structure.[7] These are:

- the objectives of the activity;
- the intensity of participation;
- the instruments of participation;
- the wider surround or environment which influences the participation process;
- the specific arena within which the participation process operates;
- identification of the primary actors;
- the roles, agendas and relationships of the different actors;
- the point of input into the participation process, and who decides this;
- the practical implementation of the participation framework;
- the differing needs of the community;
- the needs of the other actors.

Once the elements have been identified, they need to be related to the different components of the structure, and weighted in some way. For example, some may be core issues, others may be only peripheral or even descriptive, and some may not be at all relevant. Two of the elements, namely the wider environment and the specific arena, are already accounted for, as they also constitute a component and sub-component, respectively, of the conceptual framework. This leaves nine elements to be allocated. However, because the wider environment generates three different operational arenas of community participation, and the interaction between the elements and the structure is not necessarily the same for all three arenas, the process of allocation will need to be carried out separately for each of the three operational arenas. By definition, no community participation can operate within the arena of exclusion.

BUILDING AN IMPLEMENTATION STRATEGY WITHIN THE ARENA OF CONSENSUS

The arena of consensus is the only one of the three operating arenas sited in a complex environment. This makes it the most likely arena to utilize all the remaining elements. Having carried out the allocation within this arena the same process can then be repeated for the arenas of inclusion and confrontation.

Customizing the Conceptual Framework: step I

Effective implementation of an activity requires a balance between idealism and pragmatism; between what is desired and what is, practically, achievable. In striking a balance between these two, it is necessary first to define what constitutes the ideal, so that there is a goal against which the implementation strategy can be measured. This is defined as customizing of the conceptual framework and comprises a two-stage process. The first step involves identifying those elements which encapsulate the key issues of the participation process within a specific arena. At the same time there has to be a recognition that every activity has unique features which are specific to that particular situation. This means that this first step is concerned with generalities; it needs to replicable for all activities regardless of sector or geographical areas.

The complexity of the arena of consensus is reflected by an increase in the number of variables in the decision-making process as well as the fact that there are political, economic and technical implications to any decisions which are made, which impact on areas outside the immediate proximity of the activity. For this reason other actors become involved in making those decisions; it is no longer the preserve of the government and a community-based representative organization alone. Nor are these other actors all 'external' to the community. The stresses generated within the community mean that the community itself can divide, not necessarily destructively, and be represented by more than one organization.

At first sight the result appears to be a wide and diverse group of primary actors, which makes the decision-making process inoperable. In practice, these actors can be divided into collective representative groups, which in turn can be divided into seven categories. Firstly, there are politicians and officials at different levels of government. Secondly, there will be national and regional opposition groupings, operating both within and outside the formal political structures. Thirdly, there will be the local community organizations and interest groups. These may be supported by a range of NGOs, the fourth group, while any or all of these parties may draw on the services of technical and/or managerial professionals, the fifth group. There will often be a financial interest, represented by financial institutions and funding agencies. This is the sixth group. And, finally, in many projects and programmes there will be a strong parastatal and/or private sector commercial interest, the seventh and last group of actors. This list of actor groups represents the first element defining the customized conceptual framework.

Each of these actor groups brings with them not only their own interpretation of the needs of the programme/project, but also their own expectations of the result or output. In this analysis of the conceptual framework, Paul[8] used the term objectives, but this is unsatisfactory for two reasons. Firstly, an objective already has specificity, and, as argued earlier, the conceptual framework needs to deal with generalities. The second problem is one which illustrates a fundamental flaw occurring in many existing analyses of community participation, which is sub-conscious bias. From where does an objective develop? A development project is not a scientific exercise in which variables can be controlled. The interpretation of an event in development cannot exist independently of personal circumstance and individual rationality. An analysis of Paul's objectives shows them to be heavily weighted in favour of the World Bank view of development, who in this case also happens to be the client for the report. This example is illustrative and does not reflect Paul's motives in any way. There is no intended bias in Paul's work. It is the act of defining an objective which is itself selective. Equally, this argument can be applied to any group of actors. The failing is not limited to funding agencies.

What is needed in this situation is a recognition of the bias and personal agendas of different groups of actors. Thus a better term to use, which recognizes that subjectivity, is need. This may, in turn, be divided into four broad categories:

1   the needs of the community;
2   the needs of the project;
3   the needs of the state (ie needs dictated by national policy); and
4   the needs of other actors.

Each of these may be fairly complex and diverse in itself. The elements described, ie the categories of needs, and their associated groups of actors, together constitute the basis of the customized conceptual framework. A useful way of representing this framework is that of a two-dimensional matrix, as illustrated in Figure 9.1. The horizontal axis lists the major needs to be satisfied by such a project, whereas the vertical axis identifies the key groups of actors involved in the project and links them to the needs. This in turn provides the basis for the second step.

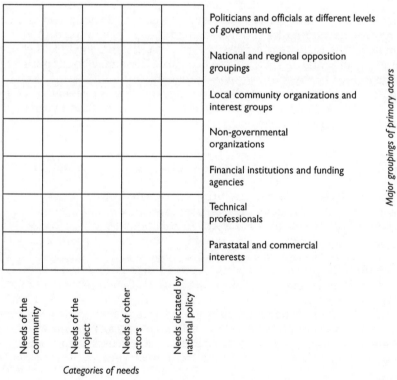

Figure 9.1 *Matrix of categories of needs and actors*

Customizing the Conceptual Framework: step 2

Up to this point everything which has been described relating to the community participation process can be described in terms of generalities. So, firstly, whatever the activity, there will be one of four arenas which will be appropriate to the community participation process associated with that activity. Within the arena of consensus, the key elements become the major actor groups and the different categories of need. This is where the generalities end. Beyond this point everything related to the participation process becomes activity-specific. For example, the generalized relationship between actors and needs has to be made activity-specific and no two sets of actors or needs will be the same for different projects or programmes.

So the second step in customizing the conceptual framework is to identify the specific actors and particular needs which are relevant to the project in question. Figure 9.2 is an illustrative example of the typical relationship between actors and needs in urban infrastructure provision projects in South Africa.

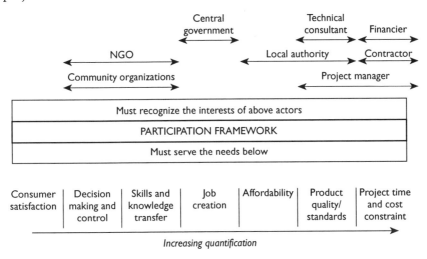

Figure 9.2 *Relationship between objectives and actors in the provision of urban infrastructure*

The needs of the different actors are listed sequentially from left to right in terms of increasing quantification. The more easily a need can be quantified, the greater the weighting it receives among external actors (especially technical and financial actors). This bias, which probably reflects the most difficult aspect of the participation process, needs to be overcome. This is actually the crux of the debate about community participation in projects specifically, because it calls for the qualitative needs of communities to be placed on a par with the quantitative needs of technocrats. Thus it is the debate between quantitative and qualitative criteria, rather than between means and ends, which is the pivotal issue.

Even where the actors agree the full list of needs and their inclusion for equal consideration, they will retain their own priorities, which suit their own agendas. A process of negotiation is then required to achieve a commonly agreed list of priorities for the project. To achieve success, two basic principles, which define the basis of the relationship between needs and actors, need to be adopted by all parties. These are: (1) that all primary actors have an equal role in the decision-making process; and (2) that all needs should begin with an equal weighting and then be prioritized by agreement among all the actors. Both of these represent a radical departure from the existing orthodoxy of community participation. Firstly, there has to be a recognition of the rights of outside actors. Experience from South Africa indicates that community organizations will recognize and accept this principle after discussion; the real opposition is more likely to come from government and radical NGOs.

Secondly, this means that there may be more than one representative group from the community, with different groups representing different interests. Again, all have an equal place in the negotiations.

There are three major areas in the development of the working model where serious problems with the potential to disrupt the participation process can occur. These relate to (1) the point of entry of the community into the decision-making process; (2) the acceptance, by all the actors, of the principle of equal treatment of needs; and (3) dealing with the fact that some actors may have more than one need. These are now dealt with in turn.

Point of Input of the Community

This whole area is one of immense confusion. The problem is that there are really three issues relating to community involvement which are often used interchangeably, but which are very different. These are the point of input; the form of community representation; and the intensity of community involvement.

Ideally the community is involved in the decision-making process from the beginning, and for a project to exist there has to be a person or group claiming to be the representative of the community. What is critical to the success of the community participation process is the legitimacy of this representation.

A detailed social survey may provide all the important information on community needs and community dynamics, but this leads to the issue of who plans, controls and interprets the survey. Resolution of this issue (discussed in detail in Chapter 13) is critical. A further problem, based on South African experience,[9] is that community organizations which have previously led a political struggle often see themselves as the sole representatives of their communities, having won this right in the struggle. Community organizations have to recognize that this viewpoint may be incompatible with the realities of complex projects and be prepared to allocate responsibility to different community groups for the wider community to participate effectively. Thus representation, which defines a complex process in which information on the community is gathered and working structures established for the different community organizations, is actually the key issue and not the point of entry per se. Although initiated at the early stage of customizing the conceptual framework, this re-allocation of responsibility within the community may well be a prolonged process extending into project implementation, as the areas of responsibilities of the different groups change in importance during the life of the project.

Finally, there is the question of intensity. Again, the way in which this is used by Paul as one of the dimensions of the conceptual framework reflects a specific interpretation of the community participation process from the perspective of an external actor. Intensity develops with the working model and is not an element of either the conceptual framework or the implementation strategy. Where it does have a role is in the evaluation of the community participation process.

Acceptance, by all the Actors, of the Principle of Equal Treatment of Needs

This was covered briefly earlier, using the example from urban upgrading. This represents potentially the most difficult factor inhibiting meaningful participation in decision-making. At the core of a problem is a difference, not only of perceptions, but of mind-set, described by Goulet[10] as the technological, political and ethical rationalities in development. Superficially, the major difference between actors appears to revolve around the issue of quantifiable output. The differences in rationality, however, combine to convert this into a deeper and more complex problem. What is needed is a new set of criteria for evaluating objectives which merge quantitative and qualitative criteria. One way of achieving this is to expand the notion of a performance specification for projects and programmes. This issue is explored in detail in Chapter 10.

Dealing with the Fact That Some Actors May Have More Than One Need

The third problem which now arises is that certain actors have more than one need. The matrix in Figure 9.1 provides the key to resolving this problem and developing a set of priorities. Once the matrix is modified to incorporate the specific actors and needs relevant to a particular project, then the process of priority setting can begin. The central feature of this process is an analysis which reflects the internal prioritization of the needs of each actor. Four levels of linkage are defined. The first is the primary (or dominant) linkage, which is identified by the sign ++. This is the need which each actor considers to be their highest priority. The second represent(s) the secondary or peripheral linkage(s), identified by the sign +, which include all of the actor's other needs. The third is that where the relationship between an actor and a particular need is neutral, which is indicated by the sign •. Finally, there is the situation where an actor may actually oppose the integration of a particular need into the participation process, a linkage which is indicated by the sign =.

The four categories are treated differently. Category one (++) is the most important and is rated highly in the decision-making process. The presence of more than one requirement by a particular actor would be handled by a process of internal priority setting in the presence of representatives of all the other actors. This would form part of the wider decision-making process carried out collectively. The presence of category four (=) is indicative of serious misunderstandings over the process and highlights potential areas of stress. The aim must be to remove all opposition linkages by a process of education of the actors involved. It is important that each actor recognizes the validity of the needs of the other parties before the negotiation process on prioritization is started. One important outcome of this process is that one specific type of community organization may not be able to represent the diverse community needs adequately. Hence more than one community organization may be required. The actual process of priority setting can be carried out through appropriate mediation techniques, which leads to the fourth problem area, the nature of the participation support mechanisms.

Instrument of Community Participation

Effective community participation almost always requires some form of intervention by outside parties. The result has been an over-emphasis on what Paul describes as the instruments of community participation, ie the organizational form which provides the support. Again, this is an indication of the subconscious bias which derives from a specific rationality. It is not the instrument which is important as the purpose of the intervention. In the arena of consensus, with the working model described earlier, several different forms of intervention may be required. Firstly, there may be a need for a mediating role, chairing the meetings of actors. Secondly, there could be an educational and/or training role in assisting community organizations with technical and economic details. Finally, there may need to be an internal co-ordinating role among the various community groupings. Each of these will require different skills and a different relationship with the actors. This question of intervention is expanded in the next section and discussed in detail in Chapter 13.

The working model then deals with three elements of the community participation process. In the first the detailed list of common objectives is identified and prioritized. The second deals with the point of input of the community into the process, recognizing that this term is inappropriate and that the real issue is the form of community representation in the process. The third element, namely the intensity of participation, is similarly inappropriate and is replaced with the form of intervention.

The process of developing the working model just described represents the ideal condition, where there is complete openness between parties, full access to information and equality among the parties. But then the working model is, intentionally, idealistic. It represents a set of working principles which all parties agree to as the basis for the project, as being necessary for meaningful community participation and, as discussed at the beginning of this section, is the first part of a two-stage process. In a practical situation the weaknesses of this ideal situation will be highlighted and compromises will have to be made. This takes place in the second phase of the implementation strategy, which determines the working model for implementation.

Hierarchy of Needs and Objectives: the Basis of Implementation

Once the conceptual framework has been customized for a specific activity, and an activity-specific matrix drawn up, then the process can proceed to the next step. Implementation of a community participation programme is an interactive process. Therefore it cannot be described in terms of a linear system such as the project cycle, but needs to be described in terms of an iterative system and the heart of this system is the working model. To commence this iterative process there has to be a starting point and this is not yet available.

Evolution of the Working Model: the Basis of a Successful Implementation Strategy

Two elements are central to this exercise: the relationship between the different actors and the parts that each actor will play in the implementation process. In theory the roles and relationships should follow through from the agreement of principle reached in the working model. In practice, the various actors are governed by various constraints (which will be different for the different actors), which can limit their ability to follow through the principles agreed. In developing the methodology of implementation, the constraints need to be identified. Once this is done, then either (1) corrective measures can be taken which will remove the constraint; or (2) there will need to be a compromise to the agreed principles which will enable the project to proceed.

The working model was studied through a series of case studies carried out in South Africa, which are discussed in detail in Chapter 11. Although the projects described in these case studies were specific in their application, the types of constraints which they identified reflect fundamental issues which occur in all development-related activities. As such, they summarize the problems which constrain effective implementation in all spheres of activity. There are four types of constraint.

1 Parties reneging on their commitments, as agreed in the working model. This may be caused by poor internal communication or by fear of the outcome of the process which has been set in motion. It is most likely to affect government linked actors. For example, political leaders may refuse to sanction agreements made by officials or by lower levels of government.
2 Parties being faced with internal conflicts which were not recognized at an earlier stage. This constraint is most likely to affect communities. There comes a point in a project where communities have to be represented by specific bodies. This is the point at which a project begins to coalesce and take form and all the different needs surrounding that project begin to emerge. This is where the question of community heterogeneity comes into play, because it is at this point that the different needs within the community will also begin to emerge. The form of representation of the community within the decision-making structures has to accommodate that diversity of

needs and interests. If the form of representation agreed at an early stage is inappropriate or undemocratic, then often the resulting tensions will only manifest themselves at the implementation stage.

3   Parties being unable to fulfil their functions due to external factors outside their control. This is the greatest impediment to full community involvement in decision-making on complex projects and can arise even though all parties agree shared principles and actively wish to translate these into practice. The factors preventing this fall into two categories: financial management and skills capacity. Financial responsibility for the project is a critical force driving the community to demand resources, knowledge and skills which are an essential component of the associated management function. The issues of shared decision-making and shared financial responsibility are inseparable. Yet because many lending agencies are constrained in whom they lend to, and many community organizations do not have a track record of financial management, the opportunities for community organizations to gain this financial experience often do not exist. The second factor is the large gap which exists, in terms of technical knowledge, skills and expertise, between technical professionals and community organizations. This severely constrains the community groups and prevents them from assuming their roles and taking their share of the responsibility. The primary focus of training should be aimed at redressing this imbalance.

4   A lack of understanding of the role of appropriate instruments of community participation for complex projects. As described earlier there are two distinct roles required of external instruments of participation. One is to provide not only training, but also expertise to community organizations in the performance of the latter's role in managing the project. This is a support service which requires a partisan agenda on the part of the support organizations. The other role involves managing the interaction between the parties as they set priorities and define their roles. This requires an independent, non-partisan actor. A failure to recognize the distinction between the different roles will weaken the capacity of communities to participate fully in implementation.

The creation of the working model is a complex exercise which is achieved through the iterative process illustrated in Figure 9.3. The first working model will generally reflect an idealistic situation which is strongly community-focused. In defining the roles of different actors this will bring out some of the constraints described earlier. There will need to be an assessment of capacity and an assessment of the impact that the constraints have on both the activity and community participation process. This in turn can affect the hierarchy of needs and objectives which will then modify the working model. This is where the balance between idealism and pragmatism becomes important. The full objectives of the participation process may not be achieved, but equally this can apply to the activity. What is important is not the output per se, but the way in which the decisions are reached. This is measured in the final component of the structure, which is the evaluation.

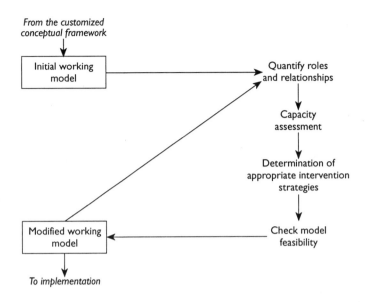

Figure 9.3 *Evolution of the working model for the implementation of community participation*

EVALUATING THE COMMUNITY PARTICIPATION PROCESS

The key to achieving successful community participation in activities lies in an understanding of the interaction between the activity and the involvement of people in that activity. The view that community participation is an input into a project, to improve effectiveness or efficiency, as suggested by Paul,[11] is not sustainable in the long term. However, neither is the project there to support or enhance community participation per se. The fact that it is there for the benefit of the wider community is not synonymous with being there for its own sake, ie as an end in itself. In reality, both the activity itself, particularly when carried out under conditions of extreme resource constraints, and the community participation are complex processes.

This requires a different approach to evaluation which (1) recognizes that what is being evaluated is the interaction between two complex processes; and (2) reflects the nature of this interaction. Both processes need to be evaluated separately, while recognizing the impact that each has on the other. Thus the success of the activity should be judged, not by technical and economic criteria alone, but also by the degree to which the project has managed to satisfy the hierarchy of needs identified in the working model.

The success of the community participation process, on the other hand, uses different indicators and there are two of these. The first indicator is the degree to which the prioritizing of needs is achieved through consensus. This reflects the success of the transition from the matrix of needs and actors to the achievement of a common hierarchy of needs and objectives. The second indicator is the intensity with which the community has been involved in project implementation, reflecting the transition from the idealized state to practical implementation, and thereby measures the effectiveness and appropriateness of the implementation strategy. Thus the element of intensity, which was previously considered an element of the conceptual framework,[12] is actually an evaluation tool which measures the success of the transition from a theoretical ideal of participation to the implementation strategy and ongoing participation in project implementation.

SUMMARY OF THE RELATIONSHIP BETWEEN ELEMENTS AND THE STRUCTURE OF COMMUNITY PARTICIPATION

There is a complex relationship between the elements of community participation and the structure of the participation process itself. Although all 11 elements identified in previously published work are used, there are certain modifications which have to be made. The first of these is an expansion of the implementation strategy. This can now be seen to consist of two parts, customizing the conceptual framework and developing the working model, as shown in Figure 9.3.

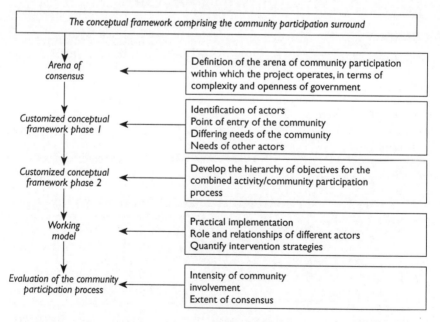

Figure 9.4 *Relationship between the elements and the structure of the participation process*

The second modification is to the elements themselves. There are 11 elements in total. Of these, nine of the original elements have been used in their existing form, whereas two have been modified. What was 'instruments of participation' becomes 'intervention strategies', whereas 'the point of entry of the community' becomes 'forms of community representation'.

The way in which these 11 elements relate to the structure is illustrated in Figure 9.4. This is a very different scenario to that mapped out by any of the previous models. Although this theory highlights the importance of the conceptual framework in the participation process, it also illustrates the much wider and more complex relationship which exists between the two constituent parts of the process, namely the structure and the elements. For the first time it defines community participation in terms of a process cycle and shows how this can also be used to monitor and evaluate the community participation process. This community participation process cycle has similarities to, and can parallel, the project cycle, but is nonetheless distinct from it. The project cycle is a misnomer, as it is much more of a linear model. The community participation process cycle, on the other hand, is exactly that. It is cyclical in its structure and makes extensive use of iterative feedback loops.

COMMUNITY PARTICIPATION IN THE ARENA OF INCLUSION

The activities which form the basis for community participation in the arena of inclusion are much more strongly community-orientated than are those operating in the arena of consensus. In this situation external actors do not operate independently, but are aligned either to the government or the community. This reduces the elements which are applicable and thereby simplifies the structure.

The historical debate on community participation in this arena has arisen from the way in which communities interact with the project cycle, which in turn stems from the growth of projects as the dominant form of activity. This can be seen in the means and end debate, as well as the structure of Paul's conceptual framework, with its five objectives. Creating a structure from within the arena of inclusion leads to a different approach to understanding participation which overcomes the problems arising from these diverse interpretations while explaining why and how they occur.

The structure of community participation within the arena of inclusion is broadly similar to that of the arena of consensus, but much simpler, both in respect of the working model and of the number of active elements. Essentially, however, it has the same two central components of conceptual framework and implementation strategy. The implementation strategy retains the two sub-components relating to the customizing of the conceptual framework and the development of the working model, although both of these will be simpler than within the arena of concensus.

Conceptual Framework

The conceptual model comprises two elements, actors and objectives. In the first, the actors are reduced to two, the government and the community, and the choice has to be made between active and passive involvement on the part of the government. The second element differs from that for the arena of consensus. Because operation in this arena is focused on the community and practised through the medium of an activity, the primary interaction should be between the community and the activity. As the role of the activity is to enhance the community in some way, whether materially, physically or qualitatively, the conceptual framework should deal with the identification of the community need.

The real value of the conceptual framework in the arena of inclusion lies not so much in its identification of elements per se, because these are relatively simple.

Instead it is in determining whether the participation process is situated in the correct arena. For example, the role of the funding agency in this arena should be to support a community project without constraining the project with its own agenda. If it is unable to do this, then either the participation process is operating in the incorrect arena and should be sited in the arena of consensus where the funder would be a partner in the decision-making process, or the funding agency does not have a clear understanding of its own role. Other examples of the wrong choice of arena are given in the section on customizing the conceptual framework.

Implementation Strategy

Customizing the Conceptual Framework: Role of the Government

To operate in this arena (of inclusion) at all, the government has to be broadly supportive of the participatory process. What needs to be determined is whether this support will be active or passive. This should be done when customizing the conceptual framework. Thus a community development activity, for example, which is strongly linked to social programmes, would tend to have active government involvement. This would be the basis of many self-help schemes in the education and health sectors. A community management activity, on the other hand, with its strong linkage to project-based development, would be more likely to have passive support. Rural water and sanitation programmes are a good example of the latter. Here there is a clear national policy within which the projects are situated.

There are also situations where the two can be combined. Farming systems and community conservation provide two example of this hybrid approach. There will be a strong economic basis for these types of hybrid schemes. Essentially they are relying on a financial return to the community to provide the incentive for involvement which takes the place of participation in the decision-making process.

In this situation the government role may be a mix of active and passive. Thus it may, for example, provide extension and other support services, which are active components. It may also recognize the role of the community in management and delegate much of the decision-making, taking a more passive role in this area.

There is clearly a danger here of a lack of clear definition in the government role which could create difficulties in the government/community relationship later. In addition, this hybrid role may be more suited to some areas, eg farming systems, where the venture is essentially commercial, than in other areas, such as community conservation. Here there is a mix of objectives which may include, but is not limited to, commercial objectives: there are strong environmental constraints, issues of multiple land use, and diverse external interests to name but three. In this type of situation there is a real danger that the activity designated for the arena of inclusion is actually in the wrong arena and should be more correctly placed within the arena of consensus.

Customizing the Conceptual Framework: Interaction Between the Community and the Project

The essence of community participation in the arena of inclusion is that there should be no distinction between the activity and the community participation process. In other words, the activity is both a means to an end (providing an output in the form of, for example, a product) and an end in itself (community growth and development). The two should not be separable, but should operate in a symbiotic relationship. If this cannot be achieved, then this is an indicator that the activity should be situated within the arena of consensus. It is the recognition of this symbiotic relationship which forms the basis for the success of community management.

As a result, there is no multiple objective for activities in this arena. Because the activity is community-related, the objectives relate to the satisfaction of the needs of the community, but because the activity relates to a homogeneous group (as determined through the first phase of the analysis relating to activity parameters), these will be limited and there should be no necessity for a hierarchy of objectives. Paul's objectives are useful in this regard in identifying the different factors which need to be taken into account in determining how the activity will be implemented to achieve the stated community objective. They should not be used as the basis of either/or decision-making, however. If they are, then this is a further indicator of a problem in the choice of arena.

What is required, rather than a hierarchy of objectives, is an equitable cost benefit analysis. In many activities in this arena, particularly those relating to physical services (eg water supply), there is a skewed cost-benefit relationship within the community which is defined by gender. Because many societies tend to be strongly patriarchal, the decisions will generally be taken by men, whereas the 'cost', which is borne predominantly by women, is not taken into account. This can often be to the detriment of the community as a whole. Hence gender relationships become the most important issue to be resolved by the community for activities in this arena.

The Working Model

This component of the structure has two elements, roles of the different actors and choice of appropriate intervention strategies. Because there are only the two sets of dominant actors this is simplified, but its importance is not diminished because of that. For not only are there the two primary parties to be dealt with, but the role of supporting actors also needs to be clearly defined.

The government role is dependent on whether its primary relationship to the community is active or passive. If it is active, then there needs to be a clear understanding of what responsibility lies with the community and what lies with the government.

This is equally true for the community, but the community also needs to have a clear understanding of the internal relationships, primarily those related to gender.

This is a topic which has been covered extensively by other workers[14] and will not be repeated here. It has to be recognized that this is the most important facet of the community participation process in the arena of inclusion, and effective community participation is not possible unless this issue is addressed satisfactorily.

This leaves the external actors. Although their role in this arena is supportive, it needs to be clearly defined. There is a need to recognize the primacy of communities and to enshrine this in the project. The best way to do this is through the use of written contracts. This should apply to all actors, be they NGOs, funders, development professionals or commercial interests.

The second element of the working model is the intervention strategy. Because the focus of the activity in this arena is community-based, the intervention strategy should be designed to be supportive. Again, there are many publications dealing with this issue, which is highly relevant here. This relates both to the obtaining of information, where the work on participatory rural appraisal is of primary interest (see, for example, the extensive work of the IIED on this subject), and to the training and education itself (the work of Srinivasan, discussed earlier, is extremely useful in this). This issue of intervention strategies is explored in greater detail in Chapter 13.

Evaluating the Community Participation Process

Because the community needs and the project needs are conflated, it is difficult to evaluate the two separately. Hence also the difficulty in defining success. This confusion led to distinction between directive and non-directive forms of participation in the 1960s[15] and the later distinction between manipulation of the community versus community control over the project in the 1980s.[16] What needs to be evaluated from a community participation perspective is the success of the intervention strategies in achieving the objective outlined in the conceptual framework. The elements used to measure this success are the intensity of the participation process and the satisfaction of the community.

INTERACTION BETWEEN THE ARENAS OF CONSENSUS AND INCLUSION

There is no clear dividing line between the two operating arenas of consensus and inclusion. The degree of complexity is incremental, so that it is difficult to define the point at which one changes to the other. To this must be added the effect of growth in competence and capacity within a community. As the community tackles small problems successfully, so it will move towards larger and more projects. Finally, there is the external impetus towards change. There is a limit to which development can be broken down into individual projects and this point has now been reached. Increasingly, there is a recognition of the interactive nature of development, as illustrated by the outcome of the 1992 Rio de Janeiro World Summit on the Environment. From this point onwards the situation will be reversed and the signs of this are already apparent, for example, in the growing reluctance of the World Bank to sanction projects without an environmental impact assessment. The result is that community participation in increasing numbers of projects and programmes will be situated within the arena of consensus. It is therefore important to understand the interaction between these two arenas.

The major point to note is that they represent fundamentally different philosophies. In the arena of inclusion the needs of the local community are paramount and the whole process of participation is built around achieving the objectives of the community. This process functions within a pre-determined policy framework, with the result that the activity can be addressed within clearly defined boundaries. This is not so with community participation in the arena of consensus. There the cross-boundary interactions are an integral part of the decision-making process. The community's needs are important, but so are the external needs, and all must be given equal weighting.

Given these differences it is not possible to move from one to the other along a continuum, a conclusion which may be difficult for many people working in the field of community participation to accept, given the strong historical basis for the continuum at the centre of the participation process. The outcome is that, although it is possible to place projects operating within the arena of inclusion within a wider programme or activity within the arena of consensus, it is not possible to move the other way without a significant mind-shift. This means that extending a successful community management project, for example, to incorporate activities in other sectors, could result in failure if this extension shifts the activity from one arena (inclusion) to the other (consensus).

This has major implications for those who continue to view community participation solely from within the narrow UNRISD definition, for example, without recognizing that the constraints of this definition restrict its validity to the arena of inclusion. On the other hand, it is valuable to both communities and external actors in clarifying their situation. For communities, understanding the relationship between the two arenas allows the notion of manipulation to be quantified for the first time (Figure 9.5). On the one hand, there is the more obvious form of manipulation, which takes place in the zone between the arenas of inclusion and confrontation. This is the classic form of manipulation whereby governments use the participation process to exert patronage or to obtain physical inputs from communities. The second zone is more diffuse and therefore less obvious and lies between the arenas of inclusion and consensus. In this instance community management, for example, may appear to give communities a wide degree of control in managing their own affairs. Meanwhile the reality is that the government has taken all the policy decisions which both define and constrain the community's limits of action, with the primary objective of relieving the state of a potential financial burden. This is not necessarily unacceptable if the decision has been made with the knowledge and agreement of the local communities, but constitutes a form of manipulation if it has been made unilaterally.

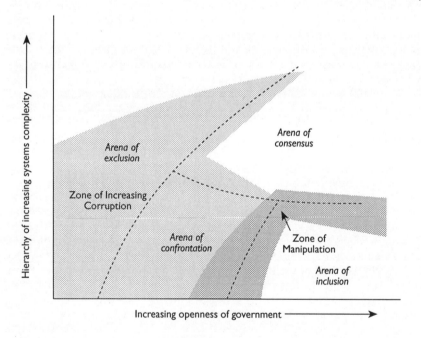

Figure 9.5 *Potential zones of manipulation and corruption in community participation*

The second area of benefit is that which helps external actors to define their own position. If the activity is taking place within the arena of inclusion, then the ideal situation is that the community organization is the client, responsible to the wider community. The government is providing passive support in the form of enabling legislation. The NGO and/or development professionals are contracted to the community organization, and are accountable both to the community and, through the community organization, to the funder, for the cost and effectiveness of the support structures. The funder then lends to the community organization as the client. This is already beginning to happen with many international donors. By recognizing that this situation is only applicable for projects in the arena of inclusion, this not only allows better targeting but enables communities to reject excessive funder involvement.

In the arena of consensus, on the other hand, all actors are party to the decision and can express their own needs. If the community organization takes part in this process it cannot demand the subjugation of donor needs, for example, to its own. In this situation the financial responsibility should lie with an independent project manager who is responsible to a committee representing all actors.

IMPLEMENTATION OF THE COMMUNITY PARTICIPATION PROCESS IN THE ARENA OF CONFRONTATION

The structure of the community participation process is simplest within the arena of confrontation. A good example of where to begin exploring this structure is the debate over land tenure. Where people do not have access to land, the resolution of this issue becomes a prerequisite to the resolution of all other issues of concern. In this environment there are only two actors, the government and the community organization, and the part played by the government becomes the central issue. If the needs of the government and the community differ significantly and the government refuses to acknowledge the needs of the community, then the needs of the community stand in direct opposition to the needs of the government and the project becomes the focus of a struggle for power. The only avenue for people to express their needs in this situation is through confrontation. Ultimately participation in this arena is concerned not so much with involvement in the decision-making process as with control over it.

This confrontation is the arena in which successful empowerment projects operate. The political nature of the struggle, however, means that the only way to achieve success is to unite large numbers of people which, in the absence of conscription, means a focus on one specific activity. So the elements which go to make up the components of the conceptual framework and the working model do not apply in this arena. Instead the whole focus of the struggle is on the implementation strategy. At most, the conceptual framework defines the objective of the struggle.

Thus the basis of the community participation process in this arena of confrontation defines the nature of the relationship between the two parties and sets out their roles. To implement the process the community will adopt those tactics most likely to force concessions from those in power, namely mass action, boycotts and strikes, the primary weapons of the disempowered. The strategic role of the CBO in this situation is to mobilize the wider community.

This is by its very nature a short-term strategy, which does not accommodate policy analysis nor allow longer term strategic planning. This struggle, which is the dominant issue within the community, is a relatively minor event to the government, which does not have the same constraints placed on its own strategic planning. Hence the community is rarely in a position to counter longer term measures, such as the undermining of community cohesion through patronage. As a result, participation in the arena of confrontation cannot be sustainable in the longer term.

This structure can now be used to explore the operation of projects within the arena of confrontation using the case study of FUNDASAL and the housing programme in San Salvador. Although the rationale behind FUNDASAL's actions was understandable, given the magnitude of the shelter crisis and the oppression of the government, the choice of housing as a vehicle for empowerment was doomed to failure. The primary objective was the construction of housing. This took place in a co-operative venture intended to empower local communities. Everything is fine up to this point, but then the contradictions become apparent.

The community is not independent of the government and does not have a clear issue on which to confront the government. The housing programme cannot exist in a vacuum. The community requires physical and social services if it is to improve the quality of life. Thus the situation is really no different from that of a land invasion. People were able to obtain their houses through unconventional means of their own choosing, but could not pursue a wider struggle. At one point (after the coup in 1979) Stein admits that the government closed the political space and the 'repression which occurred as of 1980 generated a brain drain in FUNDASAL that affected the highest levels of management and administration'.[17] The environment had moved into the arena of exclusion. As the space slowly opened and events continued, Stein states that 17 of the 22 communities established by FUNDASAL showed regressive symptoms in terms of consolidation; in other words, having achieved their primary objective, they had withdrawn, to differing degrees, from the struggle.

The other five communities

'had their central commissions fully functioning and the communal leadership at all levels was recognized as representative of the grass-root group. Community leaders were able to plan and evaluate their own work and had the power and ability to negotiate with different state agencies'.[18]

However, this meant that the environment had moved out of the arena of confrontation into the arena of inclusion, hence the project's similarity with land invasion as an unstable state of participation used to achieve a specific objective.

IMPLEMENTING COMMUNITY PARTICIPATION IN THE ARENA OF CONSENSUS

This chapter has developed the theory of community participation which, through the use of different arenas, is able to accommodate all the different variants of the participation process. Of these, the most complex, but also the most comprehensive, is the participation process in the arena of consensus. With a changing global economy and an increased awareness of the interaction between development and the environment, an increased number of community-based activities will have to operate in the arena of consensus. However, unlike the two other operating arenas, there is no experience to date of the problems and constraints of operating in this environment.

The third part of the book explores the problems of implementation in the arena of consensus. The book focuses on four areas which are particularly relevant to this environment, but about which there is little relevant experience, even though the topics themselves may have been dealt with extensively in other situations. The central feature of community participation which distinguishes it from the other arenas is the nature, and importance, of the interaction between a wide number of actors. The chapters which follow look at three groups of actors. The first is the development professional, examined in Chapter 10, and the second the NGO sector, discussed in Chapter 11. Both of these sectors affect the community organizations, who are also affected by the complexity of the new environment. Chapter 12 uses three case studies to explore the impact of operating in a complex environment on the community organizational structures. Chapter 13 then integrates this experience and looks at an area which is critical to the success of community participation in the arena of consensus, namely the role and nature of external interventions.

PART

Implementation of Community Participation

Role and Impact of Development Professionals

PROFESSIONALS AS PARTICIPANTS IN THE PARTICIPATION PROCESS

People who practise a professional skill, whether their knowledge lies in the fields of the social sciences, physical sciences or engineering and associated areas, have long been an integral part of the development process. Although many of them agree with the involvement of local communities in the decision-making associated with their own area of expertise, however, their interpretation of what involvement means will be different. Generally, it will take one of two forms. The first is to be supportive, directly, of the community, building up community expertise in, for example, community management of rural water supplies. Or it would be supportive of the status quo (ie the government or the funding agency). Many professionals would argue that this latter role was non-political, but this was not possible when the very process of development, and particularly the relationship between government and community, functioned as a duality.

The situation is now different. The Cold War, and the other associated causes of the dualistic confrontation scenario, are in decline. In their place there is a rapidly changing environment and an increasing shortage of skills and finance. In addition, professsionals can no longer take decisions within their own area of expertise without at least considering the wider implications, whether this is by way of a simple environmental impact assessment or through a complex socio-economic–technical multi-decision-making computer model. This gives professionals a power, but also a responsibility, which they did not have before. Their client is no longer this or that government department or agency, although this may still be with whom they have a contract. It is now with the user group, government and funder, with account being taken of the interests of even more external actors.

In this situation professionals will have to develop new approaches to decision-making and learn to be part of a wider forum which takes into account a multiplicity of interests. This will mean not only a widening of their knowledge base, but also a significant shift in their mind-set. This chapter will explore what this means in practical terms. It uses as an example the urban engineer/planner, as these are the most commonly used professionals in urban management. It would be equally valid to use a physical scientist in a biodiversity programme, or any one of the many other professional groups that operate within the different sectors of development. The case study used here is taken from South Africa, where planners and civil engineers have been heavily involved in a process of internal change, forced on them by operation in an increasingly participatory environment. South Africa is also useful in this context because engineers and planners operate a British/US type of profession/industry relationship, where the planning and design process is carried out by professionals operating as an independent group. The engineers in particular have codes of professional practice, strong professional bodies to lobby for their interests and well-established contract documents which define their role. In addition, they interpret their brief in a manner which derives from a specific type of rationality.

The chapter can be divided into three parts. The first part looks at the changing role of the engineer/planner in an urban environment in South Africa, following on from the work discussed in Chapters 4 and 7. The second part then looks at the importance of rationality and the way in which this limits the capacity of development professionals to take part in the type of decision-making processes needed in the arena of consensus. This in turn is illustrated by a case study which comprises the third part of the chapter.

In the political transition which took place in South Africa over the period 1984 to 1994, there was a move away from the imposed political solution to the increasing urbanization taking place in the country. Instead of resorting to forced removals, the government turned, increasingly, towards the use of technical constraints to provide a justification for the continuation of segregated, two-class society. Development professionals were the group fronting this argument and were the group that civics found themselves having to engage in negotiations. In exploring this interaction, some of which has been described earlier, the full extent of the difference in perceptions was highlighted for the first time, together with the dangers which this new approach posed for communities. The technical mind-set posed the greatest threat to meaningful community participation in this changed environment and needed to be understood and addressed before the transition to an effective working model for implementation could be achieved. This case study illustrates clearly the clash of rationalities between community and engineer/planner and how it was possible in this situation to change the approach of the professionals to one which was able to accommodate and integrate a wide variety of different needs. This is a prerequisite first step in the move towards operating within a complex system.

THE CHANGING ROLE OF THE URBAN ENGINEER IN DEVELOPING COUNTRIES

In the same way that British colonies, including South Africa, adopted the British local authority system (Chapter 4), so they adopted the British system for the management and operation of civil engineering works, which includes physical infrastructure. This system designated an engineer for each project, who is required to be independent (ie not gaining profit from the project) and separated the functions of the design engineer from that of the construction company. The changes taking place in urban management (as described in Chapters 4 and 7) are taking engineers beyond technical management and into the arena of decision-making around social issues.

Whereas previously urban civil engineers had a very clear and specific technical task to perform in the design and construction of infrastructure, this is no longer the case. Firstly, engineers must now take cognisance of the views of three distinct groups of people: those in authority associated with the local authority; the financing institution; and the community organizations and their own professional NGOs, who oppose the local authority and seek greater involvement. In addition, the engineers must also take account of several variables which did not exist before. These are described in the following sections.

Choice of Technical Option Matched to Affordability

It is no longer adequate or acceptable for the engineer to supply the best available technology. Instead, he or she must be able to provide a full list of options, each of which provides a different level of service. This has ramifications, discussed later, which have not been fully evaluated.

Use of Different Construction Techniques

Financial institutions and governments are viewing all construction in developing countries, but specifically infrastructure provision, as a vehicle for job creation on a significant scale. This not only introduces new variables in terms of construction costing and programming, for example, labour-intensive construction, but can also affect the design itself.

Management Capability of the Client

Both Chapters 6 and 7 have illustrated the increasing centrality of the long-term viability of infrastructure in the decision-making around the initial choice of such infrastructure. Different levels of service have different implications for long-term management, as well as being closely tied to the issue of affordability far more closely than is the actual provision of infrastructure (which can be supported by a variety of capital subsidy options). This affects the design, by replacing the concept of best available technology with the concept of simplest and most easily maintained technology. It also raises the issue of the engineer becoming involved in the training of personnel for operation, as well as the ongoing operation and maintenance of the system itself.

Relationship with Other Components of the Urban System

Other components of the urban system, for example, the physical environment, resources and land management, also need to be considered. There is also a need to satisfy different clients with differing agendas and to provide technical solutions which themselves may be in conflict (eg the service which optimizes job creation may not be that which minimizes maintenance). These were not envisaged when the current series of agreements and contract documents was developed and they highlight the need to explore new structures. These are all issues which need to be taken into account in a systems approach. The implementaion of new structures is itself constrained by the problem of rigid perceptions and interpretation of need.

Matching Needs Across Different Rationalities

Chapter 8 showed how the conceptual framework for the arena of consensus sets out the actor groups and the categories of need, which the working model then quantified and defined in detail for the specific application of urban management. For this transition to take place successfully there has to be agreement between the different actors. This process begins by defining the full list of needs associated with the various actors as well as the activity itself, and then building this into a hierarchy of needs which is prioritized by consensus. This hierarchy of needs then becomes the basis for implementation. The most critical factor in determining the success of this process is the relationship between the actors.

To have reached this stage in the participation process there has to have been some agreement on the principles of participation and equality. This alone will not guarantee success, however. As well as having their own needs and their own agendas, the different actors will view the same activity in very different ways. So even though professional engineers/ planners may see that wider needs exist, which have been defined by other actors, having recognized their changing role as described in the previous section they are unable to understand and analyse this external need in the same way that they do with their own perceived interpretaion of the problem. Goulet has termed this difference in perceptions the different rationalities of development.[1] This interpretation of perceptions broadly divides outlook into three categories which reflect the different backgrounds and positions of the various actors. One of these, the political rationality, has been explored extensively, albeit indirectly, in published work on participation and is well understood. The second, 'technological rationality', is less clearly understood. Yet it is the most critical of the three in determining the success of community participation in the arena of consensus. This is because most activities in this arena will incorporate a technical component, in one form or another, at some stage during the implementation phase. An understanding of these different rationalities then becomes an essential prerequisite to successful tranisition from the conceptual framework to the working model in the arena of consensus.

DIFFERING RATIONALITIES IN DEVELOPMENT

Goulet argues that development decisions are made by three different categories of actors: technical specialists; politicians (or their bureaucratic agents) and persons pressing some special or general concern.[2] Excluding self-interest (a subsection of the third category), he argues that the first two categories of decision-makers apply distinct rationality systems, the technological and the political. Those who plead for moral values pursue ethical rationality (the third category).[3] These rationalities are defined in the following way:

> '— Technological rationality rests on the epistemological foundations of modern science ... and obeys a hard logic guided by a calculus of efficiency in the assessment of time or the utility of any object. Technological rationality's animating procedure or dominating spirit leads it to treat everything other than the goal instrumentally.
> — Politicians' veritable goal is to preserve certain institutions and rules of the game, or their special power position within those institutions. Political rationality as described here is that exhibited by persons who wield power. Aspirants to power positions however are also animated by political rationality, but their logic is frequently aimed, not at maintaining the status quo, but at destroying or altering it.
> — Ethical (or humane) rationality takes value norms as its goal, that is, the creation, nurture, or defense of certain values considered worthy for their own sake. Unlike the other forms described, ethical values takes as its absolute goal – in the light of which all else is relative – the promotion of values, not the performance of concrete tasks or the preservation of institutions or power positions. Ethical rationality draws its themes and its legitimation from two distinct, albeit usually allied, sources. The first is some holistic meaning or belief system; the second the world of daily life as experienced by people devoid of power, status or expertise. All interlocutors in decisional arenas may no doubt be motivated by ethical values in playing out their roles. But the dominant form and content of their contributions to rationality mirror their special roles and express the formal warrant they possess for engaging in decision making'.[4]

Goulet argues that,

> 'when they converge in common decision making arenas, the three rationalities impinge on one another, not in the mode of horizontal mutuality, but at cross purposes and in a vertical pattern. Each brand of thinking tends to approach the others in triumphal, reductionist fashion, and leads either to unfruitful conflict or abdication, both of which generate poor decision making'.[5]

After discussing the inter-relationships and interactions between the different rationalities, and their sociological complexity, Goulet ends by saying that

> 'Ultimately the issue is how technological reason will discourse with politics and ethics. Can the logic of efficiency join the logic of power and the logic of virtue in a

holy alliance that produces genuine development? The new discourse of the three rationalities is crucially important because development decisions themselves are crucially important'.[6]

This alliance describes the process of community participation in the arena of consensus. The problem lies in how to achieve such an alliance – that is, how to assist the different actors in recognizing, firstly, how their own perceptions are a function of their relationship and, secondly, how to acknowledge the validity of other points of view which may be based on different perceptions. The converse, of course, is also necessary with respect to community organizations. The case study which follows traces the history of a negotiation process between a community civic organization and a state employed group of development professionals, which took place over a six year period from 1987 to 1993. The crux of the negotiation focused on a difference in perceptions which was due primarily to different actors having different rationalities. It explores these differences and illustrates how a common view of the development process slowly developed over that period. The setting for the negotiation was KwaThandeka, a small African township at Amsterdam in the Mpumalanga province of South Africa.

BRIEF HISTORY OF KWATHANDEKA

The history of KwaThandeka is typical of the growth of many small towns in South Africa. Before the arrival of white settlers the local African people were farmers. In the period after the Boer War (1902) the land the inhabitants had been farming was gradually taken away through legislation. At the same time there was an ongoing debate on urban tenure for Africans. The result was the Natives (Urban Areas) Act 1923, in which the right of individual tenure for Africans in selected urban areas was removed. Amsterdam was one of the areas included in this legislation,[7] under which the new white local authority was empowered to set aside land for African occupation in defined locations, or to house them, or to require their employers to do so.[8] The 1923 Act was designed primarily to solve the housing crisis in the growing industrial urban centres, rather than addressing the needs of rural towns such as Amsterdam, and many of the latter made no provision for housing. This was the case in Amsterdam so that those evicted from the farms had to find a white farmer on whose land they would be allowed to live.[9]

The farmer who finally allowed them to stay was called Scheepers and the eldest son of each family was required to work for him, for six months without pay, to enable the family to stay on the farm. In 1930, Scheepers no longer required the son to work for him, but instead levied a rent of 20–30 cents, increased in 1936 to 35 cents. A 'village for the residence of natives' was established by the Minister of Native Affairs under the Native Urban Areas Act 1923 on 12 January 1940[10] and thereafter the farm was sold to the Transvaal Provincial Administration (TPA).[11] Between 1942 and 1984 the township was administered by the TPA, the municipality, the Peri-Urban

Board and the Administration Board, after which it was administered by a local authority set up under the Black Local Authorities Act of 1982.[12]

In 1974 the second phase of forced removals, instigated by the NP government after their election in 1948, finally reached KwaThandeka, with a proposal to move the entire community into the adjacent homeland of KaNgwane. This move was publicly rejected by the community on the grounds that they had been paying rent for a long time and they would not get their money back; that they stood to lose the houses which they had built themselves; and that the community they had come to be a part of, and the area they had lived in for a long period, would be destroyed. There ensued a long and debilitating legal battle for survival. When the black local authority was appointed in 1983 the puppet councillors continued to try to persuade people to move, but without success. The struggle continued until August 1987, when the community was told that the area had been reprieved and that they were no longer to be removed. Thus for the first time in 13 years, community attention could focus on improving conditions locally.[13]

During the same period (the late 1970s and early 1980s), there was a steady increase in rents, culminating in a 20% rent increase proposal by the newly appointed KwaThandeka local authority (KLA) in 1984. This increase had been instigated by the Eastern Transvaal Development Board, but was in fact illegal because it had not been published in the government gazette.[14] The community's response to these two actions (the rent increases and the move to KaNgwane) was to form an organization, the Amsterdam Home Committee (AHC) to oppose them and to refuse to pay rent.[15]

A further issue of concern to residents at the time was the availability of land for housing. Residents began trying to obtain additional land for housing once the threat of forced removal was withdrawn. Eighty families had either applied or were on the official list by the end of August 1987.[16] However, conflicting views were given by officials, with the township superintendent saying that 350 sites were available and officials of the Department of Constitutional Affairs saying that there was a shortage of sites.[17] Finally, in January 1988 the TPA admitted that the 350 sites were available, but stated that the stands could not be allocated because the sites could not be demarcated. Consequently, the township had to be planned, otherwise this could result in conflict between the plan and the random allocation.

In an effort to end the rent boycott in KwaThandeka and to address some of the community's needs, representatives of the TPA addressed a public meeting and requested the AHC to assist the development process for their area by providing input into this plan.[18] The AHC then called in a group of professionals, under the leadership of the author, to assist in this process.

Over the period from 1974 to 1987 there was a significant shift in the wider environment. This moved from one of confrontation to one of inclusion, but the latter was of a manipulative form, using the vehicle of black local authorities, which was unacceptable to the wider community. On the one hand there was still a State of Emergency in place and the government was trying to move the environment back towards one of suppression and control in the arena of confrontation, although the government was becoming increasingly weaker and unable to exert its will. On the other hand the community had accepted the request from the provincial administration to discuss the issue of services in a non-political context (the community accepted the legitimacy of the provincial adminis- tration while simultaneously rejecting the KLA) and were drawing the debate into the arena of consensus. This was the setting for the negotiation process which followed.

BACKGROUND TO THE KWATHANDEKA DEVELOPMENT PROGRAMME

Having been given official sanction to participate in the technical planning process it became clear that the AHC perceived that the issue of a physical plan was only one aspect of a much greater needs profile for the area and as such could not be divorced from other aspects such as services, house construction, schooling needs and even work opportunities.[19] Thus they could use participation in what was nominally a simple planning exercise as a springboard for much greater social change. Working within limited financial constraints, the group decided to limit the study to the areas of greatest need. The study therefore centred around the provision of physical and social services and housing, specifically addressing two issues:

- quantifying existing levels of service, confirming demographic data and identifying community needs (the survey); and
- identifying or quantifying the minimum levels of service required to meet individual and community needs.

The development of these study objectives was carried out in such a way as to form the basis for a long-term development plan for the township. This in turn led to a report which was submitted to the TPA and from which the data quoted in this chapter are taken.[20]

In parallel with the above, the KLA, acting with the full support of the TPA, appointed a town planner who, in 1989, submitted a township application which had been prepared without any community consulta- tion and which was opposed totally by the residents of KwaThandeka. This plan was developed using a single criterion of minimized capital costs for infrastructure provision which, if implemented, would result in multiple subdivisions of existing stands. In accepting the planner's submission the TPA ignored the community's report.

The relationship between the actors at this stage shows signs of an interesting metamorphosis. Superficially it resembles a duality, centred around the local authority and the community civic organization, but in reality it was significantly more complex. The KLA was being used by the provincial administration in support of a wider government strategy. The real power lay with the administrator, who was an ex-colleague of the planners. The planners were attempting to define their brief in a purely technical context. Finally, the AHC (Amsterdam Home Committee) was determined to wrest the initiative by questioning the basis of apartheid planning, but on the planners' own ground. The first step in this process was to develop their own database through the use of social surveys.

RESEARCH METHODOLOGY FOR THE KWATHANDEKA STUDY

Initial Survey

There is an ongoing debate about the manipulative role of surveys (see also Chapter 13). In rural programmes PRA (participatory rural appraisal) is slowly establishing itself as the dominant survey form which involves the community, but there is no ideal equivalent for urban areas. The KwaThandeka surveys used many of the techniques of PRA, although this terminology was not known at the time, and showed that it could be successfully applied.

The whole process was driven by the community and was fully interactive. In conducting the research into conditions at KwaThandeka three methods of research were used. The first of these was a series of discussions with members of the AHC.[21] The second was a mass meeting with the community, held on 28 May 1988, to discuss needs and problems. South Africa was under a State of Emergency at the time and public meetings could only be held with the written permission of the magistrate. As only one meeting was permitted, consultation with the wider community had to take place via informal meetings between community groups and individual members of the AHC.

The third method was a social survey of the township. Here, because no official plans of the area existed, and because the demographic pattern was known to comprise large numbers of extended families, every stand was visited and an attempt made to interview more than one house occupant per stand. The questionnaire comprised predominantly closed questions and was aimed, primarily, at gathering demographic information. All questions were drawn up in consultation with the AHC, the questionnaire was translated into Zulu and a pilot survey carried out among a sample group selected at random by members of the AHC. The questionnaire was then modified and a full survey carried out over a three-day period, using between five and eight briefed and trained helpers from the community. In total, 341 households were canvassed and support for the survey was strong, with only 12 people refusing to answer questions. Data were gathered on house distribution, household size distribution, age distribution, school attendance and income distribution.

Follow-up Survey

In March 1990 a firm of Town and Regional Planners appointed by the KLA (with the approval of the TPA) submitted a township establishment application for KwaThandeka to the TPA. This application proposed the multiple subdivision of stands in the area, coupled with provision for a major densification in terms of the local population. The rationale behind this plan was that optimizing plot size would increase housing densities and thereby minimize service installation costs. From their submission it was clear that the planners considered that the capital cost of services was the only criterion of importance in determining the physical planning layout. In developing their proposals the planners did not consult with the community at any stage. Instead they based their proposal solely on information provided by an aerial photograph of KwaThandeka, which they commissioned.

Physically the situation on the ground appeared to be the same as that outlined by the KLA planners, in that the survey house count was 534 dwellings, whereas the number of dwellings counted in the aerial photograph was 521. However, the way in which this situation was interpreted was totally different and provided the first indication of the potential for misunderstanding arising from different interpretations driven by different rationalities. Firstly, the planners ignored existing site boundaries and assumed that the 521 dwellings were occupying a non-demarcated piece of land, ie that KwaThandeka was an informal settlement. Secondly, they took the demand figures similar to those in the AHC survey and added these to the 521 existing sites. Thirdly, the planners made provision for a large number of additional sites, which resulted in their final plan allowing for 1841 sites in total, compared with between 534 and 713 in the survey report. The only possible reason for such a high figure had to be an allowance for an influx from surrounding white farms. This coincided with a new government strategy (rigidly enforced by the TPA) of classification of all farm workers, coupled with the forced removal of those who could not prove that they were employed (eg relatives of farm workers and disabled or retired farm workers).

This planning application was totally unacceptable to the community. Firstly, the planners failed to recognize the strong sense of ownership associated with the larger sites, which had been allocated to the registered occupants legally. Secondly, the planners assumed that many of the occupants were squatters, who would support their planning approach. The survey showed in fact that this was not so. Very few site owners actually sub-let parcels of land to outsiders. Most of the additional people living in additional dwellings on the demarcated stands were in fact related to the head of household occupying the main house. Thirdly, residents claimed that the plan, if implemented, would seriously disrupt their lives and make them poorer.

These plans, as submitted to the TPA, had major economic, social, political and technical implications but, so that these could be more clearly quantified, a second follow-up survey of the area was carried out, this time by a professional social survey company which specialized in this type of work.[22]

In the second survey 177 household interviews were conducted on one-third of the stands, with one household interviewed per stand. For this survey a household was defined as all those people living under one roof. The stands on which the interviews took place were selected using a completely random sample, with strict substitution and call back rules used in accordance with this technique.[23]

This survey elicited more information than the first in terms of the relationships between the people living on the stands and provided a more detailed breakdown of income distribution. It looked at employment levels, the reaction of people to sub-division, the use of plots for growing food/keeping animals and the economic effect on plot dwellers of losing their plots. On the basis of this data, and the previous information collected, the broader implications of the impact of the plan on the social fabric of KwaThandeka were identified and summarized in terms of their economic, social, political and technical impact.

From an economic perspective there were four major points of concern expressed, namely the effects on food production and survival, employment and income, housing and affordability in terms of infrastructure. The survey indicated a high reliance on home-grown produce in an area with a very low income distribution: 93 per cent of residents indicated that they grew their own food; 75 per cent indicated that they would suffer materially if unable to grow food; and 40 per cent indicated they would not have enough to live on if this supplementary food source was unavailable. The massive influx of new residents resulting from the provision of so many stands would lower the mean income still further as there are few job opportunities in the area, the loss of homes to road reserves etc would create unnecessary hardship and the proposed plan would not necessarily provide the lowest infrastructure cost as indicated in the planners' submission.

Socially the plan would result in a general deterioration of the health and well-being of the community and a deterioration in the quality of life of residents; the expanded site would encourage the local forced removal of farm labourers; and, finally, this influx would remove both the farm labourers' and the town people's means of support. Politically the plan had within it the seeds of major unrest, as it was so strongly opposed.

Finally, technically, the increased densities would necessitate the installation of a water-borne sewage system (given the health hazards and social unacceptability of the current bucket system). This would also necessitate water to every site. Given the socio-economic profile of KwaThandeka, such a system would not be the most economical, while the operational and maintenance cost was probably beyond the means of most residents.

These findings were submitted to the TPA in the form of a legal objection to the proposed development of KwaThandeka in May 1990[24] where they stayed, without an official response, for nine months. Finally, the TPA accepted the objection and stated that recognition would be given to the existing situation. They also stated that a new approach to planning would begin and requested the AHC's assistance in demarcating existing boundaries.[25]

In August 1991 the TPA called a further meeting at which they requested a development plan from the AHC, having produced no plans of their own.[26] After an acrimonious meeting the AHC agreed to produce a development proposal, which they did in September.[27] The proposal was based on: linking the development and the economies of KwaThandeka and Amsterdam; additional land for small-scale agriculture development; the cost and level of infrastructure; access opportunities to work and facilities; transport costs; education, health and other social facilities; and user preference. The findings of this report were presented at a meeting on 21 September 1991.[28]

At a meeting on 12 March 1992 the TPA and the Council, through their town planner, stated that they accepted the recommendations set out in this report.[29] Over the next few months meetings were held with a variety of parties, culminating in a meeting on 17 July 1992 at which the AHC agreed to reform itself as a civic organization, employ the services of an NGO specializing in small-scale agriculture and support the formation of a small farmers group.[30] This group was formed on 15 August 1992. The basis for such a major shift in perceptions, on the part of the authorities, was the development of a way of viewing the problems of KwaThandeka which integrated the quantitative and the qualitative issues involved. Once this was done the barrier which the differing rationalities had created could be broken down.

DIFFERING PERCEPTIONS OF SERVICE PROVISION

The series of meetings on KwaThandeka indicated that professionals and officials of the TPA shared a common, very clear, perception of what constituted a service. This technological perception was based on a developed world view of services, operated and maintained to provide maximum user convenience within a strong technical operational and maintenance capacity. This technicist approach viewed services in terms of their performance against the original design specification, the quality of the workmanship and materials of construction. The differing perceptions of service performance were summed up, unwittingly, by an official of the TPA, in a discussion with community representatives on service charges.[31] He stated that the principle behind the negotiations over the payment of service charges must be that people agree to pay for what they get (by way of services), ie that services must be paid for.

There are actually two statements there which express the authorities' concern about non-payment of services. The first is that 'people must pay for what they get' and the second that 'services must be paid for'.[32] Superficially these two statements appear to say the same thing. In the context of KwaThandeka, however, the two statements actually highlight a fundamental difference between the perceptions of users in the community, whose interpretation is based on the first statement, and professionals and officials, who base their actions on the second. This distinction, which has relevance for service provision in many developing countries, is one of the underlying reasons for the difference between ethical and technical rationalities.

Thus, in discussions with officials on this issue, the official view of service cost recovery was that a cost had been expended and must be recovered. Although it was acknowledged that the services generally were of poor quality and not performing satisfactorily, the officials were adamant that cost recovery remained a valid objective. When the services had been installed they had met the necessary technical criteria laid down in terms of the workmanship and materials specification, as well as the design criteria specified. The cost had been amortized over 30 years and this cost had to be recovered.

The community took a different view. To them the services were not performing their function satisfactorily and should not be paid for. However, this view was not simplistic. From discussions in both public meetings and small groups it became clear that in fact the perception of services was fairly complex and that the issue of performance of a service was viewed on several different levels.

DEFINING SERVICE PERFORMANCE

From the analysis of the services discussed earlier, together with the feedback from meetings and interviews, three components of service performance were identified. The first component centred around reliability. This reflected the level of operation and maintenance of the service as well as how effectively it met the technical design criteria. Thus it was a quantitative measure, defined as the efficiency-related component of performance. The second was the issue of health and safety. Here individuals raised the issue of health hazards in water supply, sanitation, and roads and stormwater drainage. Thus this component measured, qualitatively, the relationship between the output or capacity of a particular service compared with the need for that particular service. This was defined as the quality-related component of performance. The third component reflected how far the service went towards satisfying the needs and/or aspirations of the community, ie the socio-cultural and/or socio-political values of the community. This was termed the political component of performance. The various services available to the community in KwaThandeka were then evaluated against these criteria.

Water

The water supply in KwaThandeka was intermittent and of variable flow. The residents did not know when it would be working nor how much water would be available. The supply was therefore unreliable. The limited per capita availability made personal hygiene difficult and thereby encouraged the spread of water-borne diseases. In addition, because of the poor and intermittent supply, many people used the river to supplement their requirements. This need for regular supplementation negated any public health benefit that a potable supply might (and should) provide. Thus, although the supply was in itself of adequate quality, the net result was an unsafe water supply situation for residents. With regard to meeting needs and aspirations, the community accepted the principle of communal standpipes. The number and spacing of the standpipes, however, were not acceptable.

The water supply therefore failed to meet any of the performance criteria adequately so that the value of the supply to residents was greatly diminished. In fact, it could be argued that, as soon as people are forced to use a poor quality source of water (in this instance the river) on a regular basis, the supply of water lost all value in terms of benefiting health.

Sanitation

Although buckets were generally collected twice each week there was no fixed time for collection and the buckets were often left standing outside for prolonged periods. Furthermore the twice weekly collection was inadequate for the volume of excreta generated. Hence the system was unreliable. This inadequacy in turn causes a serious health hazard which rendered the system unsafe from a health viewpoint.

Finally, the bucket system itself was highly unpopular and failed to meet the social needs and aspirations of the community. This meant that people were being asked to pay for something they did not want. The sanitation system was therefore extremely inadequate when measured against all three of the performance criteria. As there was an efficient cheap alternative which could be easily provided (ie ventilated improved pit latrines) this meant that the sanitation system in KwaThandeka had no value to residents.

Roads and Stormwater Drainage

The condition of the roads was poor and the grading of roads infrequent. In addition, provision for the drainage of stormwater was non-existent. The overall result was a road and stormwater network which not only made accessing of houses difficult for both pedestrians and vehicles, particularly during rain, but also caused direct deterioration to houses. Measured against the criteria for performance, the road and stormwater system was deficient on all three counts.

Township Management

The role of the township management was intimately bound up with the services provided and the level of those services. In KwaThandeka, where the services had been shown to be of poor quality, this reflected on the township management and, because of his high profile, the township manager. In addition, the management structure was seen by the community as a continuation of old-style apartheid and was both unpopular and unwanted.

Township management cannot be quantified directly in terms of the performance criteria of efficiency and safety. However, as a primary function of the management was to provide and maintain services, its performance could be judged indirectly in terms of the level and quality of service provision. Measured in this way the management performance was poor.

Summary of Findings

Overall the infrastructure service in KwaThandeka, whose function should have been to improve the quality of life of residents, actually had a detrimental effect on their quality of life, negatively affecting the health, comfort and convenience of the people living there. Although all services were of low quality when judged in terms of a performance specification, the sanitation system was particularly poor as well as being totally unacceptable to the community culturally, socially and politically. The system of township management, which strongly reflects a top-down paternalistic approach, was also highly unpopular.

COMPARISON OF COST AND VALUE

The community or user perceptions of services just described allow a comparison between the different parties. From the controlling authority's viewpoint a service can be defined in terms of a monetary value which equates to the cost of amortizing and operating physical infrastructure and is based on a materials and workmanship specification. However, the preceding discussion has attempted to show that, from a user viewpoint, the perception of a service may be totally different, as it is based on a performance specification, ie how well the service performs its task.

The latter specification has a qualitative as well as a quantitative component and hence is more difficult to evaluate. Nonetheless this section has attempted to evaluate the services in KwaThandeka against a performance specification and has shown that the services provided are of poor quality. This in turn raises the issue of what is a fair payment for services.

If the performance specification is lower than the materials and workmanship specification, then this implies that, between the supplier of the service and the end user, there is a loss in the value of that service. The key issue then becomes whether the user should pay for that loss in value, when he or she has had no say in the planning, provision and ongoing operation of that service. The argument of the community, which underlies the rent boycott, is effectively that the cost to the user should be based on the value of the service he or she receives.

In KwaThandeka this implies that service charges should be almost nil, as only the water supply can justify even partial recovery. Obviously such a situation is difficult for the authorities to accept, as there are other relevant factors such as costs incurred and affordability. In KwaThandeka it was argued that this should be achieved by drawing up a performance specification in conjunction with the community. The level and operation of services to meet this performance specification could then be determined and costed. This option would imply that certain costs associated with the present services may need to be written off.

Superficially, this type of involvement in infrastructure provision on the part of the community appears to fall into Paul's category of community participation for the improvement of project effectiveness. However, bearing in mind that in KwaThandeka the proposals for upgrading came from the community, and took four years of debate before they were accepted by the authorities and their technical advisers, this is an inadequate description of what is happening. In Paul's interpretation the flow is outwards, from the project to the community; establishing a project and then seeking the involvement of the community. In KwaThandeka the direction was reversed, beginning in the community and then moving inwards to express community needs through a project, in a process of negotiation with the authorities. This is a form of engagement with the authorities which is centred on redefining the role of infrastructure and establishing procedures by which priority-setting in infrastructure is achieved. The output from the negotiation process in KwaThandeka was a recognition that broader social and economic objectives were as important in achieving these as were financial and technical objectives. The central issue to recognize, however, is that, before this could be done, the basis of the technical argument which underpinned the authorities' stance had to be addressed. The relevance of the technical argument was not questioned. What was disputed, and finally proved, was that the social and economic cost of the proposal was far greater than any savings which might be made in reduced capital expenditure. This undermining of the technical base broke down the technological rationality and allowed the debate to move onto the next phase of objectives prioritization as illustrated by the working model.

CONCLUSIONS

The KwaThandeka study shows the way in which technical professionals use the quantitative data of cost and technical specifications as the base measurement criterion. This corresponds to Goulet's 'technical rationality'.[33] The study then demonstrates that the community uses a more qualitative criterion of value, corresponding to Goulet's 'ethical rationality'.[34]

In a conventional approach to urban infrastructure provision a project will be designed on the basis of technical and financial criteria and opposed by the community using a totally different set of criteria (social, economic and political). To prevent polarization and integrate these two different rationalities a new project methodology is needed.

The basis of this process is to produce arguments for and against different project proposals (eg for each service level option) in terms of the whole range of criteria (social, economic, political, financial and technical). This can be done by carrying out a social survey which is community-driven, and which collects data on issues of importance to the community and the project, in terms of all these criteria. This step leads technical professionals to appreciate the social and value-based criteria inherent in infrastructure provision.

At present technical professionals look at what a service is, and use a relatively straightforward specification to do this, namely the quality of materials and workmanship achieved during the construction phase measured against the original design specification. Based on this perception, technical professionals tend to be preoccupied with the recovery of capital cost.

The community's measurement of the performance of different infrastructure services is based on tacit knowledge (see, for example, McCall (1987)[35] for a discussion of the concept of tacit knowledge in communities, as well as the work of Chambers *et al*, (1989)[36] and Scoones and Thompson (1994)[37] of what a service does at a particular point in time. The KwaThandeka study indicates that this tacit knowledge can be quantifiably expressed in terms of three quantifiable components of performance:

1   reliability;
2   health and safety; and
3   social, cultural and political acceptability.

These performance criteria can be quantifiably compared with the issues of operating and maintenance costs and affordability. This is the basis on which both parties (technical professionals and the community) can view infrastructure in terms of how people live with a given level of service in the long term – ie its sustainability. It is also the basis for the development of a systems approach.

The way in which the contradictions between technological and ethical rationalities was explored in KwaThandeka was made possible by the absence of a strong political agenda. Unlike the major urban centres of South Africa, such as Soweto, where the primary thrust centred around political negotiations, the negotiations at KwaThandeka centred around technical issues. The primary interaction from the community was thus with technical specialists rather than politicians. As a result it was possible to analyse differing perceptions of what constitutes a service independent of a political agenda. Thus, for example, there has never been an 'empowerment' drive behind the actions of KwaThandeka residents, in the way that there was in Soweto and other metropolitan centres. There was a rent boycott because people were dissatisfied with the services provided. In public meetings the needs expressed were for employment opportunities, water, schools, improved sanitation and roads. These needs, and frustration with the performance of existing services, constituted the driving force behind the rent boycott. This difference from the metropolitan areas was also evident in the attitudes of the community towards the different authorities. Thus the KLA was considered illegitimate and opposed by most residents, and the AHC refused to deal with councillors directly. The TPA, on the other hand, was recognized as a legal authority. The community elected a committee (the AHC) to represent their needs, but there was no indication of a desire for power or control in the sense expressed by Moser, and as practised by the civics in the PWV. This left the way open for consensus decision-making in a way which became possible in a wider context in South Africa only after the change in government policy in 1990.

This chapter has focused on a particular group of development professionals and a particular type of project. The experience, however, can be applied to a broad range of projects in different sectors with different types of professionals. The central issue is the way in which professional people interpret need from one particular perspective and have difficulty in recognizing, and giving equal weight to, other perspectives of the same problem. Yet the principle of equal weighting of need is an essential prerequisite to community participation in the arena of consensus. One way of overcoming this difference in perception is to define points of common interest which can form the basis for dialogue across the technical–social barrier. In the KwaThandeka project this proved to be the performance specification, the basis for which was a comprehensive survey and a detailed social impact assessment. Other areas may find different criteria are appropriate. Even when the difficulties associated with conflicting rationalities have been overcome, however, there is a second external actor group, whose influence within the community may be powerful and whose needs have to be reconciled with those of the other actors. The group comprises the NGO support organizations. Before examining their role, however, it is necessary first to examine the role of community-based organizations, through whom they interact with in the wider community.

11

Community Organizations and Urban Management

INTRODUCTION

The output from the conceptual framework is a set of working principles which govern the interaction between actors. However, even when this has been customized, when the various problems associated with different rationalities have been overcome and when a clear understanding has been achieved between the different parties, this is still insufficient to guarantee meaningful and effective community participation. Community participation is only meaningful if it is carried through the full cycle of the activity and into the future. So where the customized conceptual framework concerns itself primarily with determining objectives and defining relationships, the working model is concerned primarily with the determination of roles, as they will relate to the activity.

This creates a second point of potential failure. In the previous transition phase (where the conceptual framework was customized), the potential for failure focused on the conflicting needs of different actors and the way in which these play themselves out. In this second transition (evolving roles and responsibilities) the potential conflict stems from the differing needs of the specific activity being dealt with and those of the participatory process. At this stage the emphasis begins to shift from inter-relationships between different parties to the evolution of a common strategy for the activity.

The sections which follow describe three case studies which explore this evolution of roles and examines what this means in practice and, more specifically, how this influences the role of the community organizations. They are based on capital projects, but the same principles apply to the ongoing management of any activity, be it around infrastructure, and/or economic development. The implementation strategies described evolved as the projects progressed, but were based on an awareness of the need to achieve a balance of power between the different parties. The research associated with these case studies identified four key areas of potential conflict which can lead to a breakdown of the community participation process. In addition, the research highlighted the potential for conflict within the communities themselves and illustrated how communities have diverse needs which express themselves through different forms of participation. This is significant, because it clarifies an issue of fundamental difference between earlier approaches to participation which revolve around the nature and form of community participation.

Each of the three projects had community participation as its stated objective, but each interpreted this participation in a different way. All three projects were situated in the KwaZulu/Natal province of South Africa and all were funded by the Independent Development Trust (IDT) under a capital subsidy scheme discussed in greater detail in the following. The three projects were: Stafford Farm, Madadeni, near Newcastle; Sibongile, near Dundee; and Luganda, in Pinetown. Each represented a different type of urban environment. The first was close to a major urban centre (Newcastle), but actually situated across a border, within the 'homeland' of KwaZulu. The second was a conventional apartheid township whereas the third was an informal settlement, originally occupied by land invasion, which fell within the boundaries of a large white municipality. These differences had a significant impact on the community participation process in the three areas.

BRIEF INTRODUCTION TO THE IDT

In the 1990 budget an amount of R2000 million was allocated to upgrading social and physical infrastructure. Control over its expenditure was given to Justice Jan Steyn, previously head of the Urban Foundation. Steyn then set up a trust which was independent of government, comprising prominent business and academic people, to oversee the spending of this money and obtain the support of all major national political organizations.

Of this R2000 million, R750 million was allocated to urban infrastructure in a scheme whereby a sum of R7500 would be allocated as a capital subsidy for a serviced site. To ensure that the money was made available to low income families, an income ceiling of R1000 per month was placed on the main breadwinner. Applications for the subsidy could be made by any group or individual and were not limited to conventional developers or municipalities.

Within the IDT capital subsidy framework there were five major groupings of parties: the IDT as financier; CBOs (generally supported by technically based NGOs); project managers (which could represent professionals, contractors, developers or a combination of the three); local authorities; and provincial administrations. In practice, the three main players in a given project were the community organization, the local authority and the project manager. The IDT as financier theoretically remained aloof from the negotiation process, although in the projects described in this chapter the author, as IDT consultant, had to play a critical part in setting up the community participation process. Other bodies, such as the regional services councils that provided bulk services, sometimes had a peripheral role. Where this new system differed from the conventional model of local government in South Africa was in the changed relationship between these different parties.

The IDT capital subsidy scheme differs from previous funding schemes in three respects:

1   the very fact that it was a capital subsidy of a fixed amount, which enabled the system of financing to be freed from the constraints normally imposed by financial institutions, thereby opening the way for meaningful project control at a local grassroots level;
2   the emphasis placed by the IDT on community participation and control;[1] and
3   the fact that any group or organization could apply for the subsidy either on behalf of a group of residents or to develop an area for new development, provided only that the applicant (in addition to meeting the community participation requirements) had the capacity to manage the project and could obtain interim finance (the IDT provided only end-user finance; the situation of Luganda, discussed later, was an exception).

Not only did this system break the monopoly of the state structures to control the urban development process, but

1   it provided the opportunity for meaningful empowerment of the community and their representative organizations;
2   it reduced the leverage of the financier and hence his ability to interfere with the democratic process; and
3   it increased the power and influence of the technical group, described here collectively as the project manager.

Where the weakness of the system arose was in the contractual arrangements. As the IDT would only allow for one applicant (in the legal sense) this had a major impact on the balance of power. This was because the applicant became the developer, who was then the party with full financial responsibility.

In the case study projects this resulted in three different power relationships. The first case study is Stafford Farm. Although the project manager was the developer, the authoritarian nature of the KwaZulu political structure placed ultimate control over the decision-making process with the government, who viewed the local authority as an arm of central government (this is similar to the local government system of Latin America discussed in Chapter 4). The second case study is Sibongile (the apartheid township). Here the project manager was again the developer, but in this instance there was a weak local authority. This made the project manager the dominant party, albeit with a strong commitment to the principle of community participation. The third case study is Luganda (invaded land in a white municipality). Here the community organization was the developer. This was made possible because of the strong technical support it received from an NGO. Hence the community organization became the dominant party, although it was faced with a strong technical and administrative local authority.

The starting point in each instance was the principle that each community should have the maximum degree of control over the project as was possible in the given situation. Because each of the three projects had associated with it a specific approach to community participation, influenced by the circumstances described earlier, this resulted in three proposed working models, each distinct from the other two. Even though these working models had been tailored to individual proposals, the practicalities of the negotiating process around implementation resulted in significant changes having to be made to all of them. Consequently, the working models as implemented were significantly different from and, in case studies 2 and 3, far more complex than, the proposed working models. The reasons for this are discussed in the three sections which follow.

CASE STUDY 1: STAFFORD FARM, MADADENI, NEAR NEWCASTLE

Brief History

Stafford Farm is a low income extension to Madadeni, an urban area within the KwaZulu homeland adjacent to the industrial centre of Newcastle. The land was opened up, pegged and settled, without any services, in 1990 in a move to prevent illegal squatting. The application to the IDT was for service provision to 3606 sites, comprising three wards. It was accepted, initially at least, because the application showed a strong commitment to community participation from a government structure with a poor historical record of participation.

The original application for funding at Stafford Farm was made by the Town Council of Madadeni, with the assistance of a housing utility company. The Council stated specifically that they had held discussions with, and received the support of, a variety of political and other organizations in the area. They then stated that their intention would be to maintain contact with these (and other) organizations throughout the course of the project. At that time, before the democratic election, KwaZulu was semi-autonomous and was dominated by one specific political party – the Inkatha Freedom Party (IFP) – and all ministers, councillors and government officials belonged to this party. As the IFP had, in the past, shown strong antipathy to these other organizations, this willingness to have discussions in a wider forum was considered to indicate a significant shift in official thinking.

A second major statement of intent, made in the original application, was to the effect that this project would be controlled by the Madadeni Town Council. Towns in KwaZulu were, nominally, jointly controlled by the Council and the KwaZulu Ministry of the Interior, but in practice dominated by the latter. Thus the Stafford Farm application appeared indicative of a further shift in KwaZulu government thinking, in allowing the council a degree of autonomy over the development of a large project.

However, once the application had been provisionally accepted and detailed discussions started with the Council, it became clear that the original application had been misleading on two key issues. The first related to the autonomy of the applicant (the Madadeni Town Council) to pursue a project independent of (KwaZulu) Central Government and its appointed National Steering Committee for Stafford Farm. The second related to the process of interaction with a broader group of interested parties.

The KwaZulu National Steering Committee remained the controlling body for the project, through whom all issues had to be cleared. The Minister of the Interior retained final say over who would be consulted officially by the Council and what that degree of consultation would be. Discussions by the author with people in the area belonging to the local ANC, COSATU and civic branches indicated strong opposition to Council-led projects. They stated that they had not been consulted earlier and initially refused to interact in any way. These problems were made more difficult by an intractable attitude on the part of the KwaZulu government.

High-level negotiations between the KwaZulu government and the IDT failed to change this stance. Eventually, an instruction was received by the author from the IDT in Cape Town to accept the situation and to attempt to achieve a compromise. During this period, which lasted from October 1991 until the end of April 1992, all work on the project was suspended.

Negotiations were held with the progressive organizations (ie ANC, COSATU and civic branches) in the Newcastle/Madadeni area. Fortunately, Stafford Farm was not a typical upgrade situation, in that sites were already laid out and occupied (albeit with no services) and there was a reasonable degree of consensus on the desired levels of service, which were of a minimal standard. This limited the political opportunity value of the project and eventually a community participation procedure was worked out which was acceptable both to these organizations and to the Madadeni Council. In this compromise the utility company was appointed project manager and developer and took over the responsibility for informing all parties of site applicants and any action concerning the project which was deemed to affect the community. A mechanism was then developed to deal with comments and complaints from these bodies.

Although this agreement was accepted, under duress, by the progressive organizations, the level of participation which was agreed fell far below that envisaged by the IDT in its original planning as described earlier.

Model Description

The structure of a theoretical working model for this project was taken from the original project proposal submitted to the IDT. This is shown in Figure 11.1. Had this model been set out graphically in this way at the time the project was adjudicated, it would have been clear that it was impractical, given the structure and attitude of the KwaZulu government. It went beyond KwaZulu government policy in terms of its negotiation policy with other parties and it gave an independence and freedom of action to the local authority which conflicted with KwaZulu law. When this intent was stated in words, these limitations were not fully recognized,

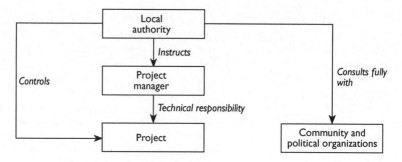

Figure 11.1 *Proposed working model for case study 1 (Stafford Farm)*

but setting it out in the form of a working model gave a firmer impression of the structure being proposed and drew out the limitations more clearly.

In this working model the project was controlled by the local authority, but responsibility for the detailed design and supervision of the project was delegated to the project manager. There was extensive liaison with other community organizations on all major issues, as well as the formation of grassroots organizations who would also be involved in the consultation process.

Implementation

The structure which was actually implemented is shown in Figure 11.2. This model is extremely common and reminiscent of a model of community development, which effectively it is. The relationship between the parties characterized by this model falls clearly into the category of participation described by Moser as a means approach. It should be recognized that this type of model is used extensively in South Africa (and elsewhere in the developing world), where it is considered by many governments to be an adequate form of participation. In this regard the project also has similarities to Paul's objective of effectiveness, whereby 'Effectiveness of a project demands that project services are congruent with beneficiary needs and preferences'.[2] Paul states that 'in all cases [where effectiveness was the objective], CP seems to have brought about a redesign of project services to better match beneficiary needs'.[3]

This statement has some validity at Stafford Farm and there are several underlying reasons for this. Firstly, the community at Stafford Farm is ethnically homogeneous. It appears from discussions with members of the community that most of the residents are members of the IFP although, according to the progressive organizations, this is because membership of the IFP was a pre-requisite for receiving a site. Also, in allocating the land, the Council moved rapidly to pre-empt a serious potential squatter problem, an action which was widely supported in the area.

Secondly, in Stafford Farm each person has a clearly defined site and the Council's policy has been to provide each family with services within two years of settling. Services are basic, comprising standpipes, ventilated

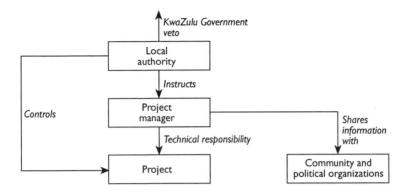

Figure 11.2 *Working model as implemented for case study 1 (Stafford Farm)*

improved pit latrines and gravel roads, whereas the electricity utility (ESCOM) has agreed to provide electricity. The project manager built a number of different toilet structures for people to choose from (this was instituted against the initial wishes of the KwaZulu government who would have preferred a single toilet option). In addition, a major employment programme was developed for the labour-based construction of toilets and water mains and the setting up of three block yards, a pre-cast concrete yard and door and window frame manufacture.

Thirdly, there are other factors working in favour of the project. The services will be provided free of charge and that the water and sanitation option is governed by technical constraints on bulk services. A higher level of service is not feasible technically at this stage, a factor which has been explained to the community and accepted. Support for the project is high and there was good attendance at mass public meetings held by the project manager's team to discuss various issues related to the transfer of land and services. The community was informed of the various technical and financial constraints on the project, but did not take part directly in any of the decision-making.

The result of this analysis, using the working model as a basis and plotting changes through the graphical relational model, is interesting because it indicates that the basic assumptions on which the model was built, which were based on a consensus form of decision, were invalid. The process was following an agenda defined by the IDT, although this was inappropriate to the environment or the project. These conditions dictated that the arena of inclusion was actually the most appropriate arena, and this is where the process came to rest. This placed the community organizations in an interesting position because they had effectively recognized this and were using the project to move towards the arena of confrontation, as indicated in Figure 8.2. Had this been recognized at the outset, then a different approach could have been taken which would have been more appropriate to the circumstances.

CASE STUDY 2: SIBONGILE, NEAR DUNDEE

Brief History

In the Natal Midlands there were two housing utility companies operating in 1991, both of whom saw the IDT scheme as an opportunity to retain their involvement in the ongoing development of the area. This case study represents a typical example of the approach taken by these companies to develop a project in association with the community. Of the 22 IDT projects approved for Natal in 1991, approximately 60% were awarded to utility companies operating a similar participation process to that described in the following.

This project application, for 600 sites to be serviced, was originally a joint application between a housing utility company and an interim Development Committee of Sibongile. However, the ultimate intention was to form a community trust before construction which would take responsibility for the project as a whole. From a community participation perspective three issues were considered important at the beginning:

1 the make-up of the Development Committee;
2 the relationship between the Development Committee and the utility company acting as project managers; and
3 the overall responsibility of the Development Committee in respect of this project.

This project was classified, according to IDT criteria, as a greenfield site for an identifiable community. This is one step up from the situation where there is no identifiable community. However, in either case, the community participation process for a greenfield site tends to be limited, primarily because there is no extant residents group with which to negotiate. In Sibongile the situation was perceived differently. Although there was no house on the site, the existing communities from which residents would be chosen were already defined. Furthermore, the housing demand was such that any decision about who would move affected the community as a whole. This created a situation which is more akin to an upgrade. The Development Committee was drawn from the whole community of Sibongile and determined that this project would be treated as a Sibongile project which involved all residents. This was a critical distinction, which is important in terms of the community participation process. In planning terminology the site was classified as greenfield and under normal circumstances development professionals would have been happy to retain this definition, with detrimental results. Fortunately, the community perception, which looked at the reality from a local political context, was different. It was perceived as an upgrade and this view was eventually accepted by all parties. This is a further example of differing rationalities.

The original Development Committee which made the application comprised members of the Council, government department professionals and local business and Church representatives. Discussions were under way with local political organizations, but no firm conclusion was reached.

Subsequently, discussions were held between the IDT representative (the author) and the various political parties, on a local level, to draw these organizations into the process. Thus by October the Committee comprised representatives of: the health department, the ANC, the Council, the ANC Youth League, civic, business, churches and the Taxi Association (which attended the meeting setting up the Interim Committee, but later withdrew). At a public meeting in October the community elected four independent representatives and this group subsequently joined the Development Committee. There was no formal IFP branch in Sibongile.

This process was repeated in all the areas where the application had been instigated by a utility company, in all instances successfully. The actual composition of the Development Committees varied and different areas took a different view on the direct involvement of national political parties. Some areas had this political party involvement and others, by mutual consent, did not. The early meetings of the Sibongile Development Committee were marked by strong tensions between two factions, one Council-led and one ANC-led. These were never fully resolved, but a workable compromise was finally accepted. This was made possible by the inclusion of the four directly elected representatives, whose presence legitimized the committee and made it extremely difficult for either of the two major groups to withdraw without being perceived to undermine a much needed housing project. At a meeting on 29 October 1990, agreement was reached to formalize the Committee and produce a constitution.

Virtually the whole of 1991 was occupied with trying to reach consensus between parties as to the detailed objectives and final composition of the Development Committee. Thus it was only from January 1992 that the real work of agreeing documentation could begin. The project manager and the Development Committee reached agreement on all project documentation, including a Community Participation Contract defining their own relationship in March 1992, and this was signed.

The contractual documentation was submitted to the IDT Head Office at the end of March and referred back with queries. It was re-submitted on 7 April 1992 for signature. In terms of participation, a mass meeting took place on 25 March 1992 to gain approval from the wider community to proceed with the development in terms of the project description. Representatives of all the main groups were present at that meeting in their capacity as Development Committee members and all supported the project openly. There was strong consensus from the meeting for the project to continue.

Model Description

The type of community participation which evolved at Sibongile places the project (and others like it) outside the normal situation for a local authority, whereby the primary relationship is between the local authority and the wider community. Sibongile was managed by a separate local authority elected in terms of the Black Local Authorities Act 1992. This authority had little perceived legitimacy and no financial resources. To receive IDT funding the project required broad-based support, which meant the formation of a committee to manage the project which was independent of the local authority. It also required proven technical expertise and the only group able to provide this was a private sector utility company operating in the area. In this instance, however, the utility company not only provided the project management expertise, but also became the developer, taking full financial responsibility for the project. The reasons for this are discussed in the section which follows.

This was not ideal, but two factors stopped this project from becoming simply a technically dominated engineering project and turned it into an alternative management model with meaningful community participation. The first was a strong commitment on the part of the utility company to full community participation, although they were not sure what this actually entailed when they first became involved. The second was strong pressure exerted by the author to provide contractual commitment to shared decision-making by the project manager and Development Committee. The outcome was the proposed working model shown in Figure 11.3.

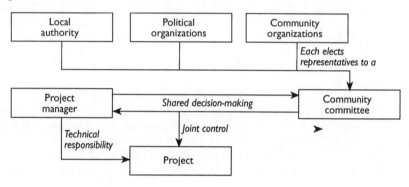

Figure 11.3 *Proposed working model for case study 2 (Sibongile)*

Implementation

When the IDT originally stated their intention to empower local communities through their involvement in, and control of, IDT funded projects, it was envisaged that many communities would be in direct control, either alone or in conjunction with project managers, of the projects in all their stages. In Sibongile, the initial intention was for the development committee to raise the finance and for the project to be a joint venture, effectively, between the development committee as developer (ie having fiscal responsibility) and the utility company, acting as project manager, having technical responsibility.

As the IDT process developed it became clear that there was a change in power relationships. The IDT was a provider of end-user finance, meaning that it would only refund the capital subsidy amount to the developer on transfer of the serviced site. Hence the developer had to provide interim finance. With no financial track record, the Development Committee was unable to achieve this. As a result, financial responsibility reverted to the utility company (which, as was stated earlier, was also the project manager), the concept of joint control receded and the Development Committee was downgraded considerably in terms of the potential for meaningful input into, as well as their ability to control, the project.

It became clear to the author that the issue of relationships was critical to the success of the community participation process. Although there were strong links from the beginning between the Council-led faction in the Development Committee in Sibongile and the utility company, the Development Committee as a whole ratified the position of the utility company as project managers to the project in October 1991. What then began to happen was that members of the Committee who were not involved originally began to question fundamental issues, such as land siting and plot size.

This was the essence of the participation process, but it soon became apparent that the disparity in knowledge and power between the project manager and the Development Committee meant that there could be no meaningful participation in the decision-making process.

This problem was rectified to some degree by a community participation agreement between the project manager and the Development Committee. There were two ways in which such agreement could be formulated. The first, adopted in other parts of Natal, would have been to insert a clause giving the committee nominal control over the project or a veto on the actions of the project manager. This was not considered adequate. A single, all-embracing clause would be difficult to enforce legally and would not overcome the problem of the disparity in the skills and knowledge base that existed between the two parties. The second option, developed by the author, was to acknowledge the difference in the financial and professional skills capacity of the two parties, but to commit the project manager to a training role over the period of the contract. All aspects of the development process would be discussed with, and thoroughly explained to, the committee. The training process was formalized by incorporating in the participation agreement a list of key decision-making issues. Primary responsibility was allocated to a given party and the second party was provided with a power of veto over any decision. The project manager would have an educational role in respect of all those items for which it had primary responsibility. The second option was adopted.

The way in which the community participation agreement evolved led a further major change to the relational model. The two parties agreed to form an executive committee to take the daily decisions and this changed the role of the Development Committee further. Those members of the Development Committee sitting on the executive gained a greater understanding of the technical process of development than did those excluded. At the same time the Development Committee, in moving out of this decision-making role, became a better vehicle for monitoring grassroots feelings about the project because of this distance from the technical decision-making process. This issue is discussed further later. These changes resulted in the proposed working model of Figure 11.3 being changed to the implementation model of Figure 11.4.

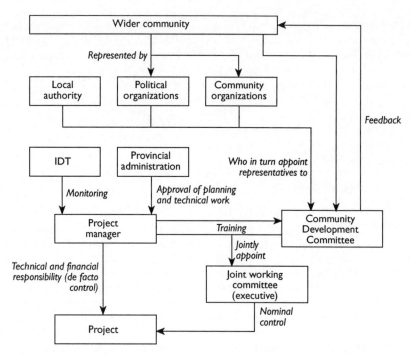

Figure 11.4 *Working model as implemented for case study 2 (Sibongile)*

CASE STUDY 3: LUGANDA, PINETOWN

Brief History

Luganda is an area of ground which, when the IDT application was made, was classified under the Group Areas Act as being an area designated for the use of people of Indian origin. Its use was therefore controlled by the House of Delegates, the Indian parliament of the apartheid tricameral legislature, although ownership of the land resided in a private development company. However, for several years it had been occupied illegally by Africans and when the project application was made there was tacit agreement that it would no longer be racially segregated. Ownership of the land was a major problem, which delayed the project for over a year. However, the details are not relevant to this discussion. The outcome was the eventual purchase from the private developer by the House of Delegates and the incorporation of the land into a white municipality – the Borough of Pinetown. The final relationship of relevance to the community participation debate was therefore a formalized land invasion area situated within a white local authority boundary.

This project application was submitted to the IDT jointly by an NGO, the Built Environment Support Group of the University of Natal (BESG) and the Luganda Residents Association (LRA). The application was for the servicing of 1861 sites. The LRA had unanimous support among residents in Luganda and maintained a high degree of community involvement in the project, with community meetings held regularly every second or third Sunday for report-back and discussion.

From the beginning it was recognized that the project had several features which would make it difficult to develop in a conventional way without fragmenting the local community. The community itself was cohesive, but relatively small. It was in constant danger of armed attack from residents living in the tribal area on the far bank of the river. Finally, once the project was fully developed, the existing population would represent only one-quarter of the total population, which meant that great care would be needed to incorporate a relatively large number of new residents without destroying existing community (social) structures. For these reasons the community wanted to retain full responsibility for the project.

Model Description

As with case study 2, this working model started from an idealistic base. The intention was that the community would 'control' and manage all aspects of the project. This is very much in line with the conventional 'ends' approach of empowerment, whereby the project objective is empowerment and all aspects of the project are built around this concept. This idealized model is shown in Figure 11.5. The only involvement of external bodies (such as Pinetown and the NPA) was anticipated to be the technical approval of planning procedures and engineering proposals. In this form the project has strong similarities to the FUNDASAL housing projects of San Salvador, discussed in Chapter 6.

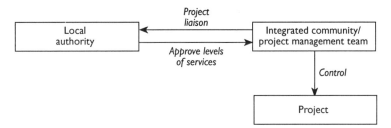

Figure 11.5 *Proposed working model for case study 3 (Luganda)*

In practice, the situation became far more complex. In the changing political environment, the CBO was prepared to work closely with the municipality, provided that this did not prevent their control of the project. At the same time the various authorities were open to a high degree of community involvement in the decision-making process. To operate in this way, the management of the project (within the community) was separated from the civic function of negotiating wider policy issues relating to the future of the community. A Development Trust was formed to control the project technically, manage its finances and hold communal assets (such as public sites and open space), as well as reporting to the IDT and other guarantors. This Trust then appointed a project manager who was responsible for the physical development of the site. All of this was made possible because the Trust was able to raise interim finance. Owing to the high political profile of the Luganda project, and the need to be seen to support some community-driven projects, the IDT had agreed to provide the guarantees which made interim financing possible.

Implementation

The approval of the project meant that Luganda residents became responsible for managing a R13 million project and this necessitated a review of community structures. The original negotiations had been initiated by the LRA, but in the intervening period the civic structure, with which the LRA was associated, had developed into a more cohesive body responsible for negotiating, at a policy level, issues such as service charges and the future of local government. During this intervening period, the Borough of Pinetown had taken over the responsibility for the ongoing maintenance of services and the future administration of the area. The Borough was therefore proposing a closer relationship with the civic on the IDT project.

The civic felt that they could be compromised in the wider political negotiating process if they were to become too closely involved with the Borough and that another body would be a more suitable vehicle to manage the IDT project (Luganda is only one of a dozen African settlements in the southern Pinetown area and there would be major negotiations taking place in the coming months on a variety of sensitive issues such as service charges, executive authority and representation on a single municipality). There was already a working committee in Luganda, at which the civic and various community groups (eg women, youth, sport and religious bodies) met to discuss the wider needs of the community, but this was also considered inappropriate. As a result, a third body was formed, namely the Luganda Development Trust (LDT).

The net result, shown in Figure 11.6, appears initially to be awkward and unwieldy, but it actually reflects a deep understanding of the complexities of the participation process on the part of the community. It also shows a project which is far removed from the FUNDASAL project. Instead of operating an empowerment project in the arena of confrontation, the community overcame attempts by the local authority to dominate the process and operate it in the arena of inclusion, and moved it fully into the arena of consensus. In doing this, however, there was a major transformation in the structure of the community organization. The Luganda project evolved naturally into three community participation components: a civic, representing the political demands of the community; a trust, taking technical and financial responsibility for a specific project; and the working committee which, in conjunction with mass meetings, was the vehicle for expressing people's needs and concerns on local issues.

The final issue to be resolved was the relationship with the Borough of Pinetown and the way in which this relationship operates within the arena of consensus. A steering committee was formed, in which general progress and issues of mutual concern could be addressed. In this way the Borough had influence over the broad policy decision-making process and retained

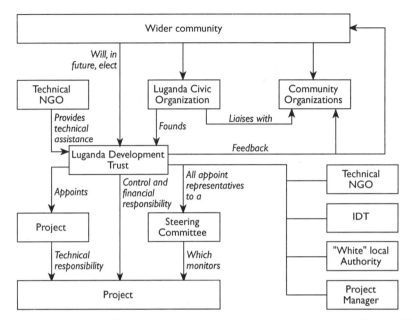

Figure 11.6 *Working model as implemented for case study 3 (Luganda)*

its legal responsibility for the project. It was committed to decision by committee, however, and therefore, in practice, it could neither dictate policy to the community nor interfere in the direct management of the project. The community thus retained a high degree of autonomy.

CONSTRAINTS TO THE ONGOING SUCCESS OF COMMUNITY PARTICIPATION DURING PROJECT IMPLEMENTATION

The implementation strategy, which results in the modification and refinement of the working model, is an iterative process, as Figure 9.3 illustrated. From the experience gained in these, and other, case studies, four potential constraints were highlighted which can prevent, or at least hinder, the successful implementation of an agreed working model. These are now described.

Unwillingness of Parties to Carry Through Agreed Commitments

Case study 1 (Stafford Farm) provides an example of this constraint, which resulted in the change in the working model structure from that illustrated in Figure 11.1 to that in Figure 11.2. In this instance the party reneging on its commitment was the Madadeni Council. The Council had stated specifically that they had held discussions with, and received the support of, a variety of political and other organizations in the area. They also stated their intention to maintain contact with these (and other) organizations throughout the course of the project. In the event they backed away from this stance under pressure from the KwaZulu central government. Two important lessons emerge from this situation. The first is that the party applying for the funding (the Madadeni Council) was not an independent agent; they were fronting for the KwaZulu government. It emerged later that this was a strategic move on the part of the KwaZulu government, who felt that they themselves would be an unacceptable applicant for IDT funding. This illustrates the need to deal with primary actors only if the subsequent negotiation process is to have a chance of success.

The second factor of importance to emerge from this case study was that the choice of the most appropriate arena was itself incorrect in this instance. At the time the full implications of working in different arenas were not recognized. The reality was that the IDT's stated requirements for community participation could only be fulfilled in the arena of consensus. Had this been recognized, then one of two courses of action could have been followed. Either projects in KwaZulu could have been excluded, a politically unacceptable condition given the state of political tension and violence in South Africa at the time, or, alternatively, the scheme could have been modified to recognize different circumstances and adopt a more pragmatic stance at the beginning. This would have prevented the KwaZulu government misleading the IDT, but would have encountered opposition with progressive organizations.

Given this polarized situation the course adopted was possibly the best available. What needs to be recognized is that the operation of community participation in the arena of consensus can only take place with the agreement of all parties. This is a factor that many outside groups, particularly in the NGO and academic fields, are reluctant to accept. The reality was that pursuing a participation strategy in the arena of inclusion was actually appropriate for this particular situation.

Internal Conflict Within Parties

This constraint applies primarily to the CBOs, although it can also affect NGOs, as the previous chapter illustrated. It is a constraint which affected the community in case studies 2 (Sibongile) and 3 (Luganda). In both instances the community organizations developed new structures (the Joint Working Committee and the Development Trust, respectively) during the negotiation process to deal with the contradictions in their respective projects and forestall internal conflict. The full implications of this change on the community organizations are discussed in the next section.

Parties Unable to Fulfil Their Functions Due to External Factors Outside Their Control

From the experience both of the South African case studies and international experience, this constraint is likely to be the major problem inhibiting meaningful community participation in the arena of consensus. The reasons for this are two-fold. Firstly, the case studies highlighted the importance of the community organizations sharing financial responsibility for the project. It is clear that such responsibility is a critical force driving the community to demand the resources, knowledge and skills which are an essential component of the associated management function. The issues of shared decision-making and shared financial responsibility are inseparable. Community management in the arena of inclusion addresses this issue by giving the full responsibility to the community, but this is not feasible in a large complex project. In terms of management, where does the community end and the local authority begin? This can only be overcome by a high degree of decentralization of both resources and responsibility, a move which is contrary to the current drive for increased centralization being pursued by the international agencies.

Secondly, the case studies highlight a large gap in technical knowledge, skills and expertise between the technical professionals and the community organizations. Case studies 2 and 3 both attempted to address this problem. Case study 2 (Sibongile) took a contractual approach, but the outcome only served to indicate that the provision of a legal framework alone is inadequate if the community members involved are not provided with the training and skills to match the scale and complexity of the problem. This was recognized but, unfortunately, the funds were not available to provide the necessary training independently and responsibility for training was given to the project manager. This did not work, not because the project manager lacked commitment, but because it conflicted with his wider interest in achieving a speedy completion of the work.

In case study 3 the knowledge transfer was more successful, but only because of the combined input of individuals from four outside parties, namely the NGO, the project manager, the local authority and the IDT. All of these, with the exception of the NGO, were exceeding their brief in contributing this support. This question of education and training is addressed further in Chapter 13.

Inappropriate External Support Structures

This issue is covered in the next chapter on NGOs, but it is valuable to summarize the experience of case studies 2 and 3 in this context. It was clear with both these projects that there were several distinct requirements for external intervention. The first was technical training. This was extensive and complex. Here the NGO's role was of primary importance. The way in which this was achieved in Luganda was to link the training to the construction programme itself. The monthly steering committee meetings provided the monitoring, as it was here that the results of the training were tested.

The second area of external intervention was in the area of practical management and this was covered more effectively by the project manager. Both case studies indicated successful skills transfer in this area, although Luganda gained a longer term benefit because of the greater size, longer time frame and more effective extension of the management function into other areas. Finally, the third area of external intervention was in the area of mediation. The IDT's community participation consultants were given a wide brief which allowed a great deal of latitude. This proved necessary. Parties of different political persuasion had to work together and a strong atmosphere of distrust had to be overcome. Once this was achieved there was an ongoing conflict of interest between the time management needs of the project and the social needs of the community. This could only have been achieved successfully by someone who was trusted by all parties and seen to be independent. Neither the NGOs, as they were constituted at the time, nor the project manager could have carried out this role.

IMPACT ON THE COMMUNITY ORGANIZATIONS

Because community participation was at the centre of these case studies, this provides a valuable insight into the relationship between communities and urban projects which has previously been lacking. Specifically, they provide a basis for exploring the relationship between the arenas of inclusion and consensus as they relate to urban management. This is particularly relevant to the first case study (Stafford Farm) and this case study will therefore be explored first before moving on to draw the distinction between this and the other two situations.

The first case study in Stafford Farm took place in an environment where the (KwaZulu) government would not allow free political expression, yet where the financier (the IDT) attempted to maximize community involvement under a project manager committed to this course of action. In addition, this project was constrained by limited technical options and by the refusal of the KwaZulu government to tolerate political opposition. The result was limited community input on issues such as the type of toilet superstructure and the location of standpipes, broad community support for the project (the level of theft, for example, was far lower than on a similar project operated by the bulk service supply authority, without any community participation, in an adjacent area of Stafford Farm) and maximizing employment and job creation opportunities.

The main factor to be recognized in discussing community participation and the role of community organizations was that the project was sited in the wrong arena, in that the initial approach was based on the assumption that the project was situated in the arena of consensus. However, the project had already been limited to one basic technical solution for all services (water, sanitation, roads, stormwater and electricity) which were broadly acceptable to most of the community of Stafford Farm. People were living on the sites and there was an agreed service charge. In other words, the level of type of participation required was not complex, so the project was actually situated in the arena of inclusion. This is not to say that it is a good example of participation within that arena. On the contrary, the model adopted was paternalistic (on the part of the government) and the most that could have been (and in fact was) achieved, was a degree of community development. However, the reality was that most people on the site appeared happy with the process as it evolved.

The response of the community organization to this project was purely political. At a local level they wanted to be a part of the management team so that residents could see that they were also responsible for providing much needed services and they could therefore gain local credibility. At the same time they used the fact that the KwaZulu government refused them full recognition to attempt to turn the IDT, openly, against the KwaZulu government. When this failed they attempted to pressurize the IDT through national political structures, writing letters of protest and arguing strongly that the IDT was not committed to the participation process. Thus they operated on two levels. At a local level they kept their involvement, but they fought the project at a national level. As described in Chapter 8, their objective was to use the project to move the participation process into the arena of confrontation, where they would be in a position to isolate the KwaZulu government and thereby gain political leverage.

Both Sibongile and Luganda were situated clearly in the arena of consensus. An exploration of these two case studies reveals the differences in the types of issues and the approach to decision-making which distinguishes the two arenas from each other. When the projects began, the community organizations dealing with the negotiation process in the two areas were situated at the two poles of the means–end continuum. In Luganda the organization was strongly politicized, being responsible for negotiating security of tenure following a land invasion. In Sibongile the organization was formed to apply for IDT funding and, under the influence of the developer who was providing the technical credibility, viewed itself as non-political and interested solely in development. By the end of the project both areas had developed similar, multi-pronged structures, but through different routes. That Luganda was more successful was due primarily to its secure positioning within the arena of consensus. In Sibongile there were pressures pulling the participation process into the arena of inclusion and this weakened the effectiveness of the community structures.

The final structures are illustrated in Figures 11.4 (Sibongile) and 11.6 (Luganda). Essentially, both have created three arms to deal with the different facets of the development process. What emerged was the recognition that no one body within the community could actually deal with the complexities of the development process effectively. This was most apparent in Luganda, where the politically based community organization foresaw that working closely with the local authority would constrain their negotiating strategy and political tactics. Potential conflicts were envisaged in:

1 negotiating a new local government management structure (political decision-making) working closely with the same controlling authority on a major project (technical decision-making); and
2 making compromise decisions on issues such as the levels of service, construction programme, type of construction techniques to be used, etc (an outcome of the community organization having full financial responsibility for the project); while
3 representing the needs and aspirations of community residents as users (ie consumers) of a service.

As a result, the newly formed civic organization continued to be the primary representative body for the residents of Luganda and retained its responsibility for negotiating wider political issues. Responsibility for technical decisions was passed to a newly formed and purpose-specific Trust which was appointed by the civic and the working committee. In the normal course of events, the election of the civic would have meant the demise of the Luganda Working Committee, as this body would have been superseded. However, this did not happen. Instead, the Luganda Working Committee took on a new role and became the primary vehicle for maintaining community contact at a grassroots level. All three bodies were available to report back at mass meetings. What had happened was that the community organizations had recognized that community participation is made up of three facets and that true empowerment in its widest sense can only take place if all of these facets are addressed satisfactorily. Thus the community needs to be involved in decision-making as part of the political structure, as part of the management structure and as users or consumers, depending on the specific application.

In Sibongile the same tensions and contradictions which arise when one organization attempts to be responsible for all three facets of the decision-making process were recognized, and a similar approach adapted. Thus the political organizations retained their own identity and took responsibility for political negotiation, while liaising with the development committee. The development committee became the grassroots link organization, a difficult in-between situation which it was able to achieve because (1) it had directly elected community representatives, thereby providing credibility in its negotiation with political organizations, and (2) it appointed the joint working committee. Finally, the Joint Working Committee took responsibility for the management decisions associated with the project. Again, all three groups agreed to report back to mass meetings.

Where the two situations of Luganda and Sibongile differed was in the inter-relationship between the three facets, and it is this issue which illustrates why effective and meaningful participation in decision-making can only take place in the arena of consensus. Superficially this difference appears to revolve around financial and managerial control, the reason why the community management approach is so popular. This is in fact only the starting point. In Luganda the community had financial responsibility for the project, whereas in Sibongile this lay with the project manager. This was only one facet, however. In both Luganda and Sibongile there was a serious lack of knowledge and experience in the community organizations, but this was addressed in both instances. In Sibongile, a community participation agreement was framed which (1) defined a training role for the project manager and (2) gave the community extensive rights of veto. The intention was to place pressure on the project manager to provide skills and knowledge training to the Development Committee. This turned out to be the wrong emphasis. The Development Committee was not sufficiently motivated to take advantage of the training opportunities. What had been created was a supply–push situation, with pressure on the project manager to provide knowledge and skills. In Luganda, what emerged was a demand-pull situation, where members of the various community organizations demanded training opportunities of their own accord. Financial control, by the community, of the project itself was only part of the reason for this demand-pull situation, however. In Sibongile the committee was dealing with a small development totally in isolation. In Luganda the development was a part of a wider process of involvement which was involved with policy. There were negotiations on service charges and on future political control. As a result the demand for knowledge came from all three of the community groups involved with the project. This was the key to success. Control over the management of the project, without involvement in the wider policy-making process, becomes simply another form of community manipulation.

Community Participation and NGOs

DIFFERENT TYPES OF NGOs AND THEIR ROLE IN DEVELOPMENT

The conventional historical analysis of community participation described earlier has resulted in a tendency to categorize and label those involved in both the participation process itself and in the wider development process. This has affected all actors to some degree, but nowhere more so than with the NGO sector. The duality of community versus state which is the outcome of the empowerment approach to community participation divides all actors into one of the two camps. Most actors, be they funding agencies, private sector groups or development professionals, are aligned with the state. This leaves the community alone with the sole exception of NGOs. This view is clearly illustrated by Cernea, writing for the World Bank, when he argues that

> 'The two fundamental actors in local development processes are the local governments and the local communities. But "community and bureaucracy are two evidently antithetical styles of social organization"... which serve to distinguish the two major protagonists in planned development, the people and the state. In the interaction between these two actors, NGOs insert themselves not as a third and different/independent actor but as an emanation and representation of the community (or of a community sub-group). Beyond their various differences, they [NGOs] appear as an organizational response, most often instrumental and sometimes political, of the community or its sub-groups, in pursuit of alternative strategies ... for local social development.[1]

The result is the perception that there is some form of symbiotic relationship between the NGO and the community which creates an ideal partnership for sustainable development. This romantic view of NGOs is a myth which, in the long term, can only be damaging to both communities and NGOs.

Problems with this view exist on two levels. One relates to the different categories of NGO and the way in which they interact both with each other and with the wider development process. This is discussed later. The second level relates to the nature of the relationship itself, as illustrated by Cernea. There is no question that many NGOs perform a valuable role in communities. At the same time it must be recognized that all organizations have their own agenda which is the basis for their existence. While this agenda is simple and clearly defined, eg to help one specific community to deal with a specific issue, then this is not a problem. As soon as they expand beyond this, however, whether through their own success or because their work already expanded beyond one community, then a potential conflict of interest exists. This was illustrated in one rural development project in the Western Transvaal region of South Africa.

During the 1980s, Mathopestad was one of the few remaining African rural settlements to retain freehold land rights within the boundaries of white South Africa. It had managed to mount a legal battle which had prevented the forced removal of its people to a homeland and, in the process, had gained a high international profile. It was therefore a prestigious community with which to be associated. Throughout the 1970s it had been supported in its struggle by an NGO, the Transvaal Rural Action Committee (TRAC), a body set up to assist black communities to fight attempts by the government to displace them. When the government finally abandoned its attempt at removal, and security of tenure was granted, the community's attention could refocus on development. Suddenly the community was inundated by NGOs from a multiplicity of sectors, all wanting to provide support to the community. There were NGOs dealing with agricultural development, with housing, water and sanitation, health, education and a variety of peripheral activities.

Each NGO wanted to be the primary support group. There was no co-ordination and several launched a campaign against TRAC to undermine their relationship with the leadership. At least one of these was funded covertly by the apartheid state. Different NGOs sought out different sectors to support in the village leadership and a system of patronage developed which caused friction and division in the community. The leadership became divided and political infighting ensued. When the international funding which was expected for Mathopestad did not materialize, many of the NGOs moved on to other communities and simply abandoned Mathopestad. The result was a community whose social structure was badly damaged and who were left fighting among themselves. This outcome raises the issue of NGO accountability.

Cernea sees local level social development as the broadest arena within which NGOs provide their contribution to communities[2] and much of the World Bank analysis is based on this premise.[3] In this situation, where the NGO is founded in a specific community, then accountability is clear. The members of the NGO are also part of the community and will be judged by their peers. This situation is changing, however. Firstly there is 'the voluntary entry of young and well-trained specialists . . . into development-related NGO activity'.[4] Secondly, there is the growth of professional trainers to satisfy the growing need for training the trainers in communities. Finally, there is the trend towards the grouping of NGOs in larger geographical or sectoral associations, which will require increased professional management. The move is therefore towards a more organized, and more professional, approach and the increased formalization of the NGO sector. These changes will have clear benefits in terms of efficiency. They are also necessary to deal with the multilateral and bilateral agencies from a position of strength.

Unfortunately, this process is likely to prise NGOs away from a position where they are fully integrated with the community, as their response to the funding agencies requires them to define, and justify, their own role as an end in itself. This in turn also increases the likelihood of the NGOs creating their own agendas and in doing so increases the need to formalize their relationship, and the nature of their accountability, with the community or communities they serve. If this does not happen, then the problems described in Mathopestad will escalate.

The whole basis of Cernea's analysis of NGOs for the World Bank was that most NGOs are grassroots organizations and for that reason these were made the focus of the paper. The earlier section showed the changes taking place within this group of NGOs, although there are other changes taking place globally which are bringing other NGOs into the development process who might previously have focused on other areas, either totally or predominantly. These changes in turn lead back to the first level at which the relationship between communities and NGOs is called into question, and which relates to the interaction between the different categories of NGO.

The NGOs may be categorized by geographical location, by their origins or by their activity content,[5] but these categorizations are becoming less relevant as most NGOs are drawn increasingly into the development process. What is a more important distinction is that which separates NGOs with an interest in policy from those with a primary interest in implementation, and this is where the second problem affecting community/NGO relationships begins to emerge.

There are two categories of NGO in particular whose involvement in development is changing the nature of NGO activity, namely environment and poverty alleviation/emergency aid. With the international Rio de Janeiro Summit on the Environment in 1992, the barriers which had kept development distinct from the wider environment were finally broken down. The position of bodies which had previously attempted to link the two areas was strengthened, while those who had previously limited their activities to the environment found themselves having to deal with development issues. These bodies came from a wide variety of backgrounds: in research (the International Institute for Environment and Development; IIED); in advocacy (Greenpeace); and in conservation (Worldwide Fund for Nature; WWF). They had different political bases, different economic bases, and widely different objectives. What they all had in common, however, was a predominant interest in policy formulation. Suddenly they all found themselves having to become more deeply involved in project implementation as the two 'areas' of the environment and development were merged. This shift will become increasingly evident in the next decade as the move towards sustainable development continues.

The transition of the emergency aid groups is slightly different, although equally dramatic. The linkage between poverty and development is evident to all of those working in the field. At a policy level organizations such as Oxfam and Christian Aid have made a major contribution to improving the development process. Their problem has been that the growth in poverty has exceeded their growth in private funding. As a result, the demand on their resources for the alleviation of poverty and for disaster relief prevents them from switching those resources to longer term development. The result is the emergence of an increasing interdependence between the funding agencies and the different international NGOs. The funding agencies recognize the effective implementation capacity of the NGOs and use them to increase their own effectiveness. The NGOs need this form of funding if they are to expand their activities to long-term development. The result is that NGOs which have a strong empathy with community needs have to deal with the contradictions inherent in taking funding agency money.

These are not just problems of conflicting agendas between funding agencies and communities. What is happening internationally is that there is an increasing overlap between policy and implementation and it is this which is causing the contradictions. In this situation it becomes essential to have a clear understanding of the distinction between the arenas of inclusion and consensus, and this is particularly important in the urban context, where both may operate in parallel. Most NGO activity, to which Cernea refers, and which plays such a vital part in development, actually operates within the arena of inclusion. The difficulty arises when the NGO transfers its activities into the arena of consensus. In this situation, the historical relationship between NGOs and communities no longer applies. Instead the NGO must recognize that there are a variety of roles to be played, in a similar way to the development professional. There will still be a need to provide support to the community organization, but then the NGO should act purely in an advisory capcity. There may be a need for the NGO to be a primary actor in its own right in the wider decision-making process, but then this must not be confused with the first role. Equally the NGO may wish to take on a mediating role, but this is different again. The point is that, when operating in the arena of consensus, one NGO cannot play a multiplicity of parts. The constraints applying to development professionals operating at this level of decision-making apply equally to NGOs.

This in turn requires a re-evaluation of the role and function of NGOs because the distinctions are not clearly understood and they may sometimes evolve from the arena of inclusion to that of consensus without the NGO being fully aware of the changes which are occurring. The section which follows examines a case study of the evolution of a purpose-built indigenous development NGO in South Africa which was caught up in this evolutionary process of change from one arena to the other. This case study illustrates many of these problems and shows how the contradictions inherent in combining policy with implementation, and independent activity with an ongoing support role to community organizations, can affect NGOs detrimentally. The following section looks at how the role of the NGOs might be adapted to overcome these contradictions and operate effectively in the arena of consensus.

DEVELOPMENT NGO SECTOR IN SOUTH AFRICA

Introduction

Lee-Smith and Stren[6] highlight the lack of indigenous development NGOs in many African countries. The use of the term in this context is wider than the World Bank definition. The reason for this is not difficult to find. To be effective, such NGOs require skills which are in short supply. They also require funding which is rarely available internally. Until recently this funding was also, with a few important exceptions, difficult to obtain internationally. South Africa was one of those exceptions. During the 1980s a significant amount of money was provided to strengthen the development NGO sector in South Africa. As a result it grew, over the decade from 1984 to 1993, to become, collectively, a powerful influence in determining the policy process in the country. Its demise in the election year of 1994 was as dramatic, and even more rapid, than its rise.

In the context of the growth of the NGO sector internationally during the present decade, and particularly the support given by international and bilateral donor agencies to this sector, which now includes encouragement for the growth of indigenous development NGOs, the South African experience is particularly relevant. As a founder member of the two largest development NGOs in South Africa, one urban-based and one rural-based, the author was able to study the operation of these organizations over time and examine their operation and the way in which they interacted with the agents of the state and with community organizations. To describe the role of development NGOs, one specific urban-based NGO, Planact, has been used as a case study.

Historical Background

Through to the end of the 1970s, the apartheid state in South Africa was able to maintain tight control over the urban population in the country. In the demarcated formal townships access was tightly controlled through rigid enforcement of the pass laws, which required every African with the right of (temporary) domicile in an urban area to carry a pass. Those without a pass were forcibly removed to the nearest homeland. Responsibility for development in those areas was the sole responsibility of the development boards and development by third parties was extremely difficult. Full segregation also meant that people who were not African were forbidden to enter townships without permission and the difference in colour made illegal entry difficult.

The smaller townships and the few remaining African rural settlements suffered a different fate. The latter were considered, literally, as black spots, to be removed totally. Similarly, the government planned that residents from the smaller townships should be moved to the nearest homeland.

This policy shaped the NGO sector in South Africa throughout the 1960s and 1970s, with the major need being assistance to help people fight forced removals, either as individuals or as communities. The dominant NGOs were therefore either legal (eg the Legal Resources Centre; LRC) or social, with the latter often having strong ties with the church (eg the Transvaal Rural Action Committee set up by the South African Council of Churches). The limiting factor was access to funding. Internal funding was negligible. Government control of the media prevented information on forced removals from reaching the white population, many of whom preferred not to know what was happening. At the same time government propaganda labelled those bodies assisting Africans to fight forced removals as communist. Thus the NGOs had to look outside the country for funding. Again this was difficult as the government attempted to prevent these organizations from functioning. The LRC set up a large international network to raise funds externally. Within the country it established a national network, but was forced to limit its work strictly to the legal issues of forced removals. This meant a gap existed in taking knowledge of their rights out to the people, providing advice and support and placing them in contact with the LRC. Hence the need for a second group of NGOs. Only the churches had the power to challenge the government and take on this role, as well as access to overseas funding through their own international church links and networks.

Growth of Development NGOs

By 1983 to 1984 the threat of forced removal started to recede and communities were able to turn their attention, for the first time, away from the struggle for survival to an examination of their own conditions. Fifteen years of neglect had left an abysmal situation as the history of KwaThandeka in Chapter 11 illustrated. In the rural towns and villages nothing had been done by way of development, whereas in the urban and metropolitan areas the limited development was totally inadequate. The new sense of permanence gave rise to new community organizations in the urban areas, whereas in the rural areas the committees which had been formed to fight forced removals began to take up wider development issues.

In looking for advice, the community groups turned first to the existing NGOs, where these existed, or to sympathetic individuals where they did not. These existing NGOs were, in the main, ill-equipped to deal with development issues, nor did they feel that they should take on this wider role as they still had to deal with the question of forced removals and the social impact of these removals. So they introduced individual development specialists to their communities. Over a period these individuals began to coalesce into groups and it was from these groups that development NGOs were born. It was only in some of the homelands that development NGOs existed before this period, but these were limited in number as homeland governments saw them as a political threat and restricted their activities.

The formation of these early NGOs coincided with a growth in interest in the urbanization process in South Africa among organizations and NGOs in Europe and the US, triggered by the publicity surrounding the formation of the new racial parliament and Black Local Authorities, and the opposition to these bodies from grassroots community organizations. The bodies in South Africa, with credibility in the community, to whom overseas groups could talk, were the church organizations on the one hand and the United Democratic Front, a newly formed umbrella organization for progressive groups, on the other. The church organizations in turn were grouped into two categories, the SACC, representing all English-speaking Protestant churches, and the South African Catholic Bishop's Conference. The outcome was an agreement between these internal bodies and the (then) European Community to set up a single body (the Khagiso Trust) which would act as a channel for all overseas development funding. This structure then provided the financial base which enabled the indigenous development NGOs to operate and grow.

The relationship between the emerging civic movement and the development NGOs was fruitful. For the first time community needs could be quantified, upgrading and land invasion planned, and improvement schemes initiated. This partnership was short-lived, however. In the first State of Emergency, introduced in 1985, all the key urban areas were targeted and the civic leadership in those areas either banned or detained. Any who escaped were driven into hiding or into exile. This action on the part of the government, which was extended by the second, nationwide State of Emergency in 1986, clearly damaged the civic movement. It also shaped the thinking of NGOs in a way which was to have negative repercussions five years later.

The NGO members themselves were not affected personally by the State of Emergency, primarily because of the way in which they were perceived, by the government, to interact with community organizations. The people targeted by the apartheid government during the States of Emergency were those with a high public profile and those who helped to build this profile. The early 1980s had seen the growth of two types of NGO. The first was the development NGO described here. The second was a category of NGO which specialized in education for organization and media presentation. The latter was perceived as a serious threat by the government and many of its members were banned and detained. The result was that development NGOs operated in a political space which allowed them a significant amount of freedom of action. The problem was that their client base had been removed. The way in which different NGOs acted under these conditions varied, but all found ways to continue operation and to grow over the period of oppression which followed.

Growth of Planact

The development NGO Planact was formally launched in 1985, in Johannesburg, by a group of development professionals working in the University of the Witwatersrand and in private practice. At the time there was a major debate about whether to link the organization formally to the university, as BESG had done in Natal, but this was rejected and the group was set up under a voluntary association constitution. The group operated on a voluntary basis, but appointed one of its membership as a full-time, paid co-ordinator in the following year. Community participation at that time could be described as classical political empowerment within the arena of confrontation. The role of the professionals was to provide the expertise in planning, engineering and architecture which would enable communities to set the development agenda for their own areas.

When this process was destroyed by the 1986 State of Emergency, Planact, through its geographical location and political network, developed slightly differently to other development NGOs. Planact, with its full-time co-ordinator, was in a position to open up avenues of communication with the union movement, and particularly (1) the National Union of Mine Workers (NUM) and (2) the Unions on the East Rand. The reason why this became possible was that community activists and community demands, in the context of organizations going underground, became articulated through the union movement. This was a two-way flow. On the one hand, the unions saw it as their responsibility and (some) were fairly receptive to taking up those issues. On the other side they were being pressurized by activists to take up community-based issues.

The outcome was that Planact's focus changed. On a practical level Planact became the adviser to the NUM in their negotiations around housing policy, a major issue in South Africa given the amount of African accommodation owned by the mines. In other areas the unions became the vehicle for the expression of frustration about the living conditions of their members. The response of Planact to these changes is clear from their structure. During this period two more full-time members were taken on, one with responsibility for education and training and one to research housing needs and alternatives in other countries, particularly those in Latin America.

By the end of 1988 the situation had begun to change again. Although there was still a State of Emergency, activists had started to come out of hiding. Arguments were required to challenge and refute the state's urbanization policies which were becoming focused on the provision of services. With alternative implementation rendered impossible by the State of Emergency, Planact focused on the policies behind the state programme and the development of alternative policies. This new direction was ill-suited to a voluntary group, particularly given the rapidly increasing workload, and Planact changed its constitution to transfer executive and administrative functions to a staff collective.

With the political transition in 1990, communities needed practical alternatives for their negotiations with the state and Planact needed to develop these alternatives. At the same time the emergence of the IDT site-and-service scheme led Planact to join with communities in applying for funding. To deal with these changes Planact reorganized itself into 'a Projects Department, responsible for direct client servicing and [a] Development Department responsible for development of policy options . . .'.[8] There was also a separate administration and finance department.

The situation in the country was changing rapidly. Local struggles were being linked to national policy, implementation was moving rapidly and there was suddenly a massive influx of private sector organizations entering the market, all supposedly committed to community participation and all offering different services to the community organizations, which 'removed the monopoly enjoyed by Planact (and its sister service organizations) over community driven support services'.[9] In response

Planact restructured yet again in 1992, dismantling the departments and replacing them with 'programmes', whose character was defined in terms of 'goals, outputs and client accountability'.[10]

This was the apogee of Planact's power. It employed 36 full-time staff dealing with almost 100 projects and was an integral part of the national consultation process. It was an adviser to the ANC, and World Bank missions could not have credibility unless they had spoken to Planact. It had been the prime mover in the establishment of an Urban Sector NGO Network in South Africa; had extensive contacts internationally with other development NGOs; and was the recognized alternative authority on the urbanization process in South Africa. It was already in decline, however. In 1993 it recognized that its restructuring was flawed[11] and changed its structure yet again, dismantling the voluntary constitution and creating a not-for-profit registered company. By then, however, many of its key people had left and its funding base was diminishing rapidly. It had not adapted either quickly enough or, more importantly, in the correct way, to the changing environment.

From Policy to Implementation: the Changing Role of the NGO

Planact recognized that it had serious problems in 1993, but attributed these primarily to structural problems within the organization. Thus its members argued, in respect of the penultimate reorganization into programmes, that

> 'Although this reorganization put in place structures which were theoretically responsible for the management of Planact's work, in practice this did not happen because the Staff Collective was still retained, along with the accompanying ethos of collective responsibility. It was therefore impossible to implement the systems which should have supported the programmatic approach'.[12]

To place the blame on structural problems is to address the symptoms while neglecting the cause. Essentially there were three underlying reasons for Planact's demise, all of which relate either to a misunderstanding of their role as an NGO, or to the contradictions which arose from their own interpretation. All of these are of general relevance to NGOs working in development.

The first of these stems from the inherent tensions and contradictions between advocacy (in this case advocacy planning, but it is equally applicable to other forms of development such as rural conservation) and practical implementation. Planact argue that they made the shift from advocacy to implementation,[13] but this was not really the case. They were in fact prevented from making this switch by self-imposed constraints. In their mission statement Planact state that their mission is 'to promote integrated community driven development'.[14] Laudable as this aim is, its achievement in these terms lies either within the arena of confrontation, which was the basis of Planact formation, or within a community management structure. As earlier parts of the book showed, neither of these are applicable, as the urban development in question sits firmly within the arena of consensus. This requires compromise, however. The community organizations were able to change and to achieve the necessary compromise, but the service organizations were not. Were they professional supporters of their clients' cause? Were they independent project managers? Were they agents of the IDT? Each of these would have required a different economic perspective and Planact was trying to be all of them at the same time. Its heart was not in these changes. Ultimately it was unable to make the transition across to being an implementing agent because that would force it to abandon its ideal as a community support organization fighting against the apartheid state.

The second reason for Planact's demise was its inability to integrate its policy work with its projects. In one restructuring the projects dominated, but this was at a time when policy was actually Planact's primary focus. The organization then shifted its emphasis to a programmatic approach just at the time when its most important work was evolving into project implementation. Planact was never really able to reconcile these two sides of its work.

Finally, the third reason for Planact's decline, which underlay the other two but was never brought into the open, was the relationship between individuals and the organization. Planact described itself as a staff collective. This is the basic structure of many development NGOs. Its premise was idealistic, namely the ethos of collective responsibility. This can, and does, occur, primarily with grassroots organizations, but the extent to which it exists in NGOs which have a strong professional component is open to question. Ultimately the aim of most individuals, particularly those are who intellectually driven, is to develop their own ideas and have those ideas accepted. This is only rarely subsumed in the collective interest. Thus the NGO provides a basis for individual power without adequate accountability and personal responsibility.

Planact was started by a group of forceful and intellectually strong individuals who supported the democratic movement at a time of extreme political oppression. There was a clear need for the service which they offered. Initially they were accountable to their constituency in the union movement and the community organizations, and this accountability was retained for their project work. The move into a policy environment created its own dynamic, however. Thus although the move into the policy area was almost inevitable in the political climate of the time, it is also true that very strongly intellectual individuals are comfortable in that policy environment.

Operating in a policy environment for an NGO which began working at a grassroots level is a dangerous area, however. Who is the NGO accountable to? The overseas funders were happy with the results and were prepared to continue funding policy work, but that is a dubious accountability. In the later stages Planact found itself in competition with the ANC's own policy groups, particularly Local Government and Water Resources, and tried to have itself made the official ANC policy adviser. The reality is that an NGO provides a position of power in the policy environment without always having concomitant responsibility. What also became clear in the period from 1990 to 1994 was the benefit of an NGO as a base from which to launch a personal move into conventional power structures. Thus there is a strong personal motivation to retain the NGO as a policy-making body, even when the collective need of the organization is to focus on project implementation.

THE NGO AND PROJECT IMPLEMENTATION IN THE ARENA OF CONSENSUS

The conflict between policy and project implementation is most acute in the arena of consensus, particularly in situations such as that found in South Africa during the political transition, where the interaction between evolving national policy played itself out at a local level. This represents an extreme example of the complexity of decision-making which affects not only NGOs but all parties involved in the community participation process. Even at the level of project implementation there are conflicts of interest affecting the NGO in the arena of consensus which do not occur in the other arenas. Some of these contradictions played themselves out in the IDT projects described in the previous chapter.

In Luganda (the land invasion area) the development NGO, BESG, had been a prime mover supporting the LRA in applying for a capital subsidy. With the division of responsibility between the civic and the Trust, BESG found itself facing the same conundrum which caused the community to separate functions. It provided the major professional support to the civic in the wider negotiation process, but was also intimately involved with the project, and therefore the Trust. This created several internal conflicts within the NGO. At one level there were those individual members who did not want the NGO to become involved in the project at all. They still saw participation in terms of a confrontational empowerment process and wanted to limit their involvement in Luganda to support of the civic in the wider political debate. This group was not successful in having their view endorsed, but they did influence the final outcome.

In Luganda the Community Trust was the developer with full financial responsibility. This forced the Trust to gain knowledge rapidly and to take meaningful responsibility for both technical and financial decision-making. However, to do this it needed technical support, and its immediate reaction was to turn to the NGO to provide this, requesting BESG to be the project manager. The NGO had its own agenda, however, part of which was described earlier, and which was a potential cause of conflict. To deal with this the NGO refused to be project manager but, at the same time, was not prepared to cut itself off from the project totally, partly because of its long-standing involvement with the community's struggle to improve their physical situation, but also because of the importance of this project nationally.

The result was that the NGO attempted to exclude itself from direct involvement in the technical decision-making process, where compromise decisions might have to be made, and to place itself as social adviser to the Community Trust. This created a dangerous situation as it separated decision-making on socio-economic issues, carried out by the Trust but advised by the NGO, from decision-making on technical issues, carried out by the Trust but advised by a newly appointed professional project manager. The possibility of conflict and polarization arising from this situation was recognized, and was overcome by all the actors (including the IDT and the municipality) agreeing (1) to provide additional technical resources to back up the Trust and (2) to share responsibility for all decisions. Although this approach proved to be valuable as a learning experience, it could provide neither a long-term nor a general solution. The use of so much technical expertise in this way would be simply too expensive and inefficient. What was really needed was a restructuring of external roles, including that of the NGO, to match the changing needs of the community.

Case study 2 (Sibongile) highlighted a different type of problem for the NGO, but one which derived from the same roots. The developer and project manager in Sibongile was a private company. It was committed to a high level of community participation and was bound by a community participation agreement to share decision-making with the community. Again, as in Luganda, there were different community structures representing different community interests, but in the case of Sibongile these also included a weak ANC grouping.

The development committee badly needed technical support and the ANC proposed BESG, the same NGO that operated in Luganda, but with a different (and more politically hardline) regional office. This was initially rejected by both the developer and other sectors of the committee, on the grounds that BESG was too partisan as an ANC support organization. After negotiation this view was softened and BESG became involved. Again, however, there was an internal conflict of interest. The ANC group, supported by BESG, argued that the site chosen for upgrading should have been situated closer to the white town of Dundee, where it would act as a link between the two areas. The outcome was that they were not able to provide the training and educational support so badly needed by the development committee because this would have compromised their political stance. There was no alternative group able to provide such support and consequently it was never forthcoming. The participation process was severely constrained and the community lost the opportunity to gain valuable experience of the physical planning process which should have been immensely valuable in later discussions with the municipality of Dundee on the creation of a single unified local authority. Long-term gain was forfeited to short-term expediency and the internal agenda of the NGO.

There was a further complication in Sibongile which also affected the dynamic. Maintaining consensus among so many diverse groups is a complex task in its own right, and one which does not apply to any great extent in the other arenas. Again the NGO saw itself as playing this key part, without recognizing the inherent contradictions of its own position. If the community participation process is to be meaningful and effective in this complex environment, there needs to be a neutral facilitator who is trusted by all parties. This is very different from the partisan role normally taken by NGOs. Yet their experience of development, and the nature of their own position outside state structures and with independent funding, places NGOs in a strong position to take on this role. This presents them with a further complication and possible inherent internal contradiction to resolve.

In Natal, BESG was eventually able to resolve many of the outlined contradictions and make the transition to an effective implementation agency working with communities. In spite of the difficulties described, it was prepared to take risks and make compromises. Part of this was also due to its geographical position in Natal, where compromise is essential to survival. This was something which eluded Planact in the Transvaal. The strong and established ANC presence created an illusion of security for Planact. As they themselves admitted, the new situation 'effectively removed the monopoly enjoyed by Planact . . over community driven support services'.[15] When coupled with the strong personal agendas of its key members, to whom organizational compromise would have meant the loss of personal political credibility, the compromises required of implementation were an anathema. When the new ANC-dominated government was installed in 1984 the key members left to take up key positions in government and government linked structures, leaving a weakened and debilitated organization to make the transition to an implementing agency.

ORGANIZATIONAL CAPACITY BUILDING AND THE ROLE OF NGOs IN THE ARENA OF CONSENSUS

One of the fundamental assumptions which underpin our current perception of development NGOs is that of the duality between the people and the state, as described by Cernea and quoted earlier. This was not always so. Community development, in its early stages, concerned itself primarily with small groups and effectively operated autonomously, although community development workers would generally be employed by one or other level of government and operated within state structures. It was only when community development moved across to developing countries that the situation changed. The community development process became a tool of government and the notion grew of communities being manipulated by governments. With moves towards empowerment and the confrontation approach, then that issue became much more one of communities claiming back power from the state and demanding a voice in decision-making processes which affected their lives. In this situation the capacity of the people to mobilize against the state was supported by the emerging NGO movement. In that respect Cernea was correct to argue that 'the mainstay of NGOs' contribution to development is . . . organizational'.[16]

This is only one aspect of NGO involvement in development, which is growing all the time. The stress which the World Bank places on (1) the organizational component and (2) the importance of 'local level social development'[17] needs to be placed in perspective. Firstly, it is applicable to community participation in the arena of inclusion; it is not applicable in the more complex arena of consensus, as this chapter has illustrated. Secondly, it fails to take into account the increasing interaction between development and the wider physical environment. Thirdly, it reflects to some extent a mould which the World Bank would like to see NGOs confined to, as this does not present a challenge to the Bank's own central position in international development. Finally, although this is linked to a degree to the last point, it fails to recognize the realities of power in development. It is insufficient for NGOs to be useful; if they are to influence change they also need to be powerful and this cannot be achieved by remaining within the limited classification outlined here.

At the same time it is essential for the NGOs themselves to recognize that their changing profile brings new obligations and responsibilities. It is no longer possible to sit outside the process and take an idealistic political stance without accepting any responsibility for the political compromise which is a necessary part of implementation. The failings described here in a South African context are equally applicable to NGOs working in the international arena. At the same time, within all of this, there is still a vital need for the traditional role of NGOs as outlined by Cernea. Indeed, most NGOs will continue to fulfill this need without becoming caught up in these contradictions. For those that do, how are these apparent contradictions to be resolved?

The most important factor is the recognition of the different arenas and what this means for NGOs. Those working in the arena of inclusion, which are concerned solely with their community clients' needs, are not affected until they begin to expand their work into the arena of consensus. This transition will usually occur when an NGO wishes to become involved in the policy formulation process. Whatever the process of transition, the NGO will have entered this arena (of consensus) when it wishes to express its own agenda in the forum of debate itself, as opposed to having its interests represented by a body speaking on behalf of NGOs as a group. This is where the contradictions will then emerge.

The nature of the development environment means that there are three distinct parts to be played by NGOs, which were mentioned briefly at the beginning of the chapter. The first is that of a community support organization, ie the traditional role. In terms of numbers, this is clearly the role of most grassroots NGOs who will continue to be involved only at this level. In playing that part, however, it needs to be recognized and accepted that they are part of one or another of the community delegations to the wider negotiation process. This means that they should be appointed and funded by the respective community organizations. If the community organization cannot afford to pay for the services of support NGOs and external funding is required, this should be channelled through the community organization.

The second role is that of influencing policy. Here the NGO would be one of the recognized actors taking part in the wider negotiation process. For this to happen there would have to be agreement from the other parties to the involvement of the NGO. The NGO would also need to have both independent funding and a clearly defined client base (outside the community) whose interests it was representing.

Finally, there is a role (although this is not limited to NGOs) in providing the facilitation/mediation to the wider group. This is a role which requires a different set of skills to those of the first two. The community support role is clearly partisan and should remain as such, whereas the second also has a clearly defined agenda. The third requires a non-partisan role which must be strictly adhered to.

The current debate on NGOs, between the World Bank and Oxfam, for example, arises to a large extent from the contradiction between the first and second roles, although that between the first and third is no less important. Currently the World Bank is placing increasing emphasis on the role of the NGO as a key player in urban infrastructure provision, because of their close working relationship with community organizations.[18] Yet this partisanship makes NGOs ill-equipped to deal with the potential conflicts and contradictions which may arise from the implementation of a complex project with multiple objectives. What becomes clear from the South African experience is that there is a massive need for technical training of community organizations and that this is a partisan function. The management of the process of community participation within the broader urban surround, on the other hand, needs to be as neutral as possible. The World Bank approach mixes these two functions and is a recipe for conflict, not only between the NGOs and the Bank but, more critically, between NGOs and their community clients.

The problems described earlier arose to a large degree because the NGOs in question could not differentiate clearly between the different roles. The difficulty many in the NGO movement face is reconciling the idealism which drives them to provide a service to communities with the desire to influence events on a personal level. The first role is still the most important for NGOs, but it requires a great deal of personal self-sacrifice. At the same time there are roles in the development process which carry, or lead to, a high level of power. On an individual project these different roles cannot be carried out by the same organization without causing a conflict of interest.

The NGOs have an important part to play in the urban development process but that can only be achieved if they are (1) prepared to define their role clearly in any given situation and (2) take an equal responsibility for the compromises which are necessary to convert ideals into effective working solutions. The need for NGOs arises from the stresses inherent in a changing environment and this need is greatest when change is most rapid. This requires NGOs to be the most flexible of all the actors involved in urban development. This is their greatest challenge.

Interventions and their Impact on the Community Participation Process

DEFINING COMMUNITY SUPPORT

As soon as a group of people participate in an activity they are faced with the need for procedures which will order the operation of that activity. On a small scale this may be generated and developed locally. Where the activity involves interaction with another party, however, particularly a bureaucracy, or where the scope of the internally generated activity is large, this will involve a degree of input by people who understand the procedures and the form and structure of the activity, but who are not necessarily directly associated with the group. The subsequent intervention in the community's activity is different from the situation described for the arena of consensus, wherein different actors are pursuing their own legitimate agendas and, in the process, interacting with the community activity.

It is the intervention, then, which is the central feature of the external involvement in the communal activity, not the description of the actor. This is an important distinction which has not been made in previously published work. It means that the starting point for exploring the nature of the external involvement is the analysis of the purpose of the intervention.

External interventions may be divided into three broad categories, which operate at different levels. The first level of intervention is that of information gathering. The purpose here is to obtain background information which will facilitate the activity. The process should be objective and non-partisan. The second level of intervention is that of community support, which seeks to assist communities in the achievement of the objectives of the activity in question. This may or may not have a partisan approach, depending on the nature of the assistance. Finally, the third level of intervention is that of facilitation and/or mediation, which uses the external intervention objectively to assist in the successful completion of the activity. This is a general categorization.

There are some interventions which seek to combine, or even integrate, different levels. These include certain forms of participatory research and participatory planning. This can be successful provided there is a clear understanding of the constraints and a recognition of the participatory arena within which the intervention is operating. The main point to recognize is that each of the three levels will have a different type of methodology/technique associated with them and that it is important to match the techniques to the level of intervention if the outcome is to be successful.

INFORMATION GATHERING IN THE ARENA OF INCLUSION

This level of intervention is research-based, interpreting the term research simply as the 'systematic collection, analysis and dissemination of information'.[1] Such research has two distinct origins. The first is anthropological, based on the system whereby an anthropologist spends several years in a community studying the language, culture and lifestyle as a trained observer. Clearly such a study is both extensive and broad, but it also has severe limitations, not least of which are the long time-frame and the fact that, however scientific the procedure adopted, it is still the work of one person. This makes it very difficult to cross-check the participant observer's findings.

The second origin is sociological and is based on the use of data collected through formal surveys of the study group. As Theis and Grady point out, survey research

> 'derives much of its popularity from its formal and standardized research techniques which produce quantifiable, representative, verifiable, and comparable data which can be statistically analyzed. Survey enumerators do not have to make many independent decisions and, if well trained, can collect the data without requiring the primary researcher to take part in the data collection in the field'.[2]

There are three main problems with this type of research when related to development work in communities. The first is that it does not necessarily achieve the truth about sensitive issues.

> 'It is not the best method for gathering information about private or otherwise sensitive matters because interviewers employed to conduct surveys might not be trusted with sensitive information, either because they are strangers to the respondents or because they are members of the same community, and might be tempted to gossip, or to use the information for personal advantage'.[3]

The second problem lies with the researchers themselves who, although conducting a scientifically based study, nonetheless bring with them their own perspective and mind-set. The historical reality of research programmes developed by white, middle-class, middle-aged researchers who failed to reach the poor and dispossessed or recognize the role of women in development is a factor which has discredited this form of research.[4]

Finally, there is the manipulative use of survey analysis in top-down development. Survey data can provide the quantitative information necessary to implement development projects developed elsewhere and with no thought given to its relevance in the specific situation, eg rural development tourism. Or it may simply be open to abuse by default, by ignoring the qualitative aspects of community needs, expectations or capabilities. Although all three of these problems create distortions it was primarily the third which, when applied in an agricultural context, created the demand for an alternative approach to information collection.

Agricultural systems can be divided into three distinct types: industrial, located mainly in industrialized countries and specialized enclaves in the less developed world; Green revolution systems, located in areas of high agricultural potential in the less developed world which are either irrigated or have stable rainfall; and 'CDR' (complex, diverse and risk-prone) , occupying rain-fed areas, hinterlands, most of sub-saharan Africa, etc.[5] For decades research focused on the first two and increasing efforts were made to force one or the other of these onto the third, often with disastrous results. Yet the third, which is increasingly important as providing the livelihood for almost 1500 million people world-wide, still requires an increased production. Increasingly, it was recognized that effective research in this area could only be achieved by working with farmers, recognizing rural people's tacit knowledge and the key part played by local innovation, and tailoring external inputs to complement rather than replace these. This in turn required new methods of obtaining information and this was the basis for a family of approaches which were to become known by the collective term of rapid rural appraisal (RRA), a 'method of grassroots research used to identify the problems, goals and strategies of households, groups and communities',[6] 'which is both quicker and more cost effective than "respectable" questionnaire surveys'[7] and yet better able to utilize qualitative inputs from the communities concerned.

In the early 1980s, RRA was still driven by researchers with the objective of more effective outside understanding of community needs and with the long-term outcome of producing plans and projects. Over the next ten years it was slowly transformed, primarily through the drive of specific NGOs, into a vehicle for the empowerment of local people with a view to achieving sustainable local action and institution. The system resulting from this transformation was known as participatory rapid (or rural) appraisal (PRA). Whereas the main innovation of RRA was the change in methodology, that of PRA was behaviour. Where RRA tapped local people's knowledge, PRA utilized their capabilities.[8] Effectively PRA merged the technique of rapid assessment procedures which had evolved from ethnographic research with the methods and principles of RRA. It is not the intention of this chapter to discuss the practice of rural appraisal in detail. A comprehensive explanation of RRA and PRA in theory and practice is to be found in the work of the Sustainable Agricultural Programme of the IIED[9,10] and that of Chambers[7] mentioned earlier. The purpose here is to explore their evolution and their relevance to different arenas of community participation.

Neither RRA nor PRA is universally applicable. Theis and Grady argue that

'Perhaps the most important considerations [in deciding whether or not PRA is appropriate for particular situations and projects] are:

- the availability of appropriate people to conduct the study,
- the degree to which project structure and decision-making are sufficiently flexible to make use of new information, and
- the intended use of the findings'.[11]

Thus

'The PRA approach seems most likely to produce positive results, in terms of a successfully mobilised community prepared to see a project through, if the project involves something which can be clearly seen to benefit the whole community, or at least a large majority of people, without harming anyone ... However, it seems clear that PRA in and of itself cannot remove major conflicts of interest, or dissolve structural inequalities, and for this reason it remains one research method among many, or, in its other role as a means of community-activation, a procedure which will work well for some communities and tasks but not for others'.[12]

This analysis, and particularly the last sentence, appears to be supported by existing evidence which links PRA and RRA to one specific arena within the wider community participation environment. The success of both RRA and PRA has been greatest in the economic area of small farmer development, but PRA in particular has begun to expand successfully into areas of social development, such as health and childcare. In this regard, however, Theis and Grady argue that 'PRA is especially well-suited for application in community development [where it] raises people's self-awareness, suggests viable solutions, and helps people analyze complex [personal] issues and problems'.[13] It has been used successfully and extensively by the AKRSP programme in Pakistan, which was analysed in Chapter 5 and shown to be a community development programme. It has had major success in India and Pakistan where there is a long history of community development; its use in Village Resource Management Planning in Kenya[14] also falls into this category. However, it has had less success in community management programmes built around physical services and it is still regarded as a tool for use in rural areas. It would therefore be ideal for use within the community development sphere of the arena of inclusion, expanding over time to encompass work in the wider sphere of this arena such as community management.

The arena of consensus provides a different environment, however. The needs of the community are balanced by outside needs and the project needs to take account of all the different requirements. Under these circumstances, PRA and RRA may have a specific role in quantifying community need, but they are not necessarily suited to identifying and quantifying wider needs. Extrapolation of PRA and RRA into the arena of consensus would therefore constitute the imposition of a form of intervention which may be totally inappropriate. To avoid this risk, the arena of consensus should be treated as totally separate from the arena of inclusion. This means returning to the standard techniques as the basis for information gathering, but structuring them in such a way that they are both compatible with, and appropriate to, decision-making in this arena. The way in which this is done is described in the next section.

INFORMATION GATHERING IN THE ARENA OF CONSENSUS

In recent years funding agencies have grown increasingly to favour the notion of a stakeholder analysis. This is a term which needs to be treated with caution. In many ways a stakeholder analysis is the antithesis of community participation, as it involves the collection of information about the community for the use and benefit of an outside party. On the other hand, because of the complex internal dynamic which characterizes large diverse communities, a knowledge of stakeholders can assist the development process. What is important is the programming of information collection and the channels of responsibility as much as the information gathering process itself. The second point to note about stakeholder analyses is that they should not be confined to the community. They should extend to all the actors likely to be influential in the activity, including the government agencies and the funding agencies. So it should take each of the different actor groups and carry out the following

- identification of the key interest groups (which may extend wider than the main actors);
- quantifying their potential for facilitation/frustration of the project;
- identification of their main agendas;
- identification of their expectations; and
- the development of appropriate strategies for the involvement of the stakeholders in the activity.

There is a fine line between paternalistic action and true consensus decision-making. Funders and development professionals will argue, correctly, that it is difficult to know the support which exists in a community for a group claiming to be representative. This does not give those parties the right to decide who should be the community representative. The analysis of the community dynamic is something which should unfold with the activity itself. In this way there will be time to adjust the community representation in line with changing circumstances. In several of the IDT projects described in Chapter 11, for example, the final composition of the community groupings was significantly different to that which submitted the original application for funding support. This was not cataclysmic, however, nor did the projects suffer in the long term. The need existed and the community was happy for an application to be made. Once accepted they were able to ensure meaningful and effective representation.

Finally, the term stakeholder analysis itself is too vague. It sounds clear enough: who are the main actors and what is their influence and role? It is difficult to determine its extent and depth. In one proposed stakeholder analysis dealing with the occupation of 1200 ha of land by informal settlement dwellers in the city of Pietermaritzburg, the proposal covered everything from a basic needs analysis to complex negotiation with political parties at a regional level.

What is needed in respect of information gathering around activities in the arena of consensus is an understanding of all the various methods of information gathering, what purpose each serves and how they interact. Superficially this too appears to be a dangerous strategy, providing the opportunity for manipulation of the community. It is therefore essential that it constitutes an integral part of the wider process of decision-making described in Chapters 8 and 9. This means that the type and level of information to be gathered is known to, and approved by, all the parties involved in the decision-making process and that the results are available to all of them. In addition, there needs to be a clear understanding of the different types of survey methodology; why each is used; and which is appropriate to the activity in question. Too often development professionals are provided with funding to carry out surveys without reference to community organizations. Just as often they do not realize the full power of the tools that they are using.

Finally, in addition to the joint control of information gathering, there needs to be a clear understanding of the role, objectives, benefits and limitations of different information gathering techniques on the part of those using the information. This is part of the training and education process discussed in the next section of the chapter.

It is not the intention of this section to discuss the detailed methodology. There are many books which deal with this topic.[15,16] Instead the chapter is concerned with the structure of the information gathering process, setting this out in a way which can be integrated into the development of the working model described in Chapter 9.

Level of Complexity of Information Gathering

The information which is gathered from within communities can be classified according to the level of complexity and the sophistication of the methodology, both of which tend to be inter-related. The complexity of the information to be gathered can be divided into four categories, wherein the information becomes increasingly quantitative. The four levels of complexity are demographic data collection, socio-economic data collection, attitudes and expectations and, finally, an understanding of the wider community dynamic.

Demographic data collection represents the most basic level of information gathering. This looks at information such as the number of households, family and household composition, and population distribution in terms of age, sex, relationships etc. In the work on RRA and PRA, researchers argued that too great an emphasis was placed on the collection of raw data, which then consumed excessive time in its analysis. In the arena of consensus the collection of this data is important, partly because many of the activities falling into the arena of consensus have a physical development component which requires this information, but also because a sound quantitative understanding of the situation is an essential prerequisite to the negotiation on defining the hierarchy of needs. What needs to be avoided is the dominance of the debate by quantitative data. There is also a failing of funding agencies in this regard. It is often easier to raise money for new surveys, which can be justified as legitimate development expenditure on the funding agency's book, than to pay someone to collate existing information. No survey should be carried out until all existing sources of information have been collated and assessed. The survey information can then be designed to complement this existing information. This saves both money and, more importantly, community time, recognizing that the latter is a valuable commodity.

The gathering of socio-economic data is the second level of information gathering. This would include information on educational levels and qualifications; employment status and income; migration patterns; and expenditure patterns. Alternatively, it may be gathered specifically for a particular type of study, for example transportation planning, in which case the data would be more concerned with information pertaining to that particular issue, such as travel to work and recreation, distances travelled, cost as percentage of household income, etc. Whereas the first level of demographic data is of primary value to the development professionals, this information should be recognized to be beneficial to community organizations. It allows the community to explain their own socio-political structure and ensure that planned activities are built around this structure. In this way the first step towards integrating quantitative and qualitative data can begin.

The next level is that of attitude surveys. This begins to be more sophisticated, requiring a greater degree of subjective interpretation of results. Here again the type of information required would be geared towards the type of output.

Typically, however, it would be related to specific problems encountered by people in the community regarding issues such as infrastructure, unemployment, housing, education, social welfare, political concerns and so on. This type of survey is often considered to be a wish list, but this is a misunderstanding of the role of the attitude survey. Certainly it allows community residents the means to express their concerns, but it also provides valuable information on the status of communities, for example poverty levels and the issue of gender relationships, which should be the central component of any planning process.

Finally, there is the most complex form of information gathering, which is that aimed at gaining an in-depth knowledge and understanding of the community dynamic. As well as being more complex, in terms of its analysis and interpretation, the means of obtaining the required information are likely to be significantly more sophisticated than the other forms of information gathering. It is also likely to require the close co-operation of influential groups within the community, which in turn can make unbiased sampling more difficult. It should not be undertaken lightly, however. As an example, an in-depth study of the political, economic and social structure of the African township of Bruntville, Mooi River in South Africa was instituted to assist in the creation of a forum for negotiation on a new unitary local authority for the area. The result was to raise the profile and importance of the town's civic leader, who was also the chair of the local ANC branch. This was at a time when there was a high degree of friction between the ANC and Inkatha in the area. The study established beyond doubt the integrity and respect in which the civic leader was held by most of the residents, but also showed the extent of the antagonism between the township residents and the residents of the two male-only hostels in the town.

In the week when the civic leadership was reviewing the final draft of the study, the leader and his entire family were murdered. The level of violence in Bruntville escalated and the negotiation process had to be abandoned. This illustrates an important facet of information gathering at this level of intensity. Meaningful decision-making in the arena of consensus has to incorporate the political as well as the social and economic, although this increases the risk. The extent to which the study played a part in this murder cannot be established, and it may have happened anyway, although the timing was indicative of a relationship between the two events. The example does, however, provide an indication of the responsibility which is attached to a detailed study of urban communities. The study cannot be something apart from the community; it has to be seen as an integral part of both the participation and the development processes. This is exactly the same conclusion that was reached in the arena of inclusion and which led to creation of PRA.

Research Methodology for Information Gathering

There are several different types of techniques which can be used for information gathering and the choice of the most appropriate will depend, to a large extent, on the level of information required. Gathering meaningful and comprehensive information from within a community is expensive and time consuming. To obtain the maximum benefit this should only be used once all existing sources of information have been identified and the results of the search analysed. This is the first division then, between information which is gathered indirectly and that which is gathered directly.

Indirect Research

Indirect research implies the collection of information about a community which is gathered without having direct contact with that community. This preliminary search may actually be sufficient for the project or it may provide some of the information. At the least it will indicate what further information is required. It also has a second function, which is to supplement or cross-check knowledge of the community dynamic. It can help to fill in knowledge gaps, or to prepare the interview questions by highlighting issues of controversy or major concern.

There are several ways in which this indirect research can be performed. It can draw on personal and public records which exist about the community. It can use government statistics. It can use previously gathered research obtained directly by others. Finally, it can use source material which relates to specific activities which took place within the community, for example engineering records of specific projects such as a water supply.

Typical sources of such information might be newspapers, government departments or publications (eg census), service organizations, publications, archives, school and hospital records, previously commissioned survey work and interviews with individuals peripheral to, or knowledgable about, the area in question. Problems associated with this type of information gathering are that it may be dated, there may not be sufficient knowledge of source reliability (eg previous surveys) or the source type itself yields unreliable data (eg the census). All these issues need to be assessed when deciding how much reliability to place in external data, or whether internal data should supplement external data. There is also the difficulty of merging data from different sources to be taken into account.

Direct Research

The direct surveys involved the interaction with members of the community and there are different ways of doing this which reflect increasing levels of sophistication. The first three levels of sophistication are all part of the questionnaire carried out through interviews with members of the community, chosen generally on the basis of the random distribution of a statistically meaningful target population. Such a population may cover the whole community or it may be targeted to address a specific market (eg women with children addressing the issue of education needs). Finally, the target group might be pre-screened, with an initial scan and a follow up in-depth survey of selected groups.

The simplest form of survey is the questionnaire which asks closed questions only. In this type of survey the questionnaire would comprise a series of questions which can only be answered by a single word which is unambiguous. This may be yes/no; it may be a number (eg how many children, what is your age); or it may be an answer fitting a pre-determined bracket (eg male/female). This type of questionnaire can provide the bulk of the information for the demographic survey and base data for the socio-economic data collection.

The second form is the questionnaire which asks semi-open questions. This term is used to describe a question which, although it is not pre-determined, nonetheless elicits an answer for which there are only a limited number of options. Generally, all of these would be related to a specific topic and expressed though the description of a place or object. Examples of this type of semi-open question would be: what is the source of the water supply; what is the main centre where shopping is done, which would result in a list of towns or suburbs; what is the main mode of transport used for a particular activity. These answers can then be grouped and there is no subjective component to the answer. A second form of semi-open question is that which asks for levels of satisfaction and/or dissatisfaction, with the answer grouped into pre-determined categories. The semi-open question does provide the person constructing the survey to apply a degree of bias through the type of question which is asked. The use of semi-open questions provides the bulk of the information for the socio-economic survey.

The third form is the questionnaire which asks open questions. This is asking for a subjective opinion, but is limited to a specific area or activity. For example, having asked for the level of satisfaction or dissatisfaction with the water supply, a question may go on and ask 'why do you say that for the water supply?' The interviewer must then use a measure of judgement to group answers into a reasonable number of viewpoints which are commonly shared to provide a list of the main points of concern. Clearly there is a much greater degree of subjectivity with this type of question, both in the way that an interviewee chooses to answer the question and in the interpretation that the analyst places on the answer. There is also even greater opportunity for bias to be applied in formulating questions than exists with the other forms of questionnaire. Nonetheless this open question format is essential for attitude surveys.

In carrying out complex attitude surveys and, even more importantly, trying to gain a knowledge of community dynamics, the use of random sampling is generally insufficient. Two other forms of survey are available to supplement the random sample in this instance. These are individual interviews and group interviews, both of which have different purposes, as the way in which people answer questions in the two situations is very different. The first is more likely to present an individual standpoint, whereas the second, recognizing that individual answers will reflect peer pressure, actively seeks a collective viewpoint.

The individual interview needs to be well structured if it is to be effective. By definition interviews with a limited number of individuals below a minimum sample size are not statistically significant, so that the information gathered is purely qualitative. Nonetheless such information can be extremely valuable, particularly when used in conjunction with a random survey. This technique is used for two main purposes:

1   as a means of finding out very specific information within a target area eg who are considered key individuals, what are areas of potential conflict; and
2   to gain greater in-depth knowledge about specific issues, eg household expenditure patterns for different income local families or details of the political structure.

In carrying out an individual interview, the analyst should know what information is required before the interview and should prepare an interview sheet in the form of a checklist of points. The interviewee would then be led through this in conversational form rather than in question and answer format. This requires a higher level of skill from the person carrying out the interview than does the straight questionnaire, which requires only a numerator. There are several benefits to individual interviews. From the greater level of detail obtained the individual interview can be used effectively to build a cross-referencing system from which one can gain a much wider understanding of what is happening within a community. So, for example, in establishing who is important it is useful to find out not only which names arise most often, but also the context within which they arise and the feelings associated with those names. This establishes clearly the parts that different people play within the community and the degree of power that they hold.

Depending on needs, the interview could take a variety of forms from a skim type interview, through semi in-depth, which might be expected to last one to two hours, through to a full in-depth interview which would be both well structured and very detailed. The difference between the latter two is less in terms of issues covered (ie both are likely to be similar in this regard) than in the amount of detail required.

The role of group interviews is different. These seek collective views, which tend to have a much stronger bias towards influence and power than do individual interviews. This reflects the needs of groups to continually replenish, and preferably to widen, their membership base. It will also indicate the degree of co-operation which may be expected from groups towards a particular line of action, as well as the likelihood that a group will attempt to mobilize community support around a specific issue. Generally, if a good understanding of the community dynamic is to be gained, then it will be necessary to use all three forms of survey techniques: the random question, the individual interview and the group interview. Finally, of course, the group interview provides a means of obtaining a more official view from an organization, where an interview carried out with, say, a full committee can be taken to represent the view of the wider organization on specific issues.

Finally, there is the role of mass meetings. It may be argued that people do not speak freely at mass meetings, but the elucidation of personal views should not be their purpose. Instead the mass meeting should be used to develop accountability. In this respect it is particularly valuable in the arena of consensus. On several of the projects discussed earlier it was the mass meeting which prevented the project from collapsing. There can be several diverse groups representing community interests in the wider decision-making process. By bringing these groups together at mass meetings this places enormous peer pressure on the different organizations to work collectively rather than disruptively.

In addition to the specific forms of information gathering described here, it is also possible to use many of the techniques developed for PRA, such as social and mobility mapping, transects and ranking techniques.[17] The real difference is in the analysis and community interaction. The accountability of those gathering information in the arena of consensus is to the group of decision-makers, of whom the community representatives form only one part, albeit an important one. There also needs to be a degree of distance maintained which is the antithesis of PRA. This is because there is generally, within the negotiation leading to consensus, a high degree of conflict to be resolved. The type of learning which takes place with the community in PRA takes place in the arena of consensus with the representatives of the primary actors. This does mean that there is a danger of creating elitism within the decision-making process. This danger needs to be recognized and balanced by the education and training programme which represents the second level of intervention in the community participation process within the arena of consensus.

COMMUNITY SUPPORT THROUGH TRAINING AND EDUCATION

The area of community education and training presents one of the key distinctions between community participation processes in the arenas of inclusion and confrontation, marked by the community development and community management approaches on the one hand and the political empowerment approach on the other. Understanding this distinction is a prerequisite to the development of an education and training strategy for the arena of consensus.

Chapter 8 discussed the three micro-level education strategies of Srinivasan – didactic, conscientization or consciousness-raising, and the growth-centred approach – which she argues correspond to the three underlying behaviourial concerns of stressed, poor communities, namely coping, transforming and transcending.[18] Within these strategies the accelerating trend towards the dominance of the growth-centred approach is providing the basis for both community management and community development. In other words it is becoming the primary educational strategy supporting community participation in the arena of inclusion. Researchers, funding agency personnel and government officials refer to this as empowerment, but is it? It can certainly be described as enablement, providing people with the power to make decisions which affect their own lives. However, these decisions take place within the constraints of a wider socio-economic system which is barely affected by the local decisions of communities. That this is termed empowerment reflects a fundamental philosophical division over the primary purpose of education which is rarely debated in publications on community participation. Yet it is central to the division between political empowerment and enablement through community management and explains why the participation process in Latin America differed so radically from that in the Anglo-Saxon dominated world.

It is inconceivable that Freire, for example, could have made the same distinction that Srinivasan made between conscientization and the growth-centred approach. That is not because he did not recognize the value of the growth-centred approach. On the contrary, the notion of building and developing the self was central to his work. However, he could never have seen this taking place in a political vacuum. It was an integral part of the wider education process which saw the individual within the wider society and where questioning the structure of that society was an integral part of the process of personal growth. Education as seen in Latin America is derived from a European philosophy which integrates a knowledge of the social, economic and political environment and places it at the centre of the education process. The Anglo-Saxon model, on the other hand, places vocational education at the core and stresses the virtues of a non-political education as the basis for stability and security within a society. Thus the civil service is perceived as non-political; bishops are condemned for criticizing political decisions, even where these impact negatively on social conditions in the country; and professionals stress that decisions are based solely on technical criteria and are non-political. This viewpoint has extended to the anglophone countries of Africa, the Indian sub-continent and the Far East. Indian civil servants pride themselves on being 'non-political'. Similarly, engineers and planners in South Africa used to stress that all of their work was 'non-political' even while they were preparing new sites for the settlement of people who were being forcibly removed from their homes.

This distinction is critical to the understanding of community participation. It explains the different interpretations of empowerment. It also explains why community management can, ultimately, be no more than a transient stage (however valuable) or a sub-component of a wider participation process. Primarily it is a distinction which is required for the development of an educational intervention strategy in the arena of consensus as, in this arena, it is not possible to confine education to a vocationally dominated growth-centred approach.

In developing the structure for education and training needs in the arena of consensus, the book returns to South Africa and the field of urban development. This links back and provides continuity with the earlier work and follows the same principles as were set out in Chapter 7, where this field is used as an illustrative example. The work is based on a study of education and training needs carried out for the Peace Accord, the forerunner of the Reconstruction and Development Programme (RDP).[19]

This field makes a useful case study as the existing development process in South Africa is such a complex procedure, the understanding of which is limited to development professionals in the public and private sectors and private developers. There is a negligible understanding of the process at grassroots levels in the townships. Under the Black Local Authorities Act the state, although duplicating existing local government structures, retained a high degree of centralized control at the Provincial level and made no provision for knowledge or skills transfer downwards. Instead all administrative functions were performed by (mainly white) township managers and the executive authority of the town councils/committees was in effect negligible.

With the demise of apartheid structures such as the Black Local Authorities, and the increasing power of local democratic organizations in the early 1990s, the potential arose of building meaningful local structures which could control and run local third-tier governments, but the single most important constraint was the limited knowledge and skills base of local people described in Chapter 11. One outcome was an evaluation of education and training needs for committees and organizations involved in development issues at a local level, which would have the objective of redressing the inequalities outlined here and would lead to more effective control of the decision-making process at a local level. Studies were commissioned both locally and in the UK.

The objective of the education and training programme would be to build local beneficiary capacity which would allow for meaningful participation in, and control over, the development process. On this basis the programme would be directed towards two specific objectives. The first was to overcome the lack of understanding of the development process which then prevailed (and still does), as this was perceived to be the only way in which meaningful decisions could be taken, whereas the second was the generation of skills in various areas of development. This required the creation of a suitable framework for the programme, which would be capable of integrating short-, medium- and long-term needs, and optimizing the relationship between formal education and training. Taking these factors into account there was a clear need for intervention at four different points, as indicated in Table 13.1.

Table 13.1 *Description of intervention points and objectives*

Intervention Point	Type of intervention	Objective
1	Formal, structured education for conventional local government	A medium- to long-term strategy to provide a sound base for future local authorities
2	Lower level education and training for decision-making around development issues	A short- to medium-term strategy to fill an immediate need and provide a bridge to the higher level
3	Provision of trained facilitators for grassroots community participation	A strategy encompassing the short and long term to enhance local skills and empower local communities
4	Education and training of development professionals in community participation	To distinguish between the project cycle and the community participation process and to enhance the latter

This approach differs from the approach to education and training in the arena of inclusion in three important respects: the definition of education; the inclusion of an intermediate tier; and the formal, recognized training of development professionals.

Definition of Education

The first level of intervention relates to programmes currently being developed in several universities to cater for conventional needs in both existing and alternative local government structures (eg public administration programmes). Its primary role at that time was in supporting organizations, mainly in the metropolitan area, which already had a high degree of internal organization, as well as providing higher level civil servants. Typically these programmes would operate at the post-graduate diploma level, making them too high for the needs of, say, area and street committees, or civics in smaller towns outside the metropolitan areas.

Such programmes cannot be developed effectively within the confines of existing local government structures and need to be modified to recognize the realities which exist on the ground. The Urban Management

Programme, for example, highlights two weaknesses in this regard.[20] On the one hand there is often an over-emphasis on public administration and too little emphasis on technical planning and implementation, resulting in weak planning structures. On the other hand, there is the duplication of infrastructure planning at different levels of government and an excess of bureaucracy. Both of these can be addressed by increasing participation and introducing the further elements outlined here. They also need to be accompanied by changes in the structure of the programmes, wherein the vocational and wider socio-political education are integrated. In this specific instance (urban infrastructure management) this means examining alternative local government structures which would make use of more horizontal integration, local devolution of decision-making to area and street committees and the generation of local skills.

Inclusion of an Intermediate Tier

In the predominantly rural areas where the growth-centred approach is successful, there is a conflation of tiers. Groups are small; central government services do exist and many of the projects for which training is being applied are self-contained. This is not the case in the urban environment. The number of people involved and the number of interactive decisions which need to be made means that communities have to delegate. Although these groups have the capacity to manage programmes and projects, they cannot be effective representatives if they are non-political representatives of central government. This requires a devolution of power and a change in the relationship with government.

Such ideas are now being recommended by the Urban Management Programme.[21,22] The latter argue that

> 'A new tier of management is usually required at the community level ... often called a Community Development Committee (CDC). The CDC represents the community in all dealings with the local authority and is responsible for the day to day management of services within the community'.[23]

This concept is linked to a community management approach based on village type structures (the community being self-defined as ideally between 50 and 150 families).

The same principle can apply to larger urban areas as well as larger scale complex rural development programmes. In this instance the core problem returns. This is the community management assumption of segregation between the operational management and the political decision-making. This is a difference which separates community participation in the arena of consensus from that in the arena of inclusion. In the latter the distinction can be made. In the arena of consensus it is not possible. Management decisions cannot be contained within clearly defined boundaries set by political agendas at a higher level. Instead they have to open out to deal with policy issues. The result is a complex interaction between regional or national policy requirements and local development needs. This interaction was illustrated by the case studies of Benoni and Luganda.

In terms of training and education at this level, the key to providing the necessary inputs to community organizations lies in the integration of capital works and long-term operation and management. To date there has been a reluctance to accept the capital works stage as relevant to training, primarily because it is a one-off injection. The South African experience indicates otherwise, however. The infrastructure provision component of development represents probably the only capital rich phase of the entire process, ie it is the stage during which large amounts of money are actually invested in the area. Access to this phase thus becomes imperative if meaningful empowerment and control over the longer term development process is to take place.

The programme which was evolved in the South African case studies was designed to provide a level of knowledge which would (1) enable decision-makers to make informed decisions and not be intimidated by state or private structures; and (2) enable facilitators to be able to disseminate information downwards in an effective and meaningful way, integrating key elements into the wider education and training programme discussed earlier. To achieve these objectives whilst limiting the danger of elitism, both the elected representatives and the trainers would undertake the programme of study. The programme itself required a range of inputs, covering formal education, informal education locally and local training. The resultant output was a four-tier programme to empower democratically elected civic bodies to control the development process at a local level.

Training of Grassroots Facilitators

At this level there is a convergence of training needs between the arenas of inclusion and consensus, wherein the growth-centred approach is the central feature of the training process. The detail is covered by a number of workers who have specialized in this field, such as Srinivasan, and will not be duplicated here. The critical point to note when operating in the arena of consensus is that this growth-centred approach still needs to be integrated with a conscientization component, as well as with an ongoing process of wider education about the nature of development as it relates to the activity under consideration. Those involved with management at a local level have to carry their constituency with them. Recognizing that they will have to make difficult choices it is essential that the constituency understands the political nature of the decisions to be made.

Education and Training of Development Professionals and other Actors

When the issue of training, or control, is discussed, the emphasis is on the community as a focal point, whether it be in terms of inputs required or obligations demanded. This is a further illustration of the conditioned thinking which places participation automatically within the arena of inclusion. In the arena of consensus this dominant focus is inappropriate. Chapter 9 illustrated the importance of recognizing the needs of the other actors, but this also places obligations on those actors. In particular there is the obligation to develop the community participation process in parallel with the activity. This cannot be achieved without a clear understanding of the participation process itself. The purpose of this book has been to provide a theoretical basis for community participation. This theoretical grounding needs to be the basis on which consensus is built. It is not a prerequisite that all parties agree the purpose and objectives of community participation in any given activity. What is critical to the long-term success is the reason why they disagree. If all the parties are working empirically and have their own vision of participation encapsulated in a box, then there can be no consensus. There has to be a common theoretical basis for the debate among the key actors so that they know where the other perceptions of the process derive from and what the implications of different expectations of the process are. This provides the only basis for consensus. The first part of the education process is therefore to provide the theoretical base which creates a shared understanding of the subject.

The second area in which education/training is required is in the role of information gathering. The survey is a very powerful tool in the information gathering process, to the extent that a tendency arises to collect as much information as possible. The professionals who commission data need to understand the responsibility which goes with the collection of such data. There is not only the danger of information overkill, but the impact that surveys have on communities. This is a particular danger when development professionals discover the community survey without really understanding its social impact. There is a tendency to look on it as a purely technical device without realizing that its main strength and benefit lies in its social dimension. Thus the development professionals in particular should undergo training and be open to cross-examination by community representatives on the role and objective of any information gathering techniques likely to be used in the project.

The provision of this level of support will provide the basis for consensus building within the community, but it will not ensure success. It provides a basis for a shared understanding of the problems, but it does not prevent major differences of opinion developing over priorities, goals and targets. Resolving these issues is the objective of the third level of intervention.

MEDIATION, FACILITATION AND CONFLICT RESOLUTION

The functional operation of community participation in the arena of consensus differs significantly from that of the other two operating arenas, due primarily to the effect of having a wide number of divergent actors involved with the decision-making process. This may appear to be impractical or unwieldy at first sight. It is not. It does require, however, that the systems of management which are set up are appropriate. This in turn requires a recognition of the centrality of personal interaction which, in turn, highlights the importance of conflict resolution.

The types of projects and programmes which will be situated in the arena of consensus over the coming years will inevitably have a high conflict potential associated with them. This is because they will be dealing with, as one component of the process, some form of resource constraint. This in turn raises issues such as equity, social justice, loss of power and, most critically, change, all of which are generators of conflict. Resolving these conflicts represents the third level of external intervention. To achieve effective intervention at this level requires an understanding of two different factors (1) the nature of conflict; and (2) an understanding of the relationship between the particular form of conflict and the group dynamic. It is possible to define both of these as they apply to community participation in the arena of consensus.

Conflict resolution is an area, like community participation, where there is no satisfactory theoretical base. Nonetheless there is a growing body of publications on the topic and a growing understanding of the different forms of conflict.

The first point is that there are different types of conflict, but these are not always interpreted correctly, primarily because of misconceptions about the nature of power and power relationships. There are two common perceptions of conflict resolution. The first sees it in the form of a judicial settlement, whereas the second sees it as a form of negotiation process. In the first, resorting to law is seen as an important avenue for a weaker party to pursue a claim against a stronger, ie more powerful, party. The second is where the parties attempt to resolve the situation between themselves through some form of bargaining. The second of these is seen as being particularly relevant to disputes involving communities. In both instances the intention is to achieve a settlement to the dispute. Unfortunately, this bargaining is not always successful and the result is to develop new forms of dispute resolution, such as mediation. However, the outcome is a move to increasingly weaker forms of settlement (in the sense of less adherence to legal norms and procedures) with the result that, ultimately, there is a reversion back to direct confrontation.

Resolving this dichotomy and ensuring the effective resolution of conflicting needs requires a different approach. Firstly, it is necessary to understand exactly what form the conflict takes. Once this is done then it is essential to ensure that the correct form of intervention is applied to ensure that there is real resolution of the conflict.

There are three distinct levels of conflict.[25] All three levels can apply to activities in the arena of consensus and each requires a different form of intervention to resolve it. The first level is a management problem, where there is a conflict between people, which may be fairly strong, on ideas and priorities. Action at this level may require intervention by a third party, but the part played by this party is the facilitation of management rather than 'conflict resolution'.

The second level can be described as normal conflictual relationships. Conflict on this level occurs through misunderstanding, conflicting transitory interest and because emotions and needs are not adequately considered. Resolving this conflict may require third party input, generally from a social psychologist or social worker. This type of conflict is likely to occur in the participation process, particularly in countries such as South Africa where ethnic differences reinforce the difference in viewpoints between different actors and need to be dealt with. Unfortunately, it is often perceived as the main problem and leads to the assumption that there needs to be some form of negotiation. This is a dangerous, and often invalid, assumption which can prevent the actors from taking the analysis of the conflict further and exploring deeper concerns.

These lie at the third level, which is the form which is often most appropriate to community participation in the arena of consensus. It is termed deep-rooted conflict, but a more descriptive term is value-laden conflict. This is the type of conflict engendered by different rationalities, by the quantitative–qualitative divide and by the wide spread of cultural and financial interests involved with projects and programmes at, for example, the environment–development interface. The intervention required at this level is facilitation, but facilitation of a kind which is not well understood in a development context.

The resolution of deep-seated conflict through facilitation is based on the recognition and acceptance of three basic principles. The first of these is that the outcome should be resolution of the conflictual situation which exists between the parties, as opposed to settlement. The latter is the outcome from the court and from an arbitrator, but it represents a forced solution which will not necessarily resolve the underlying problem. This leads to the second principle: recognizing that the root cause of the dispute lies in the satisfaction of basic human needs and that this represents a set of values which cannot be curbed or made subject to a legal judgement. This requires making 'a distinction between ontological human needs which cannot be compromised, on the one hand, and individual interests, such as transitory commercial and role interests, which can be subject to negotiation, on the other'.[26] The third principle relates to the parties themselves. Sites[27] attributed effective power not to authorities, but to individuals and groups of individuals pursuing their ontological needs. This is possibly the most difficult principle to accept, as it questions the classical notion of democracy based on majority rule. This view of conflict resolution 'holds that the identity group, not the state and its institutions, is both the appropriate unit of analysis and the explanation of conflict. In other words, the assertion is that effective political power rests finally with identity groups . . . and not with authorities'.[28]

The recognition of these principles leads to a totally different perspective of conflict resolution.

> 'The awareness of needs which cannot be compromised, cannot be made subject to some legal judgement, cannot be bargained, leads logically to the development of a process that enables parties to conflicts to ascertain the hidden agenda of motivations and intentions and to explore means by which common human–societal needs can be achieved. As these needs of security, identity and human development are universal, and because their fulfilment is not dependent on limited resources, it follows that conflict resolution with win-win outcomes is possible'.[29]

This view of conflict resolution is one which is supported by an increasing amount of empirical evidence in the wider international arena.[30] It was tested, with success, in several of the case studies described earlier in the book. It was also successful in the northern Maputaland region of South Africa, where a long-standing conflict between the nature conservation body of the KwaZulu government and local community-based development organizations was resolved, laying the foundation for a joint conservation–development programme for the sub-region.

Its primary benefit lies in its implementation as it provides the first fully analytical approach to conflict resolution.

> 'It avoids the techniques of bargaining and negotiating from prepared positions . . . and the managing of conflict through some form of coercion. It is primarily analytical of the goals, values and motivations of the opposing parties. It holds that workable options and self-sustaining agreements can emerge out of this analysis'.[31]

It does this through a facilitated conflict resolution process which seeks to assist parties in dispute to deduce what alterations in structures, institutions and policies are required to enable the fulfilment of needs, which applies equally and without bias to all parties. Most importantly, it enables the parties themselves to provide the solutions to their own differences, thereby opening the way for the development of an effective working model.

PLACING INTERVENTION IN CONTEXT

Historically the role of external agents to the community participation process has been dictated by the over-riding notion of a duality between state and community. This has placed external actors in one of two roles, either as supporters of the community or as supporters of the state. Those working for the state have generally been perceived to gather knowledge about the community for external evaluation. Those working with the community, on the other hand, who are increasingly from the NGO sector, have devised ways of building local capacity as the central focus of their involvement. This in turn has extended to developing new methods of interaction, such as PRA, which integrate external and indigenous knowledge.

Even when this issue of external involvement moves out of the area of detail about what exactly is involved, to look at the purpose for that involvement, ie why have involvement, the analysis remains focused on the community. Paul, in his analysis of community participation produced for the World Bank, identified one of the three dimensions of his conceptual framework, as instruments of community participation. By this was meant 'the institutional devices used by a project to organize and sustain CP'.[32] Paul then grouped the instruments of community participation into three categories

> '(1) Field workers of the project agency. A project may use its field staff to mobilize and interact with beneficiary groups ... [...]
> (2) Community workers/committees. A project agency may draw on workers or volunteers from among beneficiaries to act as community mobilizers .. [...]
> (3) User Groups. Where the number of beneficiaries is manageable either because of the local nature of the project or the specialized nature of the group (farmers,

mothers with small children, etc), it is possible to organize viable groups of users as an instrument of CP . . '.[33]

In contrast with this approach, Srinivasan, in work published by the UNDP, adopts a people-centred approach to the same problem. On one level she explores the underlying behavioural concerns of communities, which she summarizes as coping, transforming and transcending, and argues that these 'correspond to three distinct (though not mutually exclusive) educational strategies that are currently in use at the micro level'. The strategies are correspondingly the didactic (also known as content-centred, directive, traditional or formal instruction style); conscientization or consciousness-raising; and the growth-centred approach (also known as learner orientated, non-directive or participatory strategy).[34] At a second level she sees the tools of community participation being matched to community/user needs, but this is all developed within the participatory workshop environment.[35]

These two examples are extremely useful because they in a sense represent the two poles of thinking on community participation which reflect the two agencies associated with their work, namely the World Bank and the UNDP. They also reflect the difference between external approaches to urban and rural communities.

In spite of their strongly contrasting differences in approach, the work of both researchers shares a common flaw. Both are content to place their work within a clearly defined environment, without exploring the wider applicability of their work. Paul's ideas are easier to criticize, as they are placed firmly within a framework centred around the needs of the World Bank and clearly fit within the World Bank perspective on development. However, Srinivasan's work is equally constrained. Firstly, the work is strongly sectoral, focusing on water and sanitation provision. More important is her pre-determined vision of what constitutes community participation. Although she attempts to explore different types of participation, and her proposals for training courses emphasize the need for community members to explore their own understanding of community participation, her work is clearly situated within the participation approach which can be described as community management. In this regard, her work has also been influential in building the centrality of the concept of community management in the rural water and sanitation sector. Her work also reinforces the notion of those working in the area of community management that this is the ultimate form of community participation.

This pre-determination of what constitutes community participation is an issue which has been reiterated a number of times in the book and shown to be a major constraint to expanding the role of community participation in development. It has a further limitation which is of specific relevance to this chapter. Essentially both Paul and Srinivasan are exploring different interpretations of what represents support to the community. The earlier discussion has shown that support in this form (which is predominantly training) is only one form of intervention that can be made. In practice, intervention can take place on many different levels and in many different ways. Furthermore, different interventions will be appropriate in different circumstances. The only way to provide appropriate intervention is to understand what options exist, what they do, how they are carried out, who carries them out, for whose benefit and, in addition, how they relate to the wider environment. This means that the community has to be seen as part of the wider issue and the nature of appropriate external involvement structured accordingly. This, in turn, requires a re-evaluation which goes beyond external involvement, ie who is involved and why. It requires a new analysis of the nature and purpose of intervention in the wider decision-making process.

In this new world view the community can be viewed neither from a patronizing nor from an idealized perspective. Instead the whole interactive process needs to be seen as a complex group dynamic. In this situation some things will remain the same. Community organizations will still require various forms of training and direct support. Information will still need to be collected for use by both community- and non-community actors. However, there will also be major changes. The other actors will also need new forms of training, to work in this new development paradigm. The most important change will be the recognition that underlying the whole process is a series of inter-related conflicts. These include internal conflicts within the community, conflicts between actors, conflict over resources and conflict over control. The long-term success of the community participation process will depend on recognizing, and then resolving, these conflicts. The result is a multi-level, multi-objective intervention strategy which begins with the core group and then slowly moves out to encompass sub-groups, identifying and providing the support services for each as the process expands outwards.

References

Chapter 1

1   Midgely, J (1987) 'Popular participation, statism and development' *Journal of Social Development in Africa* vol 2, no 1, pp 5–15
2   Moser, C O N (1989) 'Community participation in urban projects in the third world' *Progress in Planning* vol 32, part 2, p 81
3   Moser, C O N (1983) 'The problem of evaluating community participation in urban development' p3 in Moser, C (ed) *Evaluating Community Participation in Urban Development Projects* Development Planning Unit, Working Paper No 14, London
4   Marsden, D and Moser, C O N (1990) 'Editorial introduction: participation and housing the poor' *Community Development Journal* vol 25, no 1, p 3

Chapter 2

1   Moser, C O N (1989) 'Community participation in urban projects in the third world' *Progress in Planning* vol 32, part 2, p 79
2   UNCHS (1988) *Community Participation: A Trainer's Manual*, UNCHS, Nairobi
3   Srinivasan, L (1992) *Options for Educators: a Monograph for Decision Makers on Alternative Participatory Strategies*, PACT/CDS, New York
4   Freire, P (1972) *Pedagogy of the Oppressed*, Penguin, Harmondsworth, translated by Ramos, M B (1985) Pelican, p 96
5   Bauer, P T and Yamey, B S (1957) *The Economics of Under-Developed Countries*, Cambridge University Press, Cambridge, p vi
6   Ibid, p 9
7   Ibid, p 10
8   Hoselitz, B F (1960) 'Theories of stages of economic growth' p 193 in Hoselitz, B F, Spengler, J J, Letiche, J M, McKinley, E (eds) *Theories of Economic Growth* The Free Press of Glencoe, New York
9   Liebenstein, H (1954) *A Theory of Economic-Demographic Development* Princeton University Press, Princeton
10 Nelson, R R (1956) 'A theory of the low-level equilibrium trap' *American Economic Review* vol 46, pp 894–908
11 Ibid, p 895
12 Lewis, W A (1954) 'Economic development with unlimited supplies of labour' *Manchester School of Economics and Social Science* vol 22, pp 139–191
13 Op cit, Simpson (1987) pp 110–111
14 Ibid, p 113, quoting Rostow, W W (1956) 'The take-off into self-sustained growth' *Economic Journal* March, pp 25–48
15 Rostow, W W (1960) *The Stages of Economic Growth, a Non-Communist Manifesto* Cambridge University Press, Cambridge, p 4
16 Ibid, p 4
17 Ibid, p 4
18 Ibid, p 6
19 Ibid, p 7
20 Ibid, p 1
21 Ibid, p 2
22 Ibid, p 12–13
23 McLelland, D C (1976) *The Achieving Society* Irvington, New York, p 16

24 Ibid, p 17
25 Ibid, p 205
26 Ibid, p 391
27 Ibid, p 205
28 Hoselitz, B F (1960) *Sociological Aspects of Economic Growth* The Free Press of Glencoe, New York, p 149
29 Ibid, p 140–149
30 Moser, C O N (1983) 'The problem of evaluating community participation in urban development' p 3, in: Moser, C O N (ed) *Evaluating Community Participation in Urban Development Projects* Development Planning Unit, Working Paper No 14, London
31 Op cit, Moser (1989) p 81
32 Ibid
33 Nkunika, A I Z (1987) 'The role of popular participation in programmes of social development' *Journal of Social Development in Africa* vol 2, no 1, pp 17–28
34 Gilbert, A and Ward, P (1984) 'Community action by the urban poor: democratic involvement, community self-help or a means of social control' *World Development* vol 12, no 8, pp 769–782
35 Mayo, M (1975) 'Community development: a radical alternative' p 131, in: Bailey, R and Brake, M (eds) *Radical Social Work* Edward Arnold, London, pp 129–143
36 Marsden, D and Oakley, P (1982) 'Editorial introduction' *Community Development Journal* vol 17, no 3, pp 186–189
37 Op cit, Gilbert and Ward (1984) p 771
38 Alliband, T (1982) 'Some uses of science in community development' *Community Development Journal* vol 17, no 2, pp 141–146
39 De Kadt, E (1982) 'Community participation for health: the case of Latin America' *World Development* vol 10, no 7, pp 573–584
40 Ibid, p 572
41 Op cit, Gilbert and Ward (1984) p 771
42 Truman, H S (1949) 'Inaugural Presidential Address', 20 January 1949, quoted in *Documents on American Foreign Relations* Princeton University Press, Connecticut, 1967
43 Rodney, W (1982) *How Europe Underdeveloped Africa* Howard University Press, Washington, pp 13–14
44 Ibid, p 75
45 Ibid, p 78
46 Ibid, p 84
47 Ibid, p 87
48 Op cit, Freire (1972) p 75
49 Frank, A G (1980) *Crisis: in the World Economy* Heinemann, London
50 Ibid, p 10
51 Op cit, Freire (1972) pp 23–24
52 Ibid, p 12
53 Op cit, de Kadt (1982) p 573
54 Nturibi, D N (1982) 'Training of community development agents for popular participation' *Community Development Journal* vol 17, no 1, pp 106–119
55 Shepherd, A (1983) 'The ILO experience: community participation in decision making for basic needs' in: Moser, C O N (ed) *Evaluating Community Participation in Urban Development Projects* Development Planning Unit, Working Paper No 14, London, pp 12–17
56 Ibid, p 12, quoting from an ILO commissioned study of *Popular Participation and Basic Needs*, ILGS, 1978: para 16
57 Curtis, D, Davey, K, Hughes, A and Shepherd, A (1978) *Popular Participation and Basic Needs*, ILO Working Paper, para 19
58 UNRISD (1979) *Enquiry into Participation: a Research Approach* UNRISD, Geneva, p 8
59 Cotgrove, S (1967) *The Science of Society: an Introduction to Sociology* George Allen

and Unwin, London, pp 31–32
60   Op cit, Moser (1989)
61   Paul, S (1987) 'Community participation in development projects: the World Bank experience' *World Bank Discussion Paper No 6* World Bank, Washington
62   Abbott, J (1994) 'Community participation and its relations to community development' *Community Development Journal* vol 30, no 2, pp 158–168
63   Jones, A (1992) 'Community development training — a comparative approach' *Community Development Journal* vol 27, no 3, pp 199–210
64   Varga, T A and Vercseg, I (1992) 'An experiment in community development in the Bakony, Hungary' *Community Development Journal* vol 27, no 1, pp 50 –59
65   Oakley, P and Marsden, D (1984) *Approaches to Participation in Rural Development*, ILO, Geneva
66   Jones, J and Wiggle, I (1987) 'The concept and politics of "Integrated Community Development"' *Community Development Journal* vol 22, no 2, pp 107–117
67   Midwinter, E (1992) 'Old age and community development' *Community Development Journal* vol 27, no 3, pp 285–289
68   Ekong, E E and Sekoya, K L (1982) 'Success and failure in rural community development efforts: a study of two cases in Southwestern Nigeria' *Community Development Journal* vol 17, no 3, pp 217–224
69   Kalawole, A (1982) 'The role of grassroots participation in national development: lessons from the Kwara State of Nigeria' *Community Development Journal* vol 17, no 2, pp 121–133
70   Op cit, Oakley and Marsden (1984) p7
71   Castells, M (1983) *The City and the Grassroots: a Cross-cultural Theory of Urban Social Movements* Edward Arnold, London
72   Cernea, M M (1988) *Nongovernmental Organizations and Local Development*: World Bank Discussion Paper Number 40, World Bank, Washington, pp 11–12

Chapter 3

1   Parsons, T, Shils, E, Naegele, K D and Pitts, J R (1961) *Theories of Society: Foundations of Modern Sociological Theory*, parts I and II, The Free Press of Glencoe, New York
2   Esteva, G (1992) 'Development' p 13, in: Sachs, W (ed) *The Development Dictionary* Zed Books, London, pp 6–25
3   Ibid, p 13
4   Little, I M D (1960) *Aid to Africa: an Appraisal of UK Policy for Aid to Africa South of the Sahara* Pergamon Press, Oxford
5   Ibid, p 7–9
6   Wisner, B (1988) *Power and Need in Africa* Earthscan, London, p 32
7   Ibid, p 38
8   Op cit, Esteva (1992) p 15
9   Op cit, Wisner (1988) pp 33–34
10   ILO (1976) *Employment, Growth and Basic Needs: a One-World Problem* ILO, Geneva, p 182
11   Ibid, p 182
12   Op cit, Wisner (1988) p 34
13   Ibid, p 34
14   Ibid, p 54
15   Bauer, P T and Yamey, B S (1957) *The Economics of Under-developed Countries* Cambridge University Press, Cambridge, p 10
16   Op cit, ILO (1976) p 182
17   Op cit, Wisner (1988) p 53
18   Gish, O (1973) 'Doctor auxiliaries in Tanzania' *The Lancet* December 1, p 35
19   WHO (1981) *Global Strategy for Health for All by the Year 2000* WHO, Geneva, p 32

20 UNRISD (1979) *Inquiry into Participation – a Research Approach* UNRISD, Geneva, p 8
21 Paul, S (9187) *Community participation in development projects: the World Bank experience* World Bank Discussion Paper No 6 World Bank, Washington, p 2
22 Oakley, P and Marsden, D (1984) *Approaches to Participation in Rural Development* ILO, Geneva, p 19
23 Ibid, p 20–27
24 Moser, C O N (1983) 'The problem of evaluating community participation in urban development' p 3, in: Moser, C O N (ed) *Evaluating Community Participation in Urban Development Projects* Development Planning Unit, Working Paper No 14, London, pp 3–11
25 Op cit, Paul (1987) p 2
26 Ibid, p 20
27 Batley, R (1983) 'Participation in urban projects – meanings and possibilities' in: Moser, C O N (ed) *Evaluating Community Participation in Urban Development Projects* Development Planning Unit, Working Paper No 14, London, pp 7–11
28 Goulet, D (1989) 'Participation in development: new avenues' *World Development* vol 17, no 2, pp 165–178
29 Kidd, R and Byram, M (1982) 'Demystifying pseudo-Freirian development: the case of Laedza Batanani' *Community Development Journal* vol 17, no 2, p 97
30 Op cit, Oakley and Marsden (1984) p 19
31 Op cit, Paul (1987)
32 Ibid, p 4
33 Ibid, p v
34 Arnstein, S R (1969) 'A ladder of citizen participation' *Journal of the American Institute of Planners* vol XXXV, no 4, p 217
35 Ibid, p 217
36 Human Awareness Programme (1984) *Community Participation Study for the Urban Foundation* unpublished report, Johannesburg
37 Committee of Urban Transport Authorities (1990) 'Public Participation in land use/transport planning' *Draft UTG (Urban Transport Guide)* 11 Department of Transport, Pretoria
38 Peattie, L (1990) 'Participation: a case study of how invaders organize, negotiate and interact with government in Lima, Peru' *Environment and Urbanization* vol 2, no 1, p 19
39 Ibid, p 19
40 Op cit, Arnstein (1969) p 216
41 Ibid, p 216
42 Ibid, p 217
43 Op cit, Paul (1987)
44 Op cit, Arnstein (1969) p 217
45 Op cit, Moser (1983) p 3
46 Ibid, p 3
47 Ibid, p 3–4
48 Op cit, Moser (1989) p 84
49 Ibid, p 84
50 Op cit, Paul (1987)
51 Ibid, p 7
52 Ibid, p 16
53 Op cit, Moser (1989) p 83
54 Op cit, Paul (1987)
55 Op cit, Moser (1989)
56 Eg van Wijk (1989)
57 Korten, D (ed) (1986) *Community management: Asian Experience and Perspectives* Kumarian Press, Connecticut, p 1
58 Op cit, Paul (1987)

Chapter 4

1   Hollensteiner, M R (1977) 'People power: community participation in the planning of human settlements' *Assigning Children* no 40, pp 11–47
2   Reed, D (ed) (1993) *The Global Environment Facility: Sharing Responsibility for the Biosphere*, Vol II, World Wide Fund for Nature, Washington, pp 31–32
3   *The Economist* (1994) Aug 27
4   World Bank (1994) *World Development Report: Infrastructure for Development* Oxford University Press, New York
5   Thornley, A (1977) 'Theoretical perspectives on planning participation' *Progress in Planning* vol 7, part 1, pp 1–57
6   Batley, R and Stoker, G (eds) (1991) *Local Government in Europe. Trends and Developments* Macmillan Education, Basingstoke
7   Herzer, H and Pirez, P (1991) 'Municipal government and popular participation in Latin America' *Environment and Urbanization* vol 3, no 1, p 81
8   Ibid, p 81
9   Ibid, p 84
10   Ibid, p 83
11   Stren, R E (1991) 'Old wine in new bottles? An overview of Africa's urban problems and the "urban management" approach to dealing with them' *Environment and Urbanization* vol 3, no 1, p 18
12   Bubba, N and Lamba, D (1991) 'Local government in Kenya' *Environment and Urbanization* vol 3, no 1, pp 37–59
13   Op cit, Stren (1991) p 16
14   Op cit, Bubba (1991) p 37
15   *Report on the Sanitary Condition of the Labouring Population of Great Britain* [quoted in Fraser, D (1973) *The Evolution of the British Welfare State* Macmillan, London, p 58]
16   Ibid, p 58–75
17   Royal Commission on Local Government in the United Kingdom (1925) *First Interim Report*, pp 81–88
18   Royal Commission on Local Government in the United Kingdom (1929) *Final Interim Report*
19   Op cit, Fraser (1973) p 63
20   Royal Commission on Local Government in the United Kingdom (1925) *Second Interim Report*
21   Op cit, Bubba and Lamba (1991) p 42
22   Op cit, Stren (1991) p 10
23   Ibid, p 14
24   Lee-Smith, D and Stren, R E (1991) 'New perspectives on African urban management' *Environment and Urbanization* vol 3, no 1, pp 23–36
25   Ibid, p 24
26   Johannesburg City Council (1992a) *Financial Report 1991–1992* City Treasurer's Department, Johannesburg, p 6
27   Ibid, p 5
28   Johannesburg City Council (1992b) *Structure of Johannesburg City Council* organogram provided by the Public Relations Directorate, Johannesburg City Council, 23 November
29   Seeley, I H (1978) *Local Government Explained* Macmillan, London, p 12
30   John, P (1991) ' The restructuring of local government in England and Wales' pp 58–72 in: Batley, R and Stoker, G (eds) (1991) *Local Government in Europe. Trends and Developments* Macmillan Education, London, pp 58–72
31   Op cit, Bubba and Lamba (1991)
32   Lee, R (1993) *The Alexandra Urban Renewal Project (Phase B): an evaluation report* Development Bank of Southern Africa, Johannesburg
33   Van Ryneveld, M B (1992) 'Costs and affordability of water supply and sanitation for developing urban communities in South Africa' *International Water Supply*

Association Seminar on Water Supply and Sanitation for Developing Urban Communities Eskon College, Midrand, South Africa, 25–26 June 1992
34 Op cit, Bubba and Lamba (1991)

Chapter 5

1 Stohr, W B (1981) 'Development from below: the bottom-up periphery-inward development paradigm' in: Stohr, W B and Taylor, D R F (eds) *Development from Above or Below?* Wiley, Chichester
2 Batten, T R (1967) *The Non-directive Approach in Group and Community Work* (third impression 1975) Oxford University Press, London, p 9
3 Ibid, p 9–10
4 Warren, R L (1970) 'The context of community development' in: Cary, L J (ed) *Community Development as a Process* University of Missouri Press, Columbia, pp 32–52
5 FitzGerald, M (1980) *Urban Community Development in South Africa* McGraw- Hill, Johannesburg, p 26
6 Moughtin, C, Shalaby, T and McLintock, H (1992) 'Who Needs Development? Planning With The Poor in Third World Countries' Institute of Planning Studies, University of Nottingham, Nottingham
7 Dunham, A (1970) 'Community Development – Whither Bound?' *Community Development Journal* vol 5, no 2, April
8 De Kadt, E (1982) 'Community participation for health: the case of Latin America' *World Development* vol 10, no 7, pp 573–584
9 Op cit, FitzGerald (1980) p 29
10 Ibid, FitzGerald (1980) p 37 quoting Batten (1967) (op cit); and Biddle, W W and Biddle, L J (1965) *The Community Development Process: the Rediscovery of Local Initiative* Holt, Rinehart and Winston, New York
11 Op cit, Batten (1967) p 5
12 Ibid, p 11
13 Moser, C O N (1983) 'The problem of evaluating community participation in urban development' p 3, in: Moser C O N (ed) *Evaluating Community Participation in Urban Development Projects* Development Planning Unit, Working Paper No 14, London, pp 3–11
14 Op cit, FitzGerald (1980) p 39
15 Sanders, I T (1970) 'The concept of community development' in: Cary, L J (ed) *Community Development as a Process* University of Missouri Press, Columbia, pp 9–31
16 Ibid
17 Op cit, de Kadt (180)
18 Lackey, J S and Dersham, L (1992) 'The process is pedagogy: what does community participation teach?' *Community Development Journal* vol 27, no 3, pp 220–234
19 Op cit, Warren (1970)
20 Op cit, FitzGerald (1980) p 36
21 Khan, M H and Khan, S S (1992) *Rural Challenge in the Third World: Pakistan and the Aga Khan Rural Support Program* Greenwood Press, New York, p viii
22 Ibid
23 Ibid, p 35
24 Johnston, B F and Clark, W C (1982) *Redesigning Rural Development: a Strategic Perspective* Johns Hopkins University Press, Baltimore
25 Korten, D (1980) 'Community organization and rural development: a learning process approach' *Public Administration Review* vol 40, no 5, Ford Foundation Reprint
26 Op cit, Khan and Khan (1992) p 30–31
27 Ibid, p 31
28 Ibid, p 6–7

29   Cary, L J (1970) *Community Development as a Process* University of Missouri Press, Columbia, p 2
30   Constantino-David, K (1982) 'Issues in community organization' *Community Development Journal* vol 17, no 3, pp 190–201
31   Ekong, E E and Sekoya, K L (1982) 'Success and failure in rural community development efforts: a study of two cases in Southwestern Nigeria' *Community Development Journal* vol 17, no 3, pp 217–224
32   Ibid, p 223
33   Kalawole, A (1982) 'The role of grassroots participation in national development: lessons from the Kwara State of Nigeria' *Community Development Journal* vol 17, no 2, pp 121–133
34   Op cit, Khan and Khan (1992) p 5
35   Waseem, M (1982) 'Local power structures and the relevance of rural development strategies: a case study of Pakistan' *Community Development Journal* vol 17, no 3, pp 225–233
36   Biddle, W W and Biddle, L J (1965) *The Community Development Process: the Rediscovery of Local Initiative* Holt, Rinehart and Winston, New York p 78
37   Arnstein, S R (1969) 'A ladder of citizen participation' *Journal of the American Institute of Planners* vol XXXV, no 4, pp 216–224
38   Srinivasan, L (1993) *Tools for Community Participation: a Manual for Training Trainers in Participatory Techniques* Prowess/UNDP, Washington, p 35
39   Abbott, J (1989) 'Community participation in water supply planning: the Ramogodi Experience' *First Biennial Conference of the Water Institute of Southern Africa* Durban, May
40   Op cit, Moughtin *et al* (1992) p 58
41   Op cit, Khan and Khan (1992) p 9
42   Op cit, Khan and Khan (1992) p 52
43   Ratcliffe, S (1993) *Developing a Human Resource Management System for the Aga Khan Rural Support Programme in northern Pakistan* unpublished report for the Aga Khan Foundation, Geneva
44   Ibid, p 15
45   Op cit, Khan and Khan (1992) p 53
46   Paul, S (9187) 'Community participation in development projects: the World Bank experience' *World Bank Discussion Paper No 6* World Bank, Washington, p 2
47   Batten, T R (1957) *Communities and their Development* (fourth impression 1964) Oxford University Press, London
48   Op cit, Batten (1967)
49   Morris, R (1970) 'The role of the agent in the community development process' in: Cary, L J (ed) *Community Development as a Process* University of Missouri Press, Columbia, pp 171–194
50   Jones, A (1992) 'Community development training — a comparative approach' *Community Development Journal* vol 27, no 3, pp 199–210
51   Srinivasan, L (1992) *Options for Educators: a Monograph for Decision Makers on Alternative Participatory Techniques* PACT/CDS, New York, p 6

Chapter 6

1   Freire, P (1972) *Pedagogy of the Oppressed* Penguin, Harmondsworth [translated by Ramos, M B (1985)] Pelican, p 15
2   Ibid, p 12
3   Ibid, p 128
4   Ibid, pp 135–150
5   UNRISD (1979) *Inquiry into Participation – a Research Approach* UNRISD, Geneva, p 8
6   Shepherd, A (1983) 'The ILO experience: community participation in decision making for basic needs' in: Moser, C O N (ed) *Evaluating Community Participation*

in Urban Development Projects Development Planning Unit, Working Paper No 14, London, pp 12–17

7   De Kadt, E (1982) 'Community participation for health: the case of Latin America' *World Development* vol 10, no 7, pp 573–584

8   De Kadt (1976) quoted in de Kadt, E (1982) 'Community participation for health: the case of Latin America' *World Development* vol 10, no 7, pp 573–584

9   Skinner, R J (1982) 'Self-help, community organization and politics: Villa el Salvador, Lima' in: Ward, P (ed) *Self-help housing: a Critique* Mansell, London, pp 209–229

10 Skinner, R J (1983) 'Government experience: a Peruvian popular participation policy and experiences in sites-and-services: Villa el Salvador' in: Moser, C O N (ed) *Evaluating Community Participation in Urban Development Projects* Development Planning Unit, Working Paper No 14, London, pp 34–45

11 Peattie, L (1990) 'Participation: a case study of how invaders organize, negotiate and interact with government in Lima, Peru' *Environment and Urbanization* vol 2, no 1, pp 19–30

12 Op cit, Skinner (1983) p 36

13 Ibid, p 36

14 Castells, M (1983) *The City and the Grassroots: a Cross-cultural Theory of Urban Social Movements* Edward Arnold, London

15 Ibid, p 176

16 Ibid, p 327

17 Ibid, p 328

18 Davenport, R (1991) 'Historical background of the apartheid city to 1948' in: Swilling, M, Humphries, R and Shubane, K (eds) *Apartheid City in Transition* Oxford University Press, Cape Town, pp 1–18

19 Davies, R, O'Meara, D and Diamini, S (1984) *The Struggle for South Africa – a Reference Guide to Movements, Organisations and Institutions*, vol 1 and 2, Zed Books, London, p 287

20 Ibid, pp 289–290

21 Ibid, p 307

22 Helliker, K, Roux, A and White, R (1987) '"Asithengi!" Recent consumer boycotts' in: South African Research Service (ed) *South African Review IV* Raven Press, Johannesburg, pp 33–51

23 McCarthy, G and Swilling, M (1984) 'Transport and political resistance' in: South African Research Service (ed) *South African Review II* Raven Press, Johannesburg, pp 26–44

24 Swilling, M (1986) 'Stayaways, urban protest and the state' in: South African Research Service (ed) *South African Review II* Raven Press, Johannesburg, pp 20–50

25 Cooper, C and Ensor, L (1981) *REBCO: a Black Mass Movement* South African Institute of Race Relations, Johannesburg

26 Ibid, pp 39–48

27 Grest, J and Hughes, H (1984) 'State strategy and popular response at the local level' in: South African Research Service (ed) *South African Review II* Raven Press, Johannesburg, pp 45–64

28 Op cit, Castells (1983) p 209

29 Op cit, Castells (1983) p 328

30 Ibid, pp 173–212

31 Ibid, p 326

32 Ibid, p 194

33 Op cit, Castells (1983) p 191

34 Cuenya, B, Armus, D, Di Loreto, M and Penalva, S (1990a) 'Land invasions and grassroots organization: the Quilmes settlements in Greater Buenos Aires, Argentina' *Environment and Urbanization* vol 2, no 1, pp 61–74

35 Cuenya, B, Armus, D, Di Loreto, M and Penalva, S (1990b) 'Community action to address housing and health problems: the case of San Martin in Buenos Aires, Argentina' in: Hardoy, J E and Satterthwaite, S (eds) *The Poor Die Young: Housing*

and *Health in the Third World* Earthscan, London, pp 25–55
36 Op cit, Cuenya *et al* (1990a)
37 Ibid, p 71
38 Ibid, p 71
39 Ward, P M and Gilbert, A G (1983) 'Comparative Government Experience: Who Wants Participation?' in: Moser, C O N (ed) *Evaluating Community Participation in Urban Development Projects* Development Planning Unit Working Paper no 14, London
40 Op cit, Castells (1983) p 324
41 Chaskalson, M, Jochelson, K and Seekings, J (1987) 'Rent boycotts and the urban political economy' in: South African Research Service (ed) *South African Review II* Raven Press, Johannesburg, pp 54–74
42 Abbott, J (1994a) *The theory and practice of community participation in the provision of urban infrastructure* Unpublished PhD Thesis, University of the Witwatersrand, Johannesburg
43 Seekings, J (1988) 'Political mobilization in the black townships of the Transvaal' in: Frankel, P H, Pines, N and Swilling, M (eds) State, *Resistance and Change in South Africa* Croom Helm, London, pp 197–228, quoting Castells (1983)
44 Op cit, Abbott (1994a) p 218
45 Morris, P (1980) *Soweto* unpublished paper, Urban Foundation, Johannesburg, p 16
46 Ecopian Consortium (1979) *Development Guidance System for Soweto Council and Diepmeadow Council* unpublished report, February, p iii
47 Planact (1989) *The Soweto Rent Boycott* a report commissioned by the Soweto Delegation, Johannesburg
48 Abbott, J, Fine, P and Oelofse, M (1988) *Service or Charade: a Critical Evaluation of Infrastructure Provision in the KwaThandeka, Amsterdam, Eastern Transvaal* unpublished report prepared for the Amsterdam Home Committee, Johannesburg
49 Op cit, Chaskelson *et al* (1987) p 56
50 Op cit, Abbott (1994)
51 Op cit, Cuenya *et al* (1990a)
52 Gilbert, A and Ward, P (1984b) 'Community participation in upgrading irregular settlements: the community response' *World Development* vol 12, no 9, pp 913–922
53 Gilbert, A and Ward, P (1985) *Housing, the State and the Poor: Policy and Practice in Three Latin American Cities* Cambridge University Press, Cambridge
54 Op cit, Ward and Gilbert (1983)
55 Stein, A (1990) 'Critical issues in community participation in self-help housing programmes. The experience of FUNDASAL' *Community Development Journal* vol 25, no 1, pp 21–30
56 Ibid, p 21
57 Ibid, p 24
58 Ibid, p 23
59 Ibid, p 22
60 Ibid, p 27
61 Ibid, p 27
62 Ibid, p 26
63 Op cit, Stein (1990) pp 24–25
64 Ibid, pp 26–27
65 Op cit, Ward and Gilbert (1983)
66 Paul, S (1987) 'Community participation in development projects: the World Bank experience' *World Bank Discussion Paper No 6* World Bank, Washington, p 15
67 Op cit, de Kadt (1982)
68 Ibid, p 574
69 Ibid, p 572
70 Ibid
71 Op cit, Gilbert and Ward (1985) p 127

72   Knox, P (1987) *Urban Social Geography: an Introduction* Longman Scientific and Technical, Harlow
73   Op cit, Ward and Gilbert (1983) p 52
74   Ibid, p 55
75   Abbott, J (1994b) 'The decline of the urban management system in South Africa' *Environment and Urbanization* vol 6, no 2, pp 201–213
76   Op cit, de Kadt (1982) p 574
77   Op cit, Abbott (1994a)
78   Op cit, Paul (1987)

Chapter 7

1   Gilbert, A (1982) 'The housing of the urban poor' in: Gilbert, A and Gugler, J (eds) *Cities, Poverty and Development* Oxford University Press, Oxford
2   Dosi, G (1982) 'Technological paradigms and technological trajectories' *Research Policy* vol 11, no 2, pp 147–162
3   Stren, R E (1991) 'Old wine in new bottles? An overview of Africa's urban problems and the "urban management" approach to dealing with them' *Environment and Urbanization* vol 3, no 1, pp 9–22
4   Rakodi, C (1992) 'Housing markets in third world cities: research and policy into the 1990s' *World Development* vol 20, no 1, pp 39–55
5   Rakodi, C (1983) 'The World Bank experience' in: Moser, C O N (ed) *Evaluating Community Participation in Urban Development Projects* Development Planning Unit, Working Paper No 14, London, pp 18–33
6   Ibid, p 19, quoting the World Bank
7   Ibid, p 22
8   UN (1975) *Popular Participation in Decision Making for Development* E.75.IV.10, UN, New York
9   Op cit, Rakodi (1983) p 25
10 Moser, C O N (1983) 'The problem of evaluating community participation in urban development' in: Moser, C O N (ed) *Evaluating Community Participation in Urban Development Projects* Development Planning Unit, Working Paper No 14, London, pp 3–11
11 Chaskalon, M, Jochelson, K and Seekings, J (1987) 'Rent boycotts and the urban political economy' *South African Review II* Raven Press, Johannesburg, pp 54–74
12 Borraine, A (1988) 'Mamelodi township – upgrading of an oilspot' *Work in Progress*, no 56/57, pp 18–21
13 Abbott, J (1994) *The theory and practice of community participation in the provision of urban infrastructure* unpublished PhD thesis, University of the Witwatersrand, Johannesburg, p 6
14 Collinge, J (1991) 'Civics: local government from below' *Work in Progress* no 74, May, pp 8–16
15 Ibid, p 8
16 Ibid, p 8, quoting the co-ordinator of the National Interim Civics Committee, P Lephunye
17 Ibid, p 8, quoting Nkwinti
18 Op cit, Abbott (1994) pp 220–225
19 Ibid, p 6
20 Lee, R (1993) *The Alexandra Urban Renewal Project (phase B): an Evaluation Report* Development Bank of Southern Africa, Johannesburg

Chapter 8

1   Shepherd, A (1983) 'The ILO experience: community participation in decision making for basic needs' in: Moser, C O N (ed) *Evaluating Community Participation in Urban Development Projects* Development Planning Unit, Working Paper No 14, London, pp 12–17

2   Arnstein, S R (1969) 'A ladder of citizen participation' *Journal of the American Institute of Planners* vol XXXV, no 4, pp 216–224
3   Ibid, p 217
4   Abbott, J (1994) *The Theory and Practice of Community Participation in the Provision of Urban Infrastructure* unpublished PhD thesis, University of the Witwatersrand, Johannesburg
5   Gilbert, A and Ward, P (1985) *Housing, the State and the Poor: Policy and Practice in Three Latin American Cities* Cambridge University Press, Cambridge
6   Ibid
7   Khan, M H and Khan, S S (1992) *Rural Change in the Third World: Pakistan and the Aga Khan Rural Support Program* Greenwood Press, New York
8   Abbott, J (1989) 'Community participation in water supply planning: the Ramagodi experience' *First Biennial Conference of the Water Institute of Southern Africa* Durban, May
9   Abbott, J, Fine, P and Oelofse, M (1988) *Service or Charade: a Critical Evaluation of Infrastructure Provision in KwaThandeka, Amsterdam, Eastern Transvaal* unpublished report prepared for the Amsterdam Home Committee, Johannesburg, March
10   De Kadt, E (1982) 'Community participation for health: the case of Latin America' *World Development* vol 10, no, 7, pp 573–584
11   Smit, D (1990) 'Community participation: some realities' *Seminar on Community Participation in Service Provision for Township Development* University of the Witwatersrand, Johannesburg, p 1
12   Ibid, p 1
13   Srinivasan, L (1992) *Options for Educators: a Monograph for Decision Makers on Alternative Participatory Strategies* PACT/CDC, New York, p 7
14   Ibid, p 6
15   Ibid, p 7
16   Op cit, Abbott (1994)
17   Cuenya, B, Armus, D, Di Loreto, M and Penalva, S (1990a) 'Land invasions and grassroots organization: the Quilmes settlements in Greater Buenos Aires, Argentina' *Environment and Urbanization* vol 2, no 1, pp 61–74
18   Moser, C O N (1989) 'Community participation in urban projects in the third world' *Progress in Planning* vol 32, part 2, pp 71–133
19   Checkland, P (1981) *Systems Thinking, Systems Practice* John Wiley, Chichester, p 46
20   Ibid, p 78
21   Ibid, pp 74–81
22   Ibid, p 314
23   Ibid

Chapter 9

1   Paul, S (1987b) 'Community participation in World Bank projects' *Finance and Development* vol 24, no 4, pp 20–25
2   Moser, C O N (1989) 'Community participation in urban projects in the third world' *Progress in Planning* vol 32, part 2, pp 71–133
3   Ibid, p 84
4   Arnstein, S R (1969) 'A ladder of citizen participation' *Journal of the American Institute of Planners* vol XXXV, no 4, pp 216–224
5   Op cit, Moser (1989)
6   Op cit, Paul (1987)
7   Abbott, J (1994) *The Theory and Practice of Community Participation in the Provision of Urban Infrastructure* unpublished PhD thesis, University of the Witwatersrand, Johannesburg
8   Op cit, Paul (1987)
9   Op cit, Abbott (1994)
10   Goulet, D (1986) 'Three rationalities in development decision-making' *World*

Development vol 14, no 2, pp 301–317
11   Op cit, Paul (1987)
12   Ibid
13   Ibid
14   Moser, C O N (1983) 'The problem of evaluating community participation in
     urban development' in: Moser, C O N (ed) *Evaluating Community Participation in
     Urban Development Projects* Development Planning Unit, Working Paper No 14,
     London, pp 3–11
15   Batten, T R (1967) *The Non-directive Approach in Group and Community Work* (third
     impression 1975) Oxford University Press, London
16   Oakley, P and Marsden, D (1984) *Approaches to Participation in Rural Development*
     ILO, Geneva
17   Stein, A (1990) 'Critical issues in community participation in self-help housing
     programmes. The experience of FUNDASAL' *Community Development Journal* vol
     25, no 1, pp 21–30
18   Ibid, p 26

Chapter 10

1   Goulet, D (1986) 'Three rationalities in development decision-making' *World
     Development* vol 14, no 2, pp 310–317
2   Ibid, pp 301
3   Ibid, pp 301–302
4   Ibid, pp 302–304
5   Ibid, pp 304–305
6   Ibid, p 315
7   *South African Government Gazette* (1924) no 1418, p 379
8   Davenport, R (1991) 'Historical background of the apartheid city to 1948' in:
     Swilling, M, Humphries, R and Shubane, K (eds) *Apartheid City in Transition*
     Oxford University Press, Cape Town, pp 1–18
9   Fine, P L (1988) *Questions of Planning, Land and Local Government: the Case of
     KwaThandeka* MSc dissertation (unpublished), University of the Witwatersrand,
     Johannesburg, p 90
10   *South African Government Gazette* (1940) no 2721, p 58
11   Op cit, Fine (1988) p 90
12   Abbott, J, Fine, P and Oelofse, M (1988) *Service or Charade: a Critical Evaluation of
     Infrastructure Provision in KwaThandeka, Amsterdam, Eastern Transvaal* unpublished
     report prepared for the Amsterdam Home Committee, Johannesburg, March, p 2
13   Interview with the AHC, 27/04/1988
14   Op cit, Fine (1988)
15   Interview with the AHC, 27/04/1988
16   Op cit, Fine (1988)
17   Op cit, Abbott et al. (1988) p 3
18   Minutes of a meeting between residents of KwaThandeka, TRAC, LRC and Abbott
     and Fine on 31/08/1987
19   Interview with the AHC, 27/04/1988
20   Op cit, Abbott *et al.* (1988)
21   Meetings with AHC on 27/04/1988, 28/05/1988, 02/08/1988
22   Social Surveys (1990) *KwaThandeka: a Survey of Residents' Needs* an unpublished
     survey prepared for the Amsterdam Home Committee
23   Ibid, p 1
24   Abbott, J, Fine, P and Oelofse, M (1988) *Motivating report for the Objection to the
     Application for the Development of KwaThandeka, Amsterdam* unpublished report
     prepared for the Amsterdam Home Committee, Johannesburg, May
25   Minutes of a meeting between residents of TPA, AHC, LRC and Abbott on
     21/03/1991

26 Minutes of a meeting between residents of TPA, AHC, LRC and Abbott on 22/08/1991
27 Abbott, J (1991) *Pre-feasibility Planning Report* unpublished report prepared for the KwaThandeka Home Committee, Johannesburg, September
28 Minutes of a meeting between residents of TPA, AHC, LRC and Abbott on 21/09/1991
29 Minutes of a meeting between residents of TPA, AHC, LRC and Abbott on 12/03/1992
30 Minutes of a meeting between residents of TPA, AHC, LRC and Abbott on 17/07/1992
31 Notes of the meeting between residents of TPA, AHC, LRC and Abbott on 19/08/1988
32 Ibid
33 Op cit, Goulet (1986) pp 301–307
34 Ibid
35 McCall, M K (1987) 'Indigenous knowledge systems as the basis for participation: East African potentials' Working Paper no 36, Technology and Development Group, University of Twente, Enschede
36 Chambers, R, Pacey, A and Thrupp, L A (eds) (1989) *Farmer First: Farmer Innovation and Agricultural Research* Intermediate Technology Publications, London
37 Scoones, I and Thompson, J (eds) (1994) *Beyond Farmer First: Rural People's Knowledge, Agricultural Work and Extension Practice* Intermediate Technology Publications, London

Chapter 11

1 Independent Development Trust (1991) *Capital Subsidy Scheme Guidelines for Developers* unpublished document, Cape Town
2 Paul, S (1987) 'Community participation in development projects: the World Bank experience, *World Bank Discussion Paper No 6* World Bank, Washington
3 Ibid, p 20

Chapter 12

1 Cernea, M M (1988) *Nongovernmental Organizations and Local Development: World Bank Discussion Paper Number 40* World Bank, Washington, pp 11–12
2 Ibid, p 3
3 World Bank (1990) *How the World Bank Works with Nongovernmental Organizations* World Bank, Washington
4 Op cit, Cernea (1988) pp 10–11
5 Ibid, pp 9–10
6 Lee-Smith, D and Stren, R (1991) 'New Perspectives on African Urban Management' *Environment and Urbanization* vol 3, no 1, April 1991
7 Ibid, p 3
8 Ibid, p 4
9 Ibid, p 4
10 Ibid
11 Ibid
12 Ibid
13 Ibid, p 3
14 Ibid
15 Ibid, p 4
16 Op cit, Cernea (1988) p 7
17 Op cit, Cernea (1988) p 3
18 Op cit, World Bank (1990)

Chapter 13

1 Pratt, B and Loizos, P (1992) *Choosing Research Methods: Data Collection for Development Workers* Oxfam Publications, Oxford
2 Theis, J and Grady, H M (1991) *Participatory Rapid Appraisal for Community Development: a Training Manual Based on Experiences in the Middle East and North Africa*, International Institute for Environment and Development, London
3 Op cit, Pratt and Loizos (1992) p 59
4 Ibid, p 6
5 Chambers, R, Pacey, A and Thrupp, L A (eds) (1989) *Farmer First: Farmer Innovation and Agricultural Research* Intermediate Technology Publications, London
6 Op cit, Pratt and Loizos (1992) p 66
7 Chambers, R (1992) *Rural Appraisal: Rapid, Relaxed and Participatory, Institute of Development Studies, Discussion Paper No 311*, Institute of Development Studies, Sussex, p 7
8 Ibid, p 11
9 Op cit, eg Theis and Grady (1991)
10 IIED (1991) *Participatory Rural Appraisal: Proceedings of the February 1991 Bangalore PRA Trainers Workshop* International Institute for Environment and Development, London
11 Op cit, eg Theis and Grady (1991) p 36
12 Op cit, Pratt and Loizos (1992) pp 76–77
13 Op cit, eg Theis and Grady (1991) p 32
14 Op cit, Chambers (1992) p 10
15 Nichols, P (1991) *Development Guidelines 6, Social Survey Methods: a Guide for Development Workers* Oxfam, Oxford
16 Op cit, Pratt and Loizos (1992)
17 Op cit, Theis and Grady (1991) p 41
18 Srinivasan, L (1992) *Options for Educators: a Monograph for Decision Makers on Alternative Participatory Strategies* PACT/CDS, New York, pp 5–6
19 Abbott, J (1992) *Proposals for an Education and Training Programme for Local Committees and Organisations Involved in the Development Process* unpublished report prepared for the Peace Accord Development Committee
20 Fox, W F (1994) Strategic Options for Urban Infrastructure Management, Urban Management Programme Policy Paper no 17, World Bank, Washington, p 53
21 Ibid
22 Choguill, C L, Franceys, R and Cotton, C (1994) 'Building community infrastructure in the 1990s. Overcoming constraints' *Habitat International* vol 18, no 1
23 Ibid, p 7
24 Burton, J W (1987) *Resolving Deep-Rooted Conflict: a Handbook* University Press of America, Lanham, pp 14–15
25 Ibid, pp 4–5
26 Ibid, p 16
27 Ibid, p 15, quoting Sites
28 Ibid, p 23
29 Ibid, p 15
30 Ibid, p 23
31 Ibid, p 23
32 Paul, S (1987) 'Community participation in development projects: the World Bank experience' *World Bank Discussion Paper No 6* World Bank, Washington
33 Ibid, pp 5–6
34 Op cit, Srinivasan (1992) pp 5–6
35 Srinivasan, L (1993) *Tools for Community Participation: a Manual for Training Trainers in Participatory Techniques* PROWESS/UNDP, Washington

Index